Pension Reform in Europe: Process and Progress

Pension Reform in Europe: Process and Progress

Edited by
Robert Holzmann, Mitchell Orenstein,
and Michal Rutkowski

THE WORLD BANK
Washington, D.C.

© 2003 The International Bank for Reconstruction and Development / The World Bank
1818 H Street, NW
Washington, DC 20433
Telephone 202-473-1000
Internet www.worldbank.org
E-mail feedback@worldbank.org

The findings, interpretations, and conclusions expressed herein are those of the author(s) and do not necessarily reflect the views of the Board of Executive Directors of the World Bank or the governments they represent.

The World Bank does not guarantee the accuracy of the data included in this work. The boundaries, colors, denominations, and other information shown on any map in this work do not imply any judgment on the part of the World Bank concerning the legal status of any territory or the endorsement or acceptance of such boundaries.

Library of Congress Cataloging-in-Publication Data

Pension reform in Europe : process and progress / edited by Robert Holzmann, Mitchell Orenstein, and Michal Rutkowski.

    p.cm. — (Directions in development)
    Includes bibliographical references.
    ISBN 0-8213-5385-6
    1. Old age pensions—Government policy—Europe. 2. Old age pensions—Government policy—Europe, Eastern. I. Holzmann, Robert. II. Orenstein, Mitchell A. (Mitchell Alexander) III. Rutkowski, Michal. IV. Series.
    HD7105.35. E85 P45 2002
    331.25′2′094—dc21

                                                                    2002034925

Contents

Figures

Tables

Foreword

Pension Reform in Europe: Process and Progress presents seven papers on the political economy of European pension reform. They are revised versions of papers that were originally presented at a workshop jointly organized by the World Bank and the International Institute of Applied Systems Analysis (IIASA) in Laxenburg, Austria, in which senior experts from European Union (EU) member and candidate countries, other European countries, the European Commission, the World Bank, and IIASA participated. Because there is much more agreement among countries with respect to the objectives of the reform than with respect to the modalities and parameters of the reform process, *Pension Reform in Europe* focuses on the process. The papers offer some answers to pertinent and critical questions, such as what starts a reform and what makes it successful; what helps to accelerate such a reform under a common European roof; and what makes a reform sustainable in a complicated world of intergenerational contracts and competing interests?

This book is especially timely. Pension reform is an important topic that is high on the agendas of most European countries. All European countries are profoundly affected by an aging population, which is the result of lower fertility and increased life expectancy, changes in family structure, and the effects of globalization. If changes are not implemented into the current system of retirement income, a shrinking number of workers, especially younger workers, will be burdened with the responsibility of providing for an increasing number of the elderly. Unless changes are implemented fairly soon in the current retirement income systems, this burden on workers and on public budgets will become more and more overwhelming, and will result in defaults on past promises. This would hurt the very vulnerable elderly.

Clearly, major reforms are needed, and these reforms must ensure the sustainability of retirement income systems. The reform program will need to combine measures to (1) delay retirement, (2) introduce changes in the benefit structure, and (3) diversify the sources of retirement income to better balance individuals' risks. Delaying retirement requires reforms of the pension systems that would—regardless of the method of financing—provide incentives for workers to remain in the labor force longer and the capacity for them to do so. Changes in the benefit structure need to respond to changes in family structure and to the way labor markets operate in an increasingly integrated world. And increasing the diversification of income sources requires the consideration of a larger role for funded pensions.

Ironically, the very success of European pension systems in securing income adequacy in old age is making reforms more difficult today, in part because these reforms increase the fears of economic insecurity among the elderly and future retirees. Because these reforms will affect income security for the most vulnerable, measures to protect these groups are needed so that a coherence is established between the economic and social goals of the reform of retirement income systems.

Several European countries have started to introduce reforms aimed at the sustainability of their retirement income systems. These reforms include steps to strengthen the link between pension benefits and contributions; to prolong the contribution period needed to qualify for a full pension; and to diversify sources of retirement pension provision so that private pension funds play a larger role in securing adequate retirement income. European Union accession countries, such as Bulgaria, Estonia, Hungary, Latvia, and Poland, have introduced important pension reform efforts along these same lines or are about to do so. The same applies to EU countries, such as Denmark, Italy, the Netherlands, and Sweden.

Many more European countries are preparing their pension reforms and we hope that they may profit from the book and the papers its presents. While the responsibility for the views expressed in the papers belongs to the authors, and not to the conference participants or the World Bank, we believe that *Pension Reform in Europe: Process and Progress* constitutes a valuable attempt to clarify some of the most important issues—particularly those surrounding the process of reform itself—with the understanding that each country faces a different set of circumstances and constraints.

Johannes F. Linn
Vice President
Europe and Central Asia Region,
World Bank

Jean-Francois Rischard
Vice President
External Affairs (Europe),
World Bank

1
Accelerating the European Pension Reform Agenda: Need, Progress, and Conceptual Underpinnings

Robert Holzmann, Landis MacKellar, and Michal Rutkowski

Pension reform gets more attention in countries throughout Western, Central, and Eastern Europe than any other topic on the economic reform agenda, but in no area of the European policy debate has progress been more uneven. Why has reform progress been greater in some countries than in others? Why has the evident need for reform not prompted reform progress? To help accelerate the reform agenda across Europe, the contributors to this book seek to offer a better understanding of these issues.

This first chapter begins by outlining the need for comprehensive, pan-European pension reform, a need that arises from three main factors: budgetary pressure, socioeconomic change, and European economic integration. This chapter also summarizes the progress of reform to date across Europe, in part through an extensive annex that covers the 15 European Union (EU) countries, the 10 European Union accession (EUA) countries of Central and Eastern Europe, and Croatia. The annex to this chapter details recent demographic and retirement trends; the current adequacy, affordability, and sustainability of the countries' pension systems; and the directions that reforms are taking. The information gathered in the table reflects the findings of an innovative policy conference, "Learning from the Partners," that in spring 2001 brought EU and EUA country officials together in Vienna, Austria, to study one another's reform progress. Finally, we assess the "open method of coordination" that the European Commission has adopted to further the progress of pension reform Europe-wide, and we conclude that, although useful, the process may be insufficient to produce rapid and comprehensive European reform.

The other chapters in this book explore the political economy of pension reform globally to better understand what triggers reform, what shapes reform outcomes, and how reform progress is made. Those chapters were produced for a conference on the "Political Economy of Pension

Reform," held at the International Institute for Applied Systems Analysis (IIASA) at Laxenburg, outside Vienna, in tandem with the "Learning from the Partners" conference in 2001. Together, these articles constitute an important contribution to the expanding literature on the political economy of pension reform. Drawing on a variety of analytical and empirical perspectives from economics and political science, the contributors present up-to-date analyses of reform progress in Europe and Latin America and of the role that international organizations have played in furthering the pension reform agenda. We hope that this and the other chapters will motivate and inform needed pension system changes across Europe.

The Need for Rapid, Comprehensive, and Pan-European Pension Reform

The need for pension reform in the European Union and European Union Accession countries arises from three factors: First, the current high expenditure level and related budgetary pressure will only worsen, given the projected further aging of populations. Second, ongoing socioeconomic changes are rendering current provisions inadequate. Third, European economic integration and the common currency will prompt higher levels of internal and external migration, but current retirement provisions do not support this needed labor mobility.

The expenditure level for public pensions in most Western European countries is well above that of other industrial countries at a similar income level. The average pension expenditure as a percentage of gross domestic product (GDP) for the 15 EU countries in 2000 amounted to 10.4 percent. [That estimate is low because it includes only the expenditure under the projection exercise of the Economic Policy Committee (EPC 2001); the Organisation for Economic Co-operation and Development (OECD) estimate is about 1.3 percentage points higher (OECD 2002)].[2] The average for the non-European and affluent OECD countries—Australia, Canada, the Republic of Korea, Japan, New Zealand, and the United States—in 2000 was about 5.3 percent, that is, roughly half. In the EU only Ireland (4.6 percent) has similar levels. This difference is also shared by the accession countries in Central and Eastern Europe. With the exception of Romania (5.1 percent), all others have expenditure shares close to (and in Croatia, Poland, and Slovenia, well above) the EU average and hence much higher than non-European OECD countries, despite an income level of one-quarter or less. Poland's pension expenditure, at close to 15 percent of GDP, rivals that of Austria and Italy as the world's highest (figure 1.1). Population age structure does not explain the gap between these expenditure levels and those in non-European OECD countries.

Figure 1.1   Pension Expenditure in EU and Accession Countries (plus Croatia), 2000 or latest (percent of GDP)

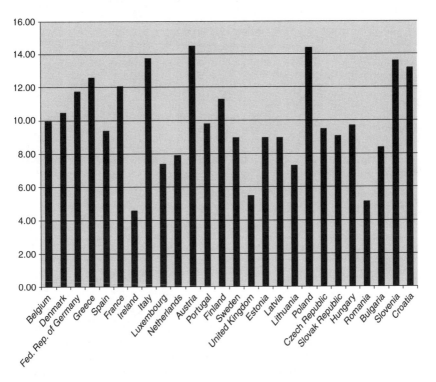

Sources: EPC (2001) and World Bank documents.

Rather, the gap reflects differences in benefit level and retirement age. The replacement rate in high-expenditure countries is generally much greater because public (largely unfunded) pensions are little supplemented by private and funded arrangements (except in Denmark, Ireland, the Netherlands, and the United Kingdom). The effective retirement age is typically low as a result of incentives for early retirement in current schemes and past deliberate labor market policy that attempted to keep the unemployment rate low. The demographic component in pension expenditure is going to increase under unreformed systems as aging in Europe accelerates.

In Europe the total fertility rate has been below replacement level (i.e. some 2.1 children per woman) since the 1970s in the west and since the 1980s in the east, and there are few signs of a rebound from the current low levels. On the other hand, life expectancy is likely to increase during the next 50 years by 4.2 years for women and 5 years for men. As a result,

Table 1.1   Projections of Old-Age Dependency in EU Member States
(ratio of people over age 64 to the working age population, percent)

Member state	2000	2010	2020	2030	2040	2050
Belgium	28.1	29.4	35.6	45.8	51.3	49.7
Denmark	24.1	27.2	33.7	39.2	44.5	41.9
Germany	26.0	32.9	36.3	46.7	54.7	53.3
Greece	28.3	31.6	35.8	41.7	51.4	58.7
Estonia	27.1	28.9	33.1	41.7	55.7	65.7
France	27.2	28.1	35.9	44.0	50.0	50.8
Ireland	19.4	19.1	24.5	30.3	36.0	44.2
Italy	28.8	33.8	39.7	49.2	63.9	66.8
Luxembourg	23.4	26.2	31.0	39.8	45.4	41.8
Netherlands	21.9	24.6	32.6	41.5	48.1	44.9
Austria	25.1	28.8	32.4	43.6	54.5	55.0
Portugal	25.1	26.7	30.3	35.0	43.1	48.7
Finland	24.5	27.5	38.9	46.9	47.4	48.1
Sweden	29.6	31.4	37.6	42.7	46.7	46.1
United Kingdom	26.4	26.9	32.0	40.2	47.0	46.1
EU15	26.7	29.8	35.1	43.8	52.4	53.4

Source: EPC (2001).

the old-age dependency ratio for the EU15 is projected to nearly double
from 27.7 percent in 2000 to 53.4 percent by 2050 (table 1.1), based on
rather optimistic assumptions about total fertility rate (assumed to rise
again to 1.8 children per women in most countries) and life expectancy
(assumed to rise less than in the past). The projections for the EU accession countries are very similar (United Nations 1998). Based on this projected change in the old-age dependency ratio, and given a no-reform
scenario, pension expenditure would roughly double.

Naturally, such a radical expenditure increase would not necessarily materialize because some reform measures have already been
enacted, and system dependency ratios (beneficiaries to contributors)
may not deteriorate to the same extent as do old-age dependency
ratios. Greater labor force participation by women is likely and that of
the elderly may increase. At least, this is the scenario put forth by the
Economic Policy Committee of the EU and by the country projections for
the period 2000 to 2050 (EPC 2001). As a result, the average EU pension
expenditure (captured under this exercise) is projected to *only* increase
from 10.4 percent of GDP in 2000 to a peak of 13.6 percent around 2040
(with a projected fall from 5.5 to 4.4 percent for the United Kingdom,
but almost a doubling for Spain from 12.6 to 24.8 percent). This moderate projected 30 percent increase in the average expenditure level
(compared with a pure demographically induced increase of some
70 percent) is estimated as a result of lower benefit ratios (average benefits

compared with GDP per capita) and higher employment ratios (employ-ment to population aged 15 to 64 years). We strongly conjecture, how-ever, that this modest increase in EU average pension expenditure levels will require major changes in the pension schemes and their incentives for enhanced labor market participation and delayed retirement deci-sions. Put differently, a further major increase in pension expenditure can only be prevented if major reforms take place. The EPC commis-sioned and published their optimistic projections as part of the politics of the EU pension reform process.

If there were no budgetary and demographic pressures for reform, however, there still would be a need for most European countries to realign their pension systems with *socioeconomic changes*. Three changes stand out: increasing female labor force participation and changing family structures, the rise in atypical employment, and the need for lifelong learning.

In the EU countries, the labor force participation of women has increased substantially in recent decades. In the formerly centrally planned countries, women's participation was very high, but it decreased during the countries' transitions to a market economy. Although there are differences among EU countries—for example, in Italy the 53 percent female labor force participation rate in 2000 was low in contrast with Denmark where the 83 percent female participation rate is almost equal to that of men—a further increase is projected for all countries. The EU average is projected to increase from 67 percent to 77 percent, whereas the participation rate for men will remain largely constant at approxi-mately 85 percent. So far this change in female labor force participation is little reflected in the pension benefit structure. The benefit rules largely reflect the traditional image of a working husband and a childcaring housewife who needs a widow's pension for her protection in old age. But eligibility for such a pension is complicated by the rising divorce rate—already some estimated 50 percent of marriages will not survive in both EU and EUA including the second or third marriages. To ensure gender neutrality, survivor's pensions in many countries have been extended to male spouses, but in order to deal with the budgetary con-sequences ceilings and tapers for the joint pension have increasingly been introduced. Only a few countries have moved in the direction of establishing independent rights for spouses, that is, the individualiza-tion of pension rights. Benefit traps for women still exist in many coun-tries where there are incentives against rejoining the labor market or remarrying when a woman becomes eligible for a survivor's pension.

A more recent development is the rise in atypical employment, that is, the reduction in full-time salaried employment and the increase in part-time employment, pseudo self-employment, and temporary employment. This development may be ascribed to globalization and competitive pressure that make full-time employment more rare, or it may be linked to more self-selected flexibility in the labor market (including the choice of retirement provisions). Whatever the reason, these atypically employed people do not fare well under many current pension schemes, which are based on the full-time employment fiction. Again, reform (and strict contribution-benefit relationships) are needed.

Finally, many pension schemes still assume the strict life-stages separation of education, work, and retirement leisure. But a modern economy and the need for lifelong learning require a pension scheme that encourages rather than impedes the mixing of those three activities—for example, going back to school after years of work, bringing (retirement) leisure forward, or taking up work again after retirement (say, from ages 70 to 72). Most current pension schemes discourage such flexibility.

The third major impetus for a pan-European pension reform approach resides in *European economic integration* and the objective of common markets for goods, services, and factors of production under a common currency—the euro. This objective has implications for the provision of retirement income: budgetary implications, the need for more labor market flexibility, and the need for enhanced labor supply in an aging population.

The concept of a stable common currency in Europe is linked with the Maastricht fiscal criteria to keep the fiscal deficit below 3 percent and public debt below 60 percent of GDP. Although the selection of the criteria may be questioned (Holzmann, Hervé, and Demmel 1996), the objective is sound: to avoid fiscal expansion that detracts from the internal and external value of the euro. To comply with the related growth and stability pact, the 12 "euroland" members engage to achieve a structural budget deficit of zero percent (to allow for fiscal expansion when cyclically needed). But many countries will not be able to achieve a zero budget deficit in a sustainable manner unless the pension system is reformed and the explicit or implicit transfers from the budget are curtailed. In Austria, for example, the pension-related deficit amounts to almost 5 percent of GDP.

Room for budgetary expansion (and contraction) is needed in a common currency area because exchange rate and interest rate policies are lost and few other instruments are available to deal with asymmetric shocks that hit some member states but not others. Given that fiscal policy in an integrated economic area is only mildly effective because of high leakages to other regions or compensating private sector savings, however, another main policy instrument has to come into play—that is, labor market flexibility through wage flexibility and migration. Empirical evidence from the United States suggests that although wage adjustment during regional crises is important, the main adjustment mechanism is migration from (temporarily) contracting to expanding regions. For Europe both wage flexibility and migration are likely to remain less important because labor markets are more rigid and there are cultural and linguistic barriers. But both mechanisms must be strengthened there if delayed adjustments after demand or supply shocks are to be avoided (à la Argentina?). One important instrument for strengthening these mechanisms does not yet exist: a pension system that allows for full labor mobility across professions and states. In many European countries, pension rules that differ for public sector and private sector workers impede mobility between the sectors. Mobility between states exists notionally for public schemes (but less in reality), but full portability for corporate and voluntary funded systems is still under discussion. Therefore the EU does not have a harmonized, even less a coordinated pension system, which characterizes other economically integrated areas under a common currency (such as the Brazil, Canada, Switzerland, and the United States). These federations or confederations exhibit many differences at state or province levels (including taxes or short-term social benefits), but they have one thing in common—a retirement income scheme.

Finally, the external value of the euro is likely to be determined or codetermined by the growth expectation of Europe (compared with the United States or other currency areas). Current-period balances or imbalances in flows of goods and services or even the net-asset positions of countries are increasingly expected to lose their importance in determining the relative price of a currency under globalization. Productivity growth can compensate only partially for the effects on GDP growth of the projected EU15 population decline (13 percent between 2000 and 2050), and higher productivity requires mechanisms to reallocate workers from shrinking to expanding sectors and regions. If aging and the declining population are not better offset through higher labor market participation, delayed retirement, and increased external migration, the impact on GDP growth will be substantial, but enhanced labor force participation and delayed retirement require appropriately reformed retirement income schemes.

In summary, countries across Europe, including current EU member states, and EU accession countries in Central, Eastern, and Southern Europe need pension reform for three reasons: increased budgetary pressures, contemporary socioeconomic changes, and European economic integration.

Where Does the Reform Effort Stand?
Learning from the Partners

Against that background and the strong need for reform of their pension systems, how do countries in Central, Eastern, and Western Europe fare? Where does the reform process stand in individual countries, and in what directions are reforms moving? To achieve a better understanding of the problems and possible solutions, the World Bank and IIASA organized a conference in Vienna in April 2001—"Learning from the Partners." The idea was to hold a conference that brought together the 15 countries from the EU and the 10 accession countries from Central and Eastern Europe (plus Croatia) to share their reform experiences and to learn innovatively from one another's reform processes. Countries were paired and each partner country served as a full peer reviewer—that is, each partner not only assessed the other's reform progress but also wrote a peer review. To enhance the learning process, countries were paired on the basis of two objectives: maximizing the reform difference (that is, pairing a reform leader and a reform laggard) and minimizing the geographical distance (that is, where possible, selecting neighboring countries). This concept proved to be a great success as was made evident by the engaging discussion and the quality of papers presented.[3] Each country's pension scheme and reform directions are summarized in the annex to this chapter.

The papers presented at the policy conference showed that both EU and EUA countries have had to adapt their pension systems in minor and often in very major ways since the extent of demographic trends have become known and appreciated. The changes have reflected the inability to finance prior commitments and the need to make pension systems more sustainable in light of forthcoming demographic developments. The changes reveal a move toward a greater role for a privately managed funded component, usually in a defined-contribution form, and the conversion of the pay-as-you-go (PAYG) components into ones that are more self-sustaining and transparent.

On closer inspection it is possible to see that two reform styles have emerged: a *parametric* style and a *paradigmatic* style. A parametric reform is an attempt to rationalize the pension system by seeking more revenues and reducing expenditures while expanding *voluntary* private pension provisions. A PAYG pillar is downsized by raising the retirement age, reducing pension indexation, and curtailing sector privileges; and a development of voluntary pension funds beyond the mandatory social security system is promoted through tax advantages, organizational assistance, tripartite agreements, and other means of administrative and public information facilitation. These among other things are happening in Austria, the Czech Republic, France, Germany, Greece, and Slovenia.

Other countries decided to change the paradigm in which pension systems operate—that is, to move away from the monopoly of a PAYG pillar within the *mandatory* social security system. A paradigmatic reform is a deep change in the fundamentals of pension provision typically caused by the introduction of a mandatory funded pension pillar, along with a seriously reformed PAYG pillar and the expansion of opportunities for voluntary retirement saving. Among other measures, this is what three-pillar Bulgaria, Croatia, Denmark, Hungary, Latvia, the Netherlands, Poland, Sweden, and the United Kingdom decided to do. So common has this reform model become that in the annex to this chapter, we sometimes refer to it merely as a "three-pillar reform."

The distinction between parametric and paradigmatic reform cuts across the EU/EUA divide. Both parametric and paradigmatic reformers can be found on either side of the disappearing fence. Paradigmatic reformers, however, tend to be more widely represented among EUA countries where, in addition to those cited above, several others are likely to follow soon—Romania and perhaps Lithuania and Slovakia. But why is it hard to find new paradigmatic reformers among EU countries?

Adopting paradigmatic reform results from the following policy conclusions: individual accounts embody desirable work and compliance incentives; funding can increase a nation's savings and investment under the right fiscal conditions; and funded accounts can accelerate the development of a nation's capital market institutions and its efficiency in capital allocation and, therefore, its economic growth rate. Those assumptions are more appealing in EUA countries where the objective is to catch up with EU countries and where they attach great importance to having a pension system conducive to growth. Their relatively underdeveloped capital markets and their scarcity of savings indicate that they would benefit from a mandatory funded pillar of the pension system more than would EU countries. Their high share of informal labor markets points to the important role of work and compliance incentives. All of those factors grouped with the lower burden of diverting revenues from a purely PAYG system to one with a funded component (usually labeled "transition costs") that results from smaller PAYG commitments for future generations, make paradigmatic reforms particularly attractive in EUA countries.

Other arguments also are commonly used to support paradigmatic reforms: The returns on capital and labor differ over time and a multipillar system thus enables individuals to diversify lifetime risks. The funded component in a multipillar pension system enables countries, especially smaller countries, to diversify their collective pension risks onto a larger economic base. Furthermore, both PAYG and funded pillars have risks and not all of the risks are the same—a partial switch would allow workers to diversify risks more beneficially. With a multipillar mandatory system, they would achieve returns based on the different kinds of assets in each pillar. In the case of the public PAYG schemes [conventional defined-benefit (DB) or notional account], the return depends solely on the growth of wages. In the new private scheme, the return depends on returns to capital. As long as these two rates of return of both systems are not fully correlated, some diversification gain is possible. Limited empirical evidence from OECD countries suggests that the correlation between the two returns is low or nonexistent, which supports the diversification argument.[4] Moreover, having experienced firsthand the political or policy risks inherent in public pension schemes, workers often are willing to spread their risks between public and private sector institutions.[5] Those arguments seem to apply equally to the EU and EUA groups.

Countries design their second pillar components differently, depending on which of those objectives they consider more important. In Denmark and the Netherlands there is a multiplicity of occupation-based funds either in DB form (the Netherlands) or defined-contribution (DC) form (Denmark). In Sweden a clearinghouse was created to channel money of the participants to asset managers and follow the investment priorities of the participants. In Hungary and Poland the second pillar is based on pension funds competing for participants' contributions.

Introducing a multipillar system with a mandatory funded component carries with it complex challenges, including conditions in terms of financial market development and in administrative and supervisory capacities. In addition, a country must have a fiscally feasible strategy for dealing with the transition costs. The transition typically will impose welfare losses over time that some countries are not prepared to legislate, and practical limits exist on how much of any shift to funding can be debt financed to match those losses over time to economic gains. These constraints, however, should not prevent countries from improving both the adequacy and the consumption-smoothing aspects of their PAYG pension systems.

The trend we see—a more willing embrace of paradigmatic reforms in EUA countries than in EU countries—may be explained by the EUA countries' need to realize the benefits of a funded pillar relatively quickly to increase savings and growth in their effort to catch up with EU countries. To some extent, their greater willingness to engage in paradigmatic reforms emphasizing personal accountability, private savings, and so forth is because EUA countries have undergone a profound ideological shift; EU countries generally have not done so. It seems inevitable, however, that with or without an ideological shift, EU countries also will have to accelerate their move beyond parametric reforms. A good recent case in point is Germany. The German parametric reform (lowering the replacement rate in the PAYG system) may contain features of a paradigmatic reform if private providers, supported and encouraged by the state and employers, step in with a significant offer that will be picked up by employers and employees. No decision has been made. Although it is less ambitious than the reforms in Denmark, Sweden, and the United Kingdom, the German reform—if successful—may guide other EU countries and some of EUA countries that decide not to take up the challenges of a paradigm shift.

The Open Method of Coordination—The Way Forward?

Despite tremendous need for reform, reform progress has been highly variable across Europe. The Commission of the European Union recently sought to accelerate pension and other policy reforms through a peer review process called the "open method of coordination." With this approach, member countries prepare and share with one another material on status, reform concept, and progress in selected policy areas, including pensions. It is assumed that pressure for further reform will be exerted by comparing reform progress and results and by identifying reform leaders and laggards. With this tool of open coordination, the EU expects to become the most competitive and knowledge-based economy in the world by 2010 (Commission of the European Union 2001). Without a doubt, introducing a peer review process shows progress in EU policy thinking, but will it be sufficient to initiate early and comprehensive reform?

Against the background of current literature on the political economy of pension reform such a peer review process suggests the following major advantages:

- It requires taking stock and presenting a baseline scenario—an illustration of the economic, budgetary, and social consequences of not reforming.
- It introduces an integrated approach that looks at, in principle, all issues related to the reform area under scrutiny.
- It informs individual member countries about different reform approaches used elsewhere in the EU and thus increases knowledge about the feasible reform set.
- It introduces reform pressure on the lagging countries by mere comparison (indirect naming and shaming).

The peer review process, which was initiated by decision of the European Council at the European summit in Lisbon on March 23–24, 2000, has hardly begun, and the Social Protection Committee (SPC) by "taking into account the work being done by the Economic Policy Committee, (...) as its first priority, [is mandated] to prepare, on the basis of a Commission communication, a study on the future evolution of social protection from a long-term point of view, giving attention to the sustainability of pension systems in different time frameworks up to 2020 and beyond, where necessary."[6] The underlying report on financial sustainability was published by the Economic Policy Committee in November 2001 (EPC 2001). The National Strategy Reports on the Future of Pension Systems were to be submitted by September 2002. The joint report by the EPC and the SPC is scheduled for spring 2003, with the results to be integrated in the Broad Economic Policy Guidelines—the EU's core of economic policy coordination—envisaged for the same year. The communication produced by the European Council in Göteborg (Council of the European Union 2001) outlines, and the guidelines published by the SPC (2002) detail, the expected content of the National Strategy Reports and, to some extent, the expected workings of the open method of coordination. The common broad objectives established by the Council are threefold, concerning the adequacy of pensions; the financial sustainability of pension systems; and the modernization of pension systems in response to changing economic needs of the economy, society, and individuals. For each of those broad goals, the following subheadings for the report are suggested: regarding adequacy, the subtopics are preventing social exclusion, maintaining living standards, and strengthening solidarity; regarding financial sustainability, they are raising employment, prolonging working lives, consolidating public finances, adjusting pension scheme parameters, and developing funded provision; regarding modernization, they are fostering labor market flexibility, gender equality, and transparency and adaptability. Common indicators to compare results are being elaborated and may not be available for use in the first National Strategy Reports.

Clearly it is too early to assess the effectiveness of this peer review approach. The approach has many attractive features, including the expected presentation in the National Strategy Reports of the translation of common objectives into national policy objectives and specific national targets, the expected presentation of the overall reform strategy, and the future use of comparable indicators. But this approach may not lead to an early, comprehensive, and pan-European reform for the following reasons:

- The method is likely to be very slow. There is a three-year gap between the initiation of a report (spring 2000) and its scheduled publication. EPC projections, which use very optimistic assumptions that are not truly baseline (as they already imply a policy change to take place), provide results that illustrate a "muddling-through" scenario and are unlikely to create major pressure for reform. If it comes at all, such pressure will have to come from domestic sources.
- The method is unlikely to lead to a comprehensive reform. Although the terms of reference expand to the analysis of social objectives, financial sustainability, and the meeting of changing social needs, the elaboration is left to the National Strategy Reports, with the EPC and SPC providing a joint summary report of the findings. That suggests the reform mood created will be parametric rather than paradigmatic.
- The method will not create a vision for a pan-European reform. Pension systems remain national agenda items. The open method

of coordination was initiated by the EU member countries to avoid any discussion about a pan-European blueprint or benchmark for pension reform. Given the diversity of pension systems in the EU, any suggestion along such lines would have elicited political opposition by member countries and an end to further common reform discussion among them. But will mere competition among European pension systems help move countries toward a more harmonized scheme?

Perhaps the entry of the EUA countries after 2004 will energize current member countries because they will become more aware of reform alternatives. Or perhaps a reform champion will emerge among European politicians to push for a reform strengthened by the EPC, as signaled in recent communications (EPC 2002). It is also possible that European politicians and the EU commission may be guided by recent lessons from the political economy of pension reform—the lessons that are the topic of this book.

The Political Economy of European Pension Reform

What lies behind the differences in pension reform approach and progress across Europe? And what are the most promising avenues for motivating and implementing needed reforms? To strengthen the Bank's understanding of the political economy of pension reform, a research workshop on potential answers was held a day prior to IIASA's policy conference in Laxenburg. The six papers presented and later revised into the chapters in this book used different methodologies to arrive at answers about reform motivation, implementation, and progress. Although they differ in methodology, they enhance our understanding of what is likely to trigger a pension reform.

The chapter by Katharina Müller begins with a careful evaluation of the political economy of policy reform literature for insights on pension reform. The literature has tended to emphasize the difficulty of enacting structural pension reform in countries with mature pension systems— difficulty resulting from the power of interest groups with stakes in the current system. Müller points out, however, that many countries in Latin America and Eastern Europe have managed to reform their pension systems radically. She investigates four cases in particular (Argentina, Bolivia, Hungary, and Poland) to identify variables that have been important in triggering reform. From the political economy literature, she identifies five likely triggers: dynamic political leadership, the role of international financial institutions, pension system crisis, intelligent reform strategy design, and the respective power or powerlessness of reform advocates and opponents. Müller emphasizes the importance of a "new pension orthodoxy" that represents a newly dominant global epistemic community (Haas 1992) in pension policy advice, and the international demonstration effects of the Chilean reform, although mostly in Latin America. Müller, however, views the domestic political process as decisive and therefore focuses attention on the domestic factors that trigger reform. She finds that political leadership is important in her four cases; that paradigmatic change is often triggered by new actors, particularly ministries of finance and economy, becoming involved in the pension policy debate; and that specific, contextual action resources often matter—for instance, the relationships between trade unions and government. In addition, she finds that economic factors are important triggers. A severe financial crisis may strengthen the hand of the ministry of finance, and high debt may enhance the leverage of international financial institutions that advocate paradigmatic reform. Müller also finds the strategy of reform design to be important, including such measures as bundling, packaging, compensation for, and sequencing of reform. Her chapter comes from a larger study and includes useful tables on reform progress in 7 Central and Eastern European (and Eurasian) countries and 10 Latin American countries.

Steven Ney's chapter shifts the emphasis decisively to Europe. He also deals with the political economy of policy reform literature, but from the perspective of previous work on Western Europe. His contribution is to apply this literature to current pan-European experience of pension reform. Ney begins, as Müller does, with the common assertion of political economy literature that systemic pension reform should be extremely difficult to achieve in democracies with strong systems of interest representation and with mature pension systems. Like Müller, Ney draws attention to the fact of systemic reform enacted in many Western, Central, and Eastern European states and offers a unique explanation that turns much of the previous political economy literature on its head. Where earlier literature emphasized that institutions of democracy render paradigmatic pension reform difficult, Ney argues that pension policy has never been very democratic. Instead he asserts that small policy networks have tended to dominate pension policymaking in Europe. Operating in backrooms and excluding those without sufficient technical expertise, these networks exercised a dominance unchallenged by normal democratic procedures. Ney posits that in the 1990s the pension debate opened to new actors with new ideas, and the breakdown of these insular and cohesive pension governance networks ensued. That change led to greater conflict among opposing camps with different pension policy discourses, ideas, and policy stories. It has destabilized pension politics, which now reflects a more unpredictable "garbage can" style of policy choice. In short, Ney argues that pension policymaking has become more prone to change as it becomes more democratic, reversing a key argument of the political economy literature that portrayed democratic processes and institutions as obstacles to change. Ney shows that more democratic political processes can help break up dominant policy networks and trigger paradigmatic reform.

The chapter by Florence Legros also deals with political economy literature, but with a different branch—the economic literature on optimal pension systems and intergenerational transfers and tradeoffs. Her contribution is to marry the literature on optimal pension schemes with the political economy literature on how choices are made and the macroeconomic consequences of those choices. In particular, she studies the conflicts between retired and nearly retired people and workers in a general equilibrium model with overlapping generations. In this model there are two key variables to be chosen: the contribution rate and the retirement age. Political authorities choose the contribution rate; households choose the retirement age. Legros finds that there are two main reasons why the retirement age may be lower than optimal in a given country, and lower than an equal sample of all individuals would choose: first, the authorities take less account of the interests of the younger generation, and second, the older generation is politically powerful and egoistic. Legros also considers the effect of a demographic shift toward greater population aging and finds this can produce a high contribution rate combined with a low retirement age. Reform, in this model, could be triggered by changes in the perceived rate of return of the pension system, the perceived effect of the pension system on real wages and capital formation, and greater voting by and political attention to the problems of the younger generation.

The chapter by Agnieszka Chlon and Marek Mora is interesting because it tests a number of political economy propositions derived from case studies and econometric models, such as the ones presented in the earlier chapters. The authors apply a survey instrument completed by a small sample of policymakers and experts in 25 reforming and non-reforming countries—and it produces some remarkable results. First, Chlon and Mora dispute the claim that the age structure of the population has much effect on paradigmatic reform decisions. They point out that both younger countries in Latin America and older countries, such as Switzerland, have launched systemic reform. They show that age-based models provide little insight into actual reform triggers and cannot explain the extent of reform, its timing, or the shift to funding. The authors also find little explanatory power in claims about the impact of institutional arrangements on pension reform. They argue that reforms have occurred equally in authoritarian and democratic countries and, among democracies, in a variety of institutional formats. Instead, Chlon and Mora emphasize the importance of ideas, particularly the spread of neoliberal ideas and the presence or absence of a reform consensus among experts and policymakers. They further emphasize the role of leadership as a key variable. The results of the authors' survey reveal a surprising lack of consensus about the positive and normative economics of pension reform. Respondents gave a wide range of definitions of what paradigmatic pension reform is, why it should be undertaken, and what effects it may have. From those responses, Chlon and Mora derive their key insight: that the primary obstacle to paradigmatic reform is lack of consensus. This means that in most countries, a long process of coalition building is required before reform can progress. In this process of coalition-building, they show that trade unions are particularly important social partners, that public opinion polls and public relations methods could be better employed in most countries, and that political leadership and the terms of ideological discourse are crucial. Chlon and Mora also present a range of challenging negative findings: that the identity of the pension reform agenda-setter is not particularly significant (whether ministry of finance or labor); that the identity of the international financial institution pushing reform does not matter much [whether the World Bank, the United States Agency for International Development, or the International Labour Organisation (ILO)]; and that domestic actors take the lead in reform. In addition to pointing up the presence or absence of policy consensus, the authors' survey emphasizes the depth of preexisting pension system crisis as an important trigger for reform.

Although the first four chapters comprehensively address the broad political economy of policy reform literature, the chapters by Tito Boeri and by Mitchell Orenstein look more specifically at the interaction between international demonstration effects and domestic policy choices. Those analyses are particularly important for global policy actors who want a stronger understanding of their impact on reform progress in developing countries.

Boeri's analysis goes beyond pension reform to encompass the broader social policy models chosen by transition countries. He presents two basic models: the Visegrad model, characterized by high social spending, greater redistribution, and a stronger emphasis on "nonemployment benefits," including social assistance, unemployment benefits, and disability benefits; and the Russian model, characterized by low spending levels, low redistribution, and a sole focus on pension spending to the near exclusion of nonemployment benefits. As a result of these different policy choices, the Visegrad countries and the Russian Federation have taken very different transition trajectories, with a much greater explosion of inequality in Russia, and very different patterns of labor market adjustment. In Russia labor market adjustment occurred primarily through wages, which fell dramatically; in the Visegrad countries, wages fell to a much lesser extent and unemployment increased.

The Baltics, Bulgaria, and Romania occupy a middle ground between those two models. Boeri emphasizes that choice of social policy models, rather than prior conditions, explains these different transition trajectories. But why were different social policy models chosen? Boeri argues that geographical proximity to the EU played a crucial role. He strongly disagrees that Russia and other countries in the Commonwealth of Independent States (CIS) desired greater inequality or did not have the means to establish systems of nonemployment benefits. Instead he shows that the CIS states' social policy crisis was caused primarily by poor tax policies in the 1990s, which allowed massive evasion and caused revenue levels to decline to approximately one-half of the levels in Central and Eastern Europe. In sum, he shows that countries with a greater chance of EU accession adopted social policy models that were more in tune with those of EU member states. So far this has helped the Visegrad countries develop better transition social policies than their CIS neighbors, but Boeri cautions against continued emulation of EU models. In countries with lower incomes, higher contribution rates, and larger gray economies, the "fatal attraction" of EU models could produce higher unemployment rates and slower growth in the years ahead. Boeri underlines the political difficulties of benefit reform, and in particular pension reform, but uses public opinion polls to show that more accurate information about the costs of current policies could help trigger paradigmatic change.

Orenstein analyzes the spread of paradigmatic pension reforms globally. Drawing on the literature concerning the diffusion of innovation, he argues that pension reforms should not be seen mainly as a result of domestic political processes, but also as a result of global patterns of ideational innovation and diffusion. Comparing the spread of paradigmatic pension reform in Latin America and in Western, Central, and Eastern Europe to the pattern of diffusion of first phase in the introduction of pension systems, he shows a number of critical similarities and differences. On average, in both waves the larger, richer, more industrial countries innovated first, and smaller, poorer countries lagged behind. Countries tended to follow the model of innovative leaders in their region, but diffusion across regions was much slower. In both waves, international organizations have played a major role, particularly in cross-regional diffusion of ideas and models. The ILO gave a major boost to pension system creation in the years after the Second World War, and the World Bank has played a leading role in diffusing paradigmatic reform in the current phase. Among the notable differences are that the first innovating country in the current phase was Chile, a middle-income country with semiperipheral status in the world economy, as opposed to Germany, the leader in the first phase. Pension system innovation is diffusing more quickly, at approximately two times the rate of first-system establishment. Cross-regional diffusion (for instance, from Latin America to Central and Eastern Europe), in particular, is occurring much faster than before and exhibiting a quicker international flow of ideas in this age of globalization. The lead international organization and content of reforms also differ. By analyzing similarities and differences between these two waves of reform, the chapter shows enduring patterns in global policy diffusion and places new developments in historical context. Orenstein puts renewed emphasis on global policy ideas and regional models as triggers of reform and suggests that the literature on political economy of policy reform has tended to overemphasize domestic triggers and not provide sufficient analysis of international trigger effects. In particular, he calls for more systematic analysis of how the internal processes of international organizations and a "global politics of attention" may affect innovation diffusion patterns.

In sum, those six chapters provide an excellent overview of the progress and process of pension reform in Europe. They elucidate patterns of reform similarity and difference in countries facing similar pressures and begin to provide a comprehensive political economy explanation of the determinants of reform. They also shed light on the role international organizations have to play in fostering change.

Notes

1. The literature consists of three main areas: First, there is literature that provides the conceptual underpinnings of the political economy of policy reform coming from political science or economics. Main references include Williamson (1994) and Rodrik (1996) for policy reforms in general, and Pierson (1994, 1996) for pension reform in particular. Second, there is literature that provides insights into policy reform through cross-regional comparison; for example, the reform processes in Latin America and Central and Eastern Europe. Main references in this area include Gillion and others (2000), James and Brooks (2001), and Müller (2000, 2001, 2002, and her chapter in this volume). Finally, there are country case studies of pension reform that try to distill lessons or apply a conceptual framework to countries for verification. Examples of the latter include Madrid (1999), Mesa-Lago (1998), and Piñera (1991) on Latin America; Müller (1999), Nelson (2001), Orenstein (2000), and Orenstein and Haas (2000) on Central and Eastern Europe; and Bonoli (2000), Hinrichs (2001), and Reynaud (2000) on Western Europe. Additional literature is provided in the chapters of this volume.

2. Using the data from the latest report by the Council of the European Union (2002), "Social Protection in Europe 2001," the public expenditure for the elderly, survivors, and disabled people (with the latter including compensation for workers' accidents) for the EU15 in 1999 amounted to 14.5 percent of GDP (of which, at maximum, 2 percentage points can be attributed to workers' accidents).

3. The revised papers can be downloaded from the World Bank's pension Website—conferences: www.worldbank.org/pensions.

4. Correlation coefficients for long time series of wage growth and equity returns were not found to be significantly different than zero in Germany, Japan, the Netherlands, the United Kingdom, and the United States (Holzmann 2000).

5. This argument was used effectively in the Polish reform effort under the label "Security through Diversity." See Office of the Plenipotentiary (1997), Góra and Rutkowski (1998), and Chlon, Góra, and Rutkowski (1999).

6. Commission of the European Communities (2000).

References

Bonoli, Giuliano. 2000. *The Politics of Pension Reform: Institutions and Policy Change in Western Europe.* Cambridge, U.K.: Cambridge University Press.

Chlon, A., M. Góra, and M. Rutkowski. 1999. "Shaping Pension Reform in Poland: Security through Diversity." Social Protection Discussion Paper 9923 (August). World Bank, Washington, D.C.

Commission of the European Communities. 2000. "Communication from the Commission to the Council, to the European Parliament and to the Economic and Social Committee." COM(2000) 622 final (20 November 2000). Brussels: European Union.

Council of the European Union. 2001. "Joint Report of the Social Protection Committee and the Economic Policy Committee on Objectives and Working Methods on the Area of Pensions: Applying the Open Method of Coordination." 14098/01/SOC469/ECOFIN334 (23 November 2001). Brussels: European Union.

———. 2002. "Social Protection in Europe 2001." 8882/02/SOC251 (16 May 2002). Brussels: European Union.

EPC (Economic Policy Committee). 2001. "Budgetary Challenges Posed by Ageing Populations: The Impact of Public Spending on Pensions, Health and Long-Term Care for the Elderly and Possible Indicators of Long-Term Financial Sustainability of Public Finances." EPC/ECFIN/655/01-EN final (24 October 2001). Brussels: European Union.

———. 2002. "Opinion on the Reform of European Pension Systems (addressed to the Ecofon Council and the Commission)." EPC/ECFIN/275-02 final (5 July 2002). Brussels: European Union.

Gillion, Colin, John Turner, Clive Bailey, and Denis Latulippe, eds. 2000. *Social Security Pensions: Development and Reform.* Geneva: International Labour Office.

Góra, M., and M. Rutkowski. 1998. "The Quest for Pension Reform: Poland's Security through Diversity." Social Protection Discussion Paper 9815 (October). World Bank, Washington, D.C.

Haas, Peter M. 1992. "Introduction: Epistemic Communities and International Policy Coordination." *International Organization* 46(1):1–35.

Hinrichs, Karl. 2001. "Ageing and Public Pension Reforms in Western Europe and North America: Patterns and Politics." In Jochen Clasen, ed., *What Future for Social Security? Debates and Reforms in National and Cross-National Perspective.* The Hague: Kluwer Law International.

Holzmann, R. 2000. "The World Bank Approach to Pension Reform." *International Social Security Review* 53(1):11–34.

Holzmann, R., Y. Hervé, and R. Demmel. 1996. "The Maastricht Fiscal Criteria: Required but Ineffective?" *Empirica* 23(1):25–58.

James, Estelle, and Sarah Brooks. 2001. "The Political Economy of Structural Pension Reform." In R. Holzmann and J. Stiglitz, eds., *New Ideas about Old-Age Security: Toward Sustainable Pension Systems in the 21st Century.* Washington, D.C.: World Bank.

Madrid, Raúl. 1999. "The New Logic of Social Security Reform: Politics and Pension Privatization in Latin America." Ph.D. dissertation, Stanford University, Stanford, Ca.

Mesa-Lago, Carmelo. 1998. "The Reform of Social Security Pensions in Latin America: Public, Private, Mixed and Parallel Systems." In Franz Ruland, ed., *Verfassung, Theorie und Praxis des Sozialstaats: Festschrift für Hans F. Zacher zum 70. Geburtstag.* Heidelberg, Germany: Müller, pp. 609–33.

Müller, Katharina. 1999. *The Political Economy of Pension Reform in Central-Eastern Europe.* Cheltenham, U.K.: Edward Elgar.

———. 2000. "Pension Privatization in Latin America." *Journal of International Development* 12:507–18.

———. 2001. "Conquistando el Este—Los Modelos Previsionales Latinoamericanos en los Países ex Socialistas." *Revista Latinoamericana de Políticas Sociales*(March):39–52.

———. 2002. "The Political Economy of Pension Reform in Central and Eastern Europe." Paper presented at the conference on "Practical Lessons in Pension Reform: Sharing the Experiences of Transition and OECD Countries," jointly organized by the OECD, the Ministry of Labour and Social Policy of Poland, and the Ministry of Foreign Affairs of the Netherlands, Warsaw, May 27–28.

Nelson, Joan M. 2001. "The Politics of Pension and Health-Care Reforms in Hungary and Poland." In János Kornai, Stephan Haggard, and Robert R. Kaufman, eds., *Reforming the State: Fiscal and Welfare Reform in Post-Socialist Countries.* Cambridge, U.K.: Cambridge University Press, pp. 235–66.

OECD (Organisation for Economic Co-operation and Development). 2002. "Fiscal Implications of Ageing: Projections of Age-Related Spending." Economics Department Working Paper 305. Paris.

Office of the Government Plenipotentiary for Social Security Reform. 1997. *Security through Diversity—Reform of the Pension System in Poland.* June. Warsaw.

Orenstein, M. 2000. "How Politics and Institutions Affect Pension Reform in Three Postcommunist Countries." Policy Research Working Paper 2310. World Bank, Washington, D.C.

Orenstein, M., and M. Haas. 2000. "The Global Politics of Attention and Social Policy Transformation in East-Central Europe." Paper presented at the American Association for the Advancement of Slavic Studies Annual Conference, Denver, November 9–12.

Pierson, Paul. 1994. *Dismantling the Welfare State? Reagan, Thatcher, and the Politics of Retrenchment.* Cambridge, U.K.: Cambridge University Press.

———. 1996. "The New Politics of the Welfare State." *World Politics* 48(January): 143–79.

Piñera, José. 1991. *El Cascabel al Gato. La Batalla por la Reforma Previsional.* Santiago de Chile: Zig-Zag.

Reynaud, Emmanuel, ed. 2000. *Social Dialogue and Pension Reform.* Geneva: ILO.

Rodrik, D. 1996. "Understanding Economic Policy Reform." *Journal of Economic Literature* 34(March):9–41.

SPC (Social Protection Committee). 2002. "National Strategy Reports on the Future of Pension Systems—Outline Guide from the Commission for the Structuring and Analysis of National Reports" (March). Brussels: European Union.

United Nations. 1998. "World Population Prospects: The 1998 Revision." New York.

Williamson, John, ed. 1994. *The Political Economy of Policy Reform.* Washington, D.C.: Institute for International Economics.

Annex

Pension Systems and Reforms in Europe: Where Are the Countries Standing?

	What are the demographic and retirement trends?	*Do pensions provide a reasonable standard of living?*	*Is pension coverage adequate?*	*Is the system affordable and sustainable?*	*What direction is reform taking?*
Austria	Even by European standards, Austria is a rapidly aging society. The old-age dependency ratio is projected to double over the next 30 years. The statutory retirement age is 65 for males and 60 for females.	The ratio of the average pension to the average net wage is approximately 70 percent.	The state PAYG pension system covers all persons who are economically active. Voluntary funded occupation schemes are available but are taken advantage of by only about 11 percent of the working population.	Under the broadest scheme, applicable to those in wage employment, the payroll contribution tax of 18.5 percent is evenly split between employer and employee, in addition to which, there is a supplemental contribution of approximately 4 percent, making for a total payroll tax rate of nearly 23 percent. Budget transfers on the order of 5 percent of GDP are required annually to balance the system.	Austria has not succeeded in reforming its pension system apart from minor parametric adjustments. Efforts to adjust the two main levers of control—the statutory retirement age and the benefit calculation formula—have been vetoed by one or another partner in Austria's highly consensual political culture. The fragmentation of the system, with different schemes covering employees, farmers, self-employed people, civil servants, and so forth, also has contributed to political gridlock.

Bulgaria	With a ratio of pensioners to working-age population close to 50 percent, Bulgaria has one of the most unfavorable demographic profiles in Europe. Reasons for this include adverse demographic trends, unemployment, and mass emigration. The effective retirement age is 63 for men and 60 for women.	Sociological evidence indicates that pensioners feel they are the most neglected segment of society. 16 percent of pensioners receive income- and assets-tested social assistance, such as winter heating subsidies. In 2001 the average pension was 34 percent of the average wage and the minimum pension (received by one-fifth of pensioners) was 16 percent. When account is taken of the fact that pensions are not taxed, the average pension is equal to 48 percent the average net wage.	About 80 percent of formal sector employees contribute to the social insurance system, as do about 50 percent of self-employed people. However, the informal sector amounts to 20–25 percent of GDP. Less than one-tenth of the population engaged in agriculture participates in the system.	Prior to reform, calculations showed a choice between increasing the payroll contribution tax to 60 percent or reducing the replacement rate to 20 percent. The reform has put the system on a sustainable basis. However, contribution rates (26.3 percent employer and 6.4 percent employee) for the first pillar remain high. Pensions amount to about 9 percent of GDP, projected to decrease to 6–7 percent by 2010. These ratios are not high by European standards. Evasion is rife: the private sector accounts for 60 percent of economic activity but only 10 percent of social security revenues.	In 1999 Bulgaria became the third transition economy to institute a three-pillar reform. This reform was precipitated by more than a 60 percent erosion in the real value of pensions during the preceding decade. The preceding system, with a complicated series of cross-subsidies and top-ups for favored workers, was widely perceived to be inequitable.

Annex, *continued*

	What are the demographic and retirement trends?	*Do pensions provide a reasonable standard of living?*	*Is pension coverage adequate?*	*Is the system affordable and sustainable?*	*What direction is reform taking?*
Croatia	The standard retirement age is being raised gradually by five years, from 60 to 65 for men and 55 to 60 for women, as part of the reform. Nonetheless, the effective retirement age in Croatia remains below the European average. The ratio of PAYG pension system contributors to beneficiaries declined from 1.6 around the year 1990 to 1.4 around 2000.	The ratio of the average pension to the average net wage is now approximately 40 percent, down from 58 percent in the early 1990s. It is estimated that about half of all pensioners over 60 receive a pension below the poverty line.	Coverage expanded rapidly in the 1990s. Close to 100 percent of the population over 60 receives pension benefits.	Pension expenditure grew rapidly during the 1990s, rising from 7 percent of GDP in 1994 to 13 percent of GDP in 1999. This was caused by the decline in the average employment rate and an increase in the ratio of the average pension to GDP per capita. Simulations of the reformed pension system suggest that pension expenditures will gradually decrease. The payroll contribution tax is approximately 19 percent, of which 14 percent goes to the state PAYG pension system and 5 percent goes to a fully funded pension system chosen by the worker. Health and other social welfare programs add another 20 percent to the payroll tax. Evasion is common and the pension system requires subsidies of up to 4 percent of GDP.	A three-pillar reform was initiated in 1998, although the second mandatory, fully funded, defined-contribution pillar took some time to get off the ground. The main difficulty is in financing the continued payment of pensions under the old system. Currently, transfers amounting to 4 percent of GDP must be made from general revenue keep the pension system afloat.

| Czech Republic | The ratio of pension system beneficiaries to contributors is expected to increase from its current level of 0.53 to a peak of 0.68 in 2020. Pensionable age is currently 60 for males and 53–57 for females; legislation has been passed to raise this to 62 for men and 57–61 for women. | The current replacement rate is approximately 45 percent. Only 2–3 percent of pensioners receive the minimum pension. | The basic first-pillar state pension system covers essentially the entire working population, 40 percent also participate in the second funded pillar. | The current payroll tax is 26 percent and pension expenditure represents 9.2 percent of GDP. Based on reasonable economic assumptions, the current system is unsustainable, with contribution rates projected to rise to 60 percent by mid-century and the pension system deficit to more than 10 percent of GDP. Even given substantial increases in the (relatively low) retirement age, the projected contribution rate would still exceed 40 percent. | The focus of pensions policy in the 1990s was on eliminating preferential treatments and inequities. Tax incentives encourage households to save in a voluntary second pillar, which has proven extremely popular. The key question facing policymakers is how to reform the first pillar in order to cope with adverse demographic trends. |

Annex, *continued*

	What are the demographic and retirement trends?	*Do pensions provide a reasonable standard of living?*	*Is pension coverage adequate?*	*Is the system affordable and sustainable?*	*What direction is reform taking?*
Denmark	The dependency rate (65+/15–64), currently 22 percent, is projected to rise to 35 percent by 2050. The effective retirement age is 62 for males and 60 for females.	Basic social assistance for the elderly is generous and the elderly poverty rate is extremely low. The first pillar of pension provision (the People's Pension) provides a low-wage employee with a 70 percent replacement rate and a high-wage worker with a 42 percent replacement rate. The People's Pension contains a basic minimum pension and various means-tested supplements.	Coverage of the basic People's Pension is 100 percent. About 75 percent of pensioners also receive income from the obligatory supplementary public labor-market scheme, and expansion of this system implies that eventually its coverage also will approach 100 percent. Defined-contribution occupational pension schemes now cover about 80 percent of workers. About 10 percent of pensioners also receive income from voluntary saving schemes.	Public pensions expenditure amounted to about 8 percent of GDP in 1995. An increase of about 2 percentage points is expected between now and 2035.	The centerpiece of the pension system continues to be the universal People's Pension financed out of general tax revenue. The general direction of reform, however, is to use the People's Pension to secure a basic income and rely on other pillars—supplementary labor pensions and private schemes—to secure income in excess of the minimum.

Estonia					
The old-age dependency ratio, 24 percent, is on a par with the ratio in the EU. (27 percent). Because of extremely low fertility rates observed during transition, however, the dependency ratio will increase rapidly. The current retirement age is 63 for men and 58 for women, with women's age scheduled to rise to 63 by 2016.	The national (minimum) pension, received by 15 percent of pensioners, is about 20 percent of the average monthly wage and is situated well below the estimated poverty line. Approximately 12 percent of pensioner households live below the poverty line, compared with about 18 percent of all households; however, pensioner households are more likely to live on the edge of poverty. The ratio of the average old-age pension to the average wage is about 40 percent.	Virtually all elderly people receive pensions—the national minimum pension for those who were not economically active.	The ratio of pensions to GDP is approximately 9 percent. The payroll tax, which finances all state pensions, including the national minimum pension, is 20 percent. Health, unemployment, and so forth, raise the total payroll tax to 33 percent.	Estonia is moving toward a three-pillar system, but the compulsory funded second pillar is only now being introduced. Reform of the first PAYG pillar, introduced in 1997, included equalizing male and female pensionable ages and implementing a standard basis for pension calculation, including reductions for early retirement.

Annex, *continued*

	What are the demographic and retirement trends?	*Do pensions provide a reasonable standard of living?*	*Is pension coverage adequate?*	*Is the system affordable and sustainable?*	*What direction is reform taking?*
Finland	The Finnish old-age dependency ratio is 25 percent, roughly on par with the EU average (27 percent). The standard age is equal for men and women at 60, but the effective retirement age in 1997 was 57 for males and 58 for females.	Old-age poverty is rare in Finland, as is poverty at all ages. The income of pensioner households averages 85 percent of the income of nonpensioner households. In 2000, only 3.7 percent of persons over 65 considered themselves poor (as opposed to 6 percent of the total population). The ratio of average net pension income to average net income is 56.6 percent (1999 data). For low-income persons the replacement rate from the combined national pension and earnings related pension exceeds 100 percent.	A national pension, financed by a combination of employer contributions and general revenue, is available to all residents. Among people over 65, 12.9 percent receive only a national pension. More than three-quarters receive a state earnings-related pension as well.	The national pension is financed by employer contributions and general taxation. The contribution rate for the main earnings-related public pension scheme is 21.8 percent, of which 4.7 percent represents the employee's contribution. The scheme is partially funded, with some elements being earmarked as PAYG financed (index adjustments, for example) and other parts being subject to explicit funding rules (disability pensions, for example). Pension assets currently amount to about 55 percent of GDP. Total pension spending in 1997 was 12.6 percent of GDP. Projections indicate that pension spending could rise to 16 percent of GDP by 2050, and the contribution rate could rise to 32 percent.	Finland used pension policy to encourage early retirement during the 1990s' economic crisis. Simulations suggest that the most effective way to slow increase in contribution rates is to raise average retirement age by two to three years in the long run. A number of parametric changes were introduced in the 1990s—increase in pensionable age, reduction in the accrual rate, lengthening of the reference period, and change in indexation rules.

| France | The old-age dependency ratio (65+/15–64) is currently approximately 20 percent and projected to rise to 50 percent by 2040. The statutory retirement age (60) is among the lowest in Europe and, according to survey results, only one-quarter of the population currently aged 45–55 wishes to work past 60. Less than one-third of men aged 55–64 are in the workforce. | France has one of the most generous pension systems in the European Union. Replacement rates range from 60 percent for high-wage workers to almost 100 percent for low wage workers. | The minimum flat-rate pension is available to all people over 65. Only 5 percent of pensioners receive the minimum flat-rate pension, which is about half the average manufacturing wage. The remainder receive benefits from the basic public schemes, from mandatory occupational supplemental schemes, and from voluntary employer-based schemes. | Pensions currently amount to about 12 percent of GDP and are projected to rise to 20 percent by 2050 in the absence of changes in the system. Current payroll contribution rates, about 20 percent, would rise to approximately 30–40 percent. A notable feature of the French system is that it is extremely complicated: there are 120 basic pension schemes and about 400 mandatory occupational schemes, all financed on a PAYG basis. | Partly because of the complicated nature of the French system, reform has been slow in coming. There is no political or social consensus on the direction reform should take. The only concrete steps taken in recent years are the establishment of a pension reserve fund and the passage of laws to facilitate voluntary private retirement saving. Resistance to lengthening the minimum contributory period is especially strong. |

Annex, *continued*

	What are the demographic and retirement trends?	Do pensions provide a reasonable standard of living?	Is pension coverage adequate?	Is the system affordable and sustainable?	What direction is reform taking?
Germany	Germany has one of the most rapidly aging European populations. The pensionable age, previously 60 for women and 65 for men, gradually is being raised to 65 for both men and women.	The current replacement rate for an "average" pensioner is approximately 72 percent.	The state PAYG pension scheme is effectively universal, and accounts for 80 percent of all pensions paid. Supplementary occupational pensions offered by employers cover about 43 percent of employees, and there is a significant third-pillar consisting of voluntary private savings.	The payroll tax to finance the PAYG state pension system is currently 19 percent. This covers 80 percent of system expenditures, and the remainder is covered by a range of state transfers and subsidies. If the current structures are extrapolated, the necessary payroll tax will be 30 percent by 2030.	Current reform efforts seek to limit increases in contribution rates by gradually reducing the replacement rate in the state pension system from 72 percent to 64 percent. In compensation, tax benefits will be offered for occupational and voluntary private pension schemes.

Greece				
The old-age dependency ratio in Greece, currently about 28 percent and expected to rise to about 50 percent by 2050, broadly tracks the EU average. Different sectors are characterized by different retirement ages, but the unifying theme is early exit from the workforce. Under the main private sector scheme, 80 percent of retirees qualify for some form of early retirement and the situation is even more extreme with respect to public sector pensions.	Public pensions are generous in Greece. In the salaried employees' private sector scheme, the minimum pension is 71 percent of minimum pay; 84 percent if the income supplement available to recipients of the minimum pension is taken into account. Pensions have grown faster than inflation since 1994 and there have been large increases in farmers' pensions since 1997. Over half of pensioners have nonpension income.	Although coverage is compulsory and covers all sectors of production, there are still problems with coverage of women with broken career histories. In addition, evasion is widespread because of poor linkage between contributions and benefits. Occupational private pension schemes do not play a significant role.	State pensions amount to about 12 percent of GDP, one of the highest ratios in the EU. Projections by the OECD show total expenditure reaching nearly 25 percent of GDP by 2035. In the main scheme covering the private sector, the payroll tax is 26 percent; 44 percent if nonpension social contributions are taken into account.	Since Greece's entry into the European Monetary Union in January 2001, pension reform has been singled out as the most important structural reform. Problems include the fragmentary nature of the system (different schemes by sector of employment, by tier of income replacement, and so forth), the inequities and administrative inefficiencies to which this fragmentation gives rise, and the need to develop further the role of the private sector.

Annex, *continued*

	What are the demographic and retirement trends?	*Do pensions provide a reasonable standard of living?*	*Is pension coverage adequate?*	*Is the system affordable and sustainable?*	*What direction is reform taking?*
Hungary	The normal retirement age is 62 for males and will gradually rise to 62 for females by 2009. The old-age dependency ratio, currently about 35 percent, is projected to reach 50 percent by the middle of the century. Nonetheless, Hungary is a relatively slow-aging country in the European context. Over half of new pensions are disability pensions.	Between 1990 and 1995 the ratio of average pension benefits to the average net wage declined from 66 percent to 61 percent. As the old first pillar is phased out, this ratio will drop further to 45 percent. There will be compensating increases, however, in the form of annuities paid from the second pillar. A means-tested elderly social benefit is available to people over 62 whose incomes are less than 50 percent of the average pension.	Pension coverage is essentially universal. About 31 percent of the Hungarian population receives some form of pension benefit.	Pensions account for about 10 percent of GDP; the deficit in the first-pillar PAYG system is approximately 1.5 percent of GDP. The combined employer–employee contribution rate is about 30 percent; for those who are members of the new, reformed system, 6 percent (8 percent by 2003) of this goes into the fully funded second pillar. Evasion of social security taxes is widespread.	Hungary, the first three-pillar reformer in Eastern Europe, embarked on pension reform in 1998. The main motivation was fiscal: between 1990 and 1995 the system dependency ratio rose from 46 percent to 76 percent because of a decline in employment and an explosion of early retirement. The reform has been enthusiastically welcomed, in fact, one of the problems is "overswitching," that is, people who would be better off remaining in the old system are switching into the new one and thereby weakening the surviving first pillar.

| Italy | The legal retirement age is flexible between a range of 57 and 65. The effective retirement age is 58 for males and 56 for women. | The average replacement rate is about 70 percent, but however, the situation is complicated because, for many pensioners, this reflects more than one pension. | A means-tested social allowance is available to people over 65. Although old-age poverty has declined over the last 30 years, a significant proportion of elderly households still live in poverty. | Pension expenditures as a share of GDP, currently about 14 percent, are projected to rise to about 15–16 percent by 2030 and decline thereafter. The current payroll contribution rate is 32.7 percent for salaried employees, of which 23.8 percent represents the employer's contribution. | The Italian pension system has undergone substantial changes since the 1990s. The 1992 ("Amato") reform reduced preferential treatment of civil servants. The 1995 ("Dini") reform tightened the link between contributions and benefits by introducing a nominal defined-contribution approach. A source of complication is, however, the very long transition period, meaning that there are three major pension regimes in operation in Italy at this time. |

Annex, *continued*

	What are the demographic and retirement trends?	*Do pensions provide a reasonable standard of living?*	*Is pension coverage adequate?*	*Is the system affordable and sustainable?*	*What direction is reform taking?*
Ireland	Ireland is distinctive in that its elderly dependency ratio is low (about 17–18 percent) and is not projected to rise significantly. Also notable is a strong increase in female labor force participation.	The ratio of the average first-pillar benefit to the average gross wage is about 33 percent.	The first pillar is essentially universal. The second pillar, however, covers only about half of all people at work (52 percent of employees, 27 percent of self-employed people).	The rate for the contributory element of the first pillar is approximately 16 percent (4 percent employee, 12 percent employer). Second-pillar contribution rates average about 10 percent of wages. Pension expenditure is less than 6 percent of GDP, a very low level for Europe.	The Irish pension system consists essentially of two pillars. The first pillar is a mandatory PAYG-financed social pension designed to ensure a minimum income. It is split into a universal basic pension (means-tested and financed out of general revenue) and a contributory scheme. The second pillar consists of voluntary occupational pension schemes. Traditionally, these were DB; new schemes, however, are almost all DC. The overall direction of pensions policy is to increase the share of the work force participating in supplemental schemes to 70 percent.

Latvia	During transition, the number of pensioners increased dramatically while the number of contributors was cut in half. The current standard pensionable age is 62 for both men and women.	The minimum pension is 51 percent of the average old-age pension and 21 percent of the average wage; people retiring before pensionable age may receive 80 percent of the minimum pension. About 5 percent of pensioners receive the minimum pension.	Close to three-quarters of the work force is covered by social insurance.	Pension expenditure, currently about 9 percent of GDP, is projected to decline to about 6 percent of GDP by 2050 because of the introduction of the nominal DC system. Without reform, the share of GDP devoted to public pension spending was expected to rise to about 16 percent. The current contribution rate is 27.5 percent, of which 2 (rising gradually to 10) percentage points are devoted to financing the new fully funded second pillar and 7.5 percent goes to financing the debt of the old pension system.	In the mid-1990s, a three-pillar system was constituted to replace the rapidly weakening Soviet-era single PAYG scheme. The second and third pillars are conventional but the first pillar is a notional DC scheme.

Annex, *continued*

	What are the demographic and retirement trends?	*Do pensions provide a reasonable standard of living?*	*Is pension coverage adequate?*	*Is the system affordable and sustainable?*	*What direction is reform taking?*
Lithuania	The nominal retirement age, formerly 55 for women and 60 for men, is being gradually raised to 60 for women and 62.5 for men. Because pensions are low, about one in six pensioners continues to hold a job. The system dependency ratio (beneficiaries to contributors) has been declining continuously despite increases in the retirement age. The main cause is not demography but declining employment.	After 30 years of contribution, an elderly person is entitled to a basic flat pension set at 110 percent of the minimum standard of living plus a supplemental earnings-related pension. The average pension is about 40 percent of the average net wage, perhaps the lowest in Eastern and Central Europe. Twenty-two percent of pensioner households are estimated to live in poverty, as opposed to 16 percent of all households.	About two-thirds of the working-age population participates in the state pension scheme. Less than one-third of farmers are covered. Coverage has been declining. Evasion is common and it is estimated that only 85 percent of contributions due are actually collected.	Pension payments amount to 78 percent of GDP and the payroll tax to finance the PAYG state pension system is 25 percent (22.5 percent employer and 2.5 percent employee). Because of recent increases in the payroll tax rate, the system is expected to run a small surplus until 2010, after which deficits are expected to reemerge unless contribution rates are increased again.	Introduction of a mandatory funded pillar is planned for the beginning of 2003, with 5 percent of the state pension contribution earmarked for a fully funded second pillar. Supplemental private pension funds (that is, third-pillar funds) were legalized in 2000 but their development has been slow.

| Luxembourg | The normal pensionable age is 65 and the pension must be taken at 68. | The current replacement rate is approximately 65 percent. | All gainfully employed people are covered by the public pension system, with a special scheme for civil servants. | The payroll tax for the basic state pension is 24 percent, split in thirds among the employer, the employee, and the state. Workers can also opt for a supplementary public pension involving a 16 percent personal contribution matched by an 8 percent state contribution. |

Annex, *continued*

	What are the demographic and retirement trends?	Do pensions provide a reasonable standard of living?	Is pension coverage adequate?	Is the system affordable and sustainable?	What direction is reform taking?
Poland		Under the old system, the ratio of average pension income to the net wage was 70 percent; under the new system, the estimated long-run replacement rate (pension over last income) for people retiring at 65 is 62 percent. Survey data reveal no substantial difference between the living standards of the working age population and the elderly. However, there is a great deal of anecdotal evidence of elderly people living in poverty. It is estimated that in 2035, 17 percent of the elderly population will be receiving the minimum pension.	The entire gainfully employed population is covered by the new system. However, a separate scheme has been maintained for farmers.	The old-age pension contribution rate is 19.5 percent, of which 12 percent goes toward financing the nominal DC (NDC) first pillar and 7 percent goes towards financing the fully-funded second pillar. Projections indicate that it will be possible to maintain the 19.5 percent old-age contribution rate. However, other contributions, which raise the total payroll tax to about 36 percent, may rise over time. The pension system deficit caused by prefunding the second pillar is covered by transfers from government amounting to about 5 percent of GDP.	The "Security through Diversity" three-pillar reform initiated in 1999 bears a marked similarity to the Swedish reform. The first pillar is a public PAYG-financed NDC system; the second pillar is a mandatory fully funded pension scheme in which individual accounts are managed by the private sector.

| Portugal | The old-age dependency, currently 22.5 percent, is projected to double by 2050. Given likely trends in labor force participation and unemployment, it is expected that the number of retirees will grow at about 1.4 percent per annum, a period over which total population is projected to remain virtually constant. Compared with other European countries, Portugal is characterized by relatively high elderly labor force participation rates (25 percent versus about 5 percent for the rest of the EU). | The ratio of average old-age pension to average after-tax salary is 43.5 percent A means-tested minimum pension is available to people whose monthly income is less than 40 percent of the minimum wage. | Separate public pension schemes cover wage employees, self-employed people, and farmers. | The total payroll tax, covering the entire range of social insurance, is 34.75 percent of wages, 11 percentage points of which are paid by the employer. Even under favorable macroeconomic assumptions, the pension system is projected to experience serious imbalances after about 2015. Total social insurance spending (pensions, family allowances, and unemployment) are presently ca 7 percent of GDP and are projected to rise to close to 9 percent by mid-century. | Apart from parametric reforms designed to strengthen system finances, dating from 2000, there has been no step toward comprehensive structural pension reform in Portugal. |

Annex, *continued*

	What are the demographic and retirement trends?	*Do pensions provide a reasonable standard of living?*	*Is pension coverage adequate?*	*Is the system affordable and sustainable?*	*What direction is reform taking?*
Romania	The proportion of the total population aged over 65 is currently 13 percent and is projected to rise to 25 percent by 2050. Romania is characterized by a very large, low-productivity agricultural sector, with a correspondingly elevated share of the population living in rural areas. The average age of retirement is 56 for men and 51 for women.	The replacement rate under the old single-pillar PAYG pension system varied between 54 percent and 85 percent. During the 1990s, however, the real value of pensions declined, mostly as a result of incomplete indexation. For an average pensioner with a full contribution record, the decline was from 64 percent of the average net wage in 1990 to 48 percent in 1998. Old-age poverty is widespread, and more than one-third of pensioners' income consists of home production.	The pre-reform single-pillar pension scheme failed to cover farmers and the nonagricultural self-employed population. Coverage nonetheless expanded dramatically during the 1990s because of shorter qualifying periods and the increase in the number of people qualifying for special privileges (hazardous occupations, and so forth) The ratio of pension beneficiaries to population aged 15–60 rose from 17 percent to 28 percent between 1990 and 1998.	Due to reductions in the contribution base associated with unemployment and evasion (about 35 percent), payroll contribution rates are extremely high. Employers contribute 32.5 percent for pensions and individuals contribute 5 percent for a mandatory supplementary pension scheme. By 2050, in the absence of reform, the total pension contribution rate would have to rise from 37.5 percent to 60 percent. Information management is at a very low level, with handwritten pension passbooks still the main means of tracking contributions.	In 2001, a three-pillar pension reform was implemented. This aims, first, to restrict entitlement by raising the pensionable age, increasing the qualifying period, and instituting rewards for deferred retirement. Coverage is to be extended to all people, including farmers. The mandatory second pillar, financed by a 10 percent payroll tax, is to be run along Chilean lines. The total contribution rate (first and second pillars combined) is not to exceed 37.5 percent.

| Slovakia | The old-age dependency ratio, currently approximately 29 percent, is projected to increase to 62 percent by 2040. Because of informalization, unemployment, delayed entry into the labor force, and disability pensions, less than half the working-age population contributes to the system. The ratio of contributors to beneficiaries, currently 1.4, is projected to decline to only 0.7–0.8. | The current ratio of average pension to average wage is about 41–42 percent. | Coverage is comparable to that in EU countries. | The current payroll contribution rate of 28 percent is insufficient to cover the costs of the system, which requires a transfer from general revenue on the order of 4–6 percent of GDP. Without structural reforms or contribution rate increases, the ratio of average pension to average wage would decline to 18–19 percent by 2040. | The main directions of reform are to strengthen the links between contributions and benefits and to achieve a benefit equal to 50 percent of the average wage while maintaining the current contribution rate. Measures to date are insufficient to achieve this. |

Annex, *continued*

	What are the demographic and retirement trends?	*Do pensions provide a reasonable standard of living?*	*Is pension coverage adequate?*	*Is the system affordable and sustainable?*	*What direction is reform taking?*
Slovenia	Slovenia's demographic indicators bear a marked resemblance to those of Italy, one of the most rapidly aging EU countries. Total population is projected to decline between 2000 and 2050 and population over 65 is projected to increase from 14 to 32 percent of the total. The current ratio of pensioners to contributors is 1.7, down from 2.5 in 189. The effective retirement age is 58 for men and 55 for women.	The replacement rate is roughly 75 percent of net wages. During the 1990s the relative welfare of pensioners increased because of mass unemployment.	Coverage is comparable to that in EU countries.	The pension payroll contribution rate is just under 25 percent (16 percent employee and 9 percent employer), but social contributions as a whole amount to 38 percent of wages—22 percent employee and 16 percent employer. Prior to the 1999 reform, it was projected that pensions might rise from 14 to 27 percent of GDP by the middle of the century. In the late 1990s, close to 4 percent of GDP had to be transferred out of general revenue to balance the pension system.	In 1992 Slovenia instituted a reform that placed its PAYG pension system more or less on the same footing as Western European systems. In 1999, an attempt to introduce a multipillar system failed to win passage and, instead, the existing PAYG single-pillar system was strengthened through parametric reforms. Among these were lengthening the reference period, reducing the accrual rate, and modifying indexation procedures. The legal bases for second and third pillars have been introduced but little has changed.

| Spain | With fertility rates among the lowest in the world (total fertility rate [TFR] 1.2), Spain faces an especially challenging demographic future. Even given gradual increase in the TFR, it is still expected that Spain's old-age dependency ratio will increase from 27.1 percent in 2000 to 65.7 percent by 2050 (compared with an EU average of 50.8 percent). The aggregate employment rate in Spain is also significantly lower (about 9 percent) than in other EU countries. | The average replacement rate in 1998 was 65 percent, relatively high compared with other EU countries. Regional governments are responsible for administering a non-contributory means-tested minimum pension. | Separate mandatory schemes cover employees, self-employed people, farmers, and public employees. About 225,000 elderly people do not qualify for any pension and receive only the minimum pension. | Currently 9–10 percent of GDP public pension spending might reach 15–20 percent by mid-century as a result of adverse demographics. This would place Spain at the top relative to GDP share of EU. The payroll contribution rate is 28 percent, of which employees contribute less than 5 percentage points. | A number of parametric changes were made in 1997 to shore up the rapidly weakening pension system. However, the Spanish pension system remains a single-pillar PAYG system. |

Annex, *continued*

	What are the demographic and retirement trends?	*Do pensions provide a reasonable standard of living?*	*Is pension coverage adequate?*	*Is the system affordable and sustainable?*	*What direction is reform taking?*
Sweden	The ratio of old-age pensioners to workers is projected to increase from 30 percent at present to over 40 percent by 2025. The official retirement age is 65 for both men and women and the effective retirement age is roughly the same.	The basic pension plus the state supplementary (earnings-related) scheme replace about 65 percent of a person's income up to a ceiling. Cash pension supplements and housing allowances are available to people with no or very low supplementary pensions.	Virtually the entire population over 65 receives some form of state pension benefit. Ninety percent of full-time employees participate in occupational and private individual pension plans that supplement the state pension.	Having peaked at 21 percent in 1993, the share of social insurance expenditure in GDP has declined to about 17 percent, approximately half of which represents old-age and survivor's pensions. The impetus for reform came from projections showing that the payroll contribution rate necessary to balance the unreformed system would rise from about 15 percent (late 1990s) to over 20 percent by 2015 and even higher thereafter. By contrast, the contribution rate to the reformed system is expected to remain in the 15–20 percent range.	Sweden was a leading European pension reformer. Starting in 1994, a fully funded pillar was instituted using 2 percent (subsequently revised to 2.5 percent) of the total payroll tax (currently 18.5 percent). In 1999 benefit calculation in the first pillar was shifted to a notional DC basis and the first benefits so calculated were paid out in 2001.

| United Kingdom | The current pensionable age is 65 for men and 60 for women; legislation is in the works to equalize at 65. Although Great Britain faces an aging society like the countries of continental Europe, the extent of aging is expected to be milder. | State pensions are meagre—the maximum basic state pension (flat-rate) was 16 percent of the average wage in 1998. The combined replacement rate from the flat-rate first tier and the earnings-related second tier, currently 35–40 percent, will decline if steps are not taken. Many pensioners depend on means-tested benefits. The Minimum Income Guarantee, a noncontributory means-tested benefit, stands at about £90 per week for an aged person living alone. The ratio of elderly to nonelderly average net income is 78 percent in Britain, compared with 94 percent in the EU. | Historically, low and moderate earners and those with an irregular work history have been inadequately covered. Introduction of "stakeholder pensions," low-cost transferable products that must be offered by every employer of more than five people, is designed to address this problem. | The state pension contribution rate is a modest 10 percent and public pension expenditure is only 4 percent of GDP. The main sustainability issues in Britain have to do with the well-being of the elderly population and growing inequality among pensioners, not with the affordability of the pension system. | Britain has opted for a minimal PAYG first-pillar public pension, placing emphasis on fully funded second- and third-pillar schemes and, for the poor, on means-tested benefits. The public–private pensions mix is currently about 60–40, and the government policy is to shift this to 40–60 by mid-century. Policy concern focuses on poorer pensioners and on meeting the needs of moderate earners. Regulation of the private pension industry is under constant review as new issues arise. |

Note: This information is based on the revised country reports which were presented at the spring 2001 policy conference, "Learning from the Partners." The information provided has not been verified for correctness. To read underlying and revised background papers, visit www.worldbank.org/pensions.

2

The Making of Pension Privatization in Latin America and Eastern Europe

Katharina Müller

Many countries around the world are facing the pressing task of old-age security reform. Yet, pension systems have long been thought difficult to reform, as they tend to create powerful clienteles. This is particularly true for pay-as-you-go (PAYG) systems, which build up long-term expectations that are hard to reverse. Some experts argue that "any pronounced challenge to the basic structure of the [pension] system is equivalent to political suicide" (Buchanan 1983, p. 340).[1] In many countries pensioners constitute a substantial part of the electorate and amount to the largest single-issue constituency. Their power is thought to increase as the population ages (Butler and Germanis 1983; Börsch-Supan 1998). The elderly also are viewed sympathetically by other voters who may perceive themselves as being indirectly hurt by cutbacks, providing for a large blame-generating potential of pension reforms (Pierson and Weaver 1993).

Although the existing pension arrangements in Western industrialized countries still show a remarkable degree of resilience (Pierson 1996, 1998), a number of Latin American and Eastern European countries have

This paper summarizes findings from the research project titled "The Political Economy of Pension Reform: Eastern Europe and Latin America in Comparison," conducted while the author was at European University Viadrina, Frankfurt (Oder), Germany. Funding by the Volkswagen Foundation is gratefully acknowledged. Without the generous help and the insights provided by Eastern European and Latin American pension experts, this project would not have been possible. Special thanks are due to Fabio Bertranou in Córdoba; Carlos Grushka and Jorge San Martino in Buenos Aires; Huáscar Cajías, Pablo Gottret, and Helga Salinas in La Paz; Mária Augusztinovics, Róbert I. Gál, and András Simonovits in Budapest; Zofia Czepulis-Rutkowska and Stanislawa Golinowska in Warsaw; and Maciej Zukowski in Poznan.

opted for full or partial pension privatization in recent years. Such reform is radical because it implies a fundamental paradigmatic departure from the previous pension system: a shift from an intergenerational contract to individual provision for old age, as well as from the state to the market as the main supplier of retirement pensions. The paradigm change inherent in radical pension reform therefore amounts to a substantial rewriting of the underlying social contract, which usually does not occur in the case of a mere change of entitlement conditions.

Under what conditions has radical pension reform proved to be politically feasible? Established institutional arrangements in the area of welfare provision are considered hard to change because they involve substantial economic, social, cognitive, and normative investment and adaptation efforts, turning into sunk costs (Pierson 1994; Götting 1998). Most political scientists, sociologists, and economists are skeptical of the idea that policymakers will engage in fundamental pension reform steps. Chile, the first country to substitute its public pension insurance with a mandatory individually fully funded (IFF) scheme, was long seen as an isolated case. The feasibility of radical pension reform was explained by the repressive, authoritarian character of the Pinochet regime (see, for example, Mesa-Lago 1998b). Yet, the pension reform dynamics that developed all over Latin America in the 1990s indicated that full or partial pension privatization was possible under democratic regimes (see table 2.1).[2] At the end of the 1990s several Eastern European transition countries followed suit (see table 2.2).[3]

Despite being geographically and culturally distant from one another, Eastern Europe and Latin America show some interesting similarities in their move to old-age security privatization. These similarities are no coincidence; they result from a unique institutional transfer from south to east. In Central and Eastern Europe, where economic transformation had put additional strain on existing pension systems, Latin American reforms have been influential, particularly the substitutive "Chilean model" and the mixed "Argentine model."[4] This chapter compares the political processes leading to pension privatization in selected Eastern European and Latin American countries, drawing on literature that concerns the political economy of policy reform and that provides some interesting insights into the political viability of radical reforms. Four cases of pension reform in Latin America and Eastern Europe will be presented, followed by an analysis of the making of pension privatization in both regions. That analysis is intended as a contribution to the political economy of pension reform, interpreting it as part of a "medium-range theory" (Merton 1948) of policy reform.

Table 2.1   A Comparison of Latin American Pension Privatizations

Characteristics	Implemented									Legislated
	Chile	Peru	Argentina	Colombia	Uruguay	Bolivia	Mexico	El Salvador	Costa Rica	Nicaragua
Public mandatory tier	Phased out	Traditional PAYG scheme; alternative to private tier	Traditional PAYG scheme; private tier complementary	Traditional PAYG scheme; alternative to private tier	Traditional PAYG scheme; private tier complementary	Closed down	Closed down	Phased out	Traditional PAYG scheme; private tier complementary	Phased out
Private mandatory tier	Individually fully funded	Individually fully funded	Individually fully funded	Individually fully funded	Individually fully funded	Individually fully funded	Individually fully funded	Individually fully funded	Individually fully funded	Individually fully funded
	Mandatory for new entrants to labor market. Other workers may opt to switch from the public tier.	Membership in either the private or the public tier is mandatory for all workers.	All workers may redirect their contribution to the private tier.	Membership in either the private or the public tier is mandatory for all workers.	Mandatory for workers earning over US$800 and optional for lower earning groups and workers above age 39 to redirect part of their contribution to the private tier.	Mandatory for all workers.	Mandatory for all workers.	Mandatory for new entrants to labor market and affiliates up to age 35. Older workers (up to age 50 for women and age 55 for men) may opt to switch from the public tier.	Mandatory for all workers.	Mandatory for all workers up to age 43.
	Individual contribution rate: 10 percent	Individual contribution rate: 8 percent	Individual contribution rate: 7.74 percent	Individual contribution rate: 2.5 percent + employer's contribution rate: 7.5 percent	Individual contribution rate: 12.27 percent	Individual contribution rate: 10 percent	Individual contribution rate: 1.125 percent + employer's contribution rate: 5.2 percent + state subsidy: 2.2 percent	Individual contribution rate: 3.25 percent + employer's contribution rate: 6.75 percent	Individual contribution rate: 1 percent + employers' contribution rate: 3.25 percent	Individual contribution rate: 4 percent + employers' contribution rate: 6.5 percent
	From 1981	From 1993	From 1994	From 1994	From 1996	From 1997	From 1997	From 1998	From 2001	From 2002
Reform type	Substitutive	Parallel	Mixed	Parallel	Mixed	Substitutive	Substitutive	Substitutive	Mixed	Substitutive

Note: No detailed information was available about the recent reforms in the Dominican Republic and Ecuador. It should be noted that although the IFF tier is dominated by private pension administrators, some countries also have publicly run pension funds.

Table 2.2   A Comparison of Post-Socialist Pension Privatizations

Characteristics	Implemented						
	Kazakhstan	Hungary	Poland	Latvia	Bulgaria	Croatia	Estonia
Public mandatory tier	Closed down	Traditional PAYG scheme; private tier complementary	NDC scheme; private tier complementary	NDC scheme; private tier complementary	Traditional PAYG scheme; private tier complementary	Traditional PAYG scheme; private tier complementary	Traditional PAYG scheme; private tier complementary
Private mandatory tier	Individually fully funded	Individually fully funded	Individually fully funded	Individually fully funded	Individually fully funded	Individually fully funded	Individually fully funded
	Mandatory for all workers.	Mandatory for new entrants to labor market and optional for other workers to redirect part of their contribution to the private tier.	Mandatory for workers below 30 years of age and optional between ages 30 and 49 to redirect part of their contribution to the private tier.	Mandatory for workers below 30 years of age and optional between ages 30 and 49 to redirect part of their contribution to the private tier.	Mandatory for all workers up to 42 years of age to redirect part of their contribution to the private tier.	Mandatory for workers below 40 years of age and optional between ages 40 and 49 to redirect their contribution to the private tier.	Mandatory for workers below 18 years of age and optional for other workers to redirect part of their contribution to the private tier.
	Individual contribution rate: 10 percent	Individual contribution rate: 6 percent	Individual contribution rate: 9 percent	Individual contribution rate to be gradually increased to 10 percent	Contribution rate yet to be defined (2–5 percent); it will be paid in equal shares by employers and employees	Contribution rate: 5 percent; to be paid in equal shares by employers and employees	Individual contribution rate: 2 percent + employer's contribution rate: 4 percent
	From 1998	From 1998	From 1999	From 2001	From 2002	From 2002	From 2002
Reform type	Substitutive	Mixed	Mixed	Mixed	Mixed	Mixed	Mixed

NDC = notional defined contribution.

Note: A mixed reform was legislated in FYR Macedonia in March 2000; the likely date of its implementation is 2004. It should be noted that although the IFF tier is dominated by private pension administrators, some countries also have publicly run pension funds.

Insights from the Political Economy of Policy Reform

This analysis approaches the political feasibility of radical pension reforms from the perspective of the political economy of policy reform. This multidisciplinary strand of research seems particularly relevant for the present study because it seeks to explain the political viability of radical, market-oriented reforms that had long been precluded by conventional wisdom, which tended to assume selfish, rent-maximizing bureaucrats and obstructionist vested interests (see Rodrik 1993; Williamson 1994a).[5] Early contributions to the political economy of policy reform literature compared failed and successful reform efforts, centering on the politics of structural adjustment programs and market-oriented reforms in industrializing countries, notably those in Latin America (for example, Bery 1990; Whitehead 1990; Krueger 1993). The focus of attention soon was extended to the Organisation for Economic and Co-operative Development countries (for example, Williamson 1994b). The growing body of literature includes works by political scientists and economists who use different methodologies: some authors hold that the only practical approach is a comparative one based on case studies; others have tried to formalize underlying explanatory models (for a review, see Rodrik 1996; Tommasi and Velasco 1996; Sturzenegger and Tommasi 1998b; Bönker 2002).

When does fundamental agenda-shifting occur in the first place? Some scholars have stressed the importance of "vigorous political leadership" (Sachs 1994, p. 503). Courageous, extraordinarily committed people (see Harberger 1993)—often market-oriented economists-as-politicians (see Williamson 1994a)—and their ability to communicate a coherent vision of the "promised land" ahead might prove crucial for radical reform (see Balcerowicz 1994; Rodrik 1994). However, the existence of these agenda-setters certainly cannot be considered sufficient to guarantee success against powerful interest groups (see Williamson and Haggard 1994; Tommasi and Velasco 1996).

Another argument focuses on the influence of the international financial institutions (IFIs), which has been reviewed from various angles. On many occasions, the International Monetary Fund (IMF) and the World Bank have acted as vital catalysts for an agenda entailing fundamental change (see Toye 1994). Their conditionalities may be interpreted as extra leverage given to reform-minded policymakers (see Sachs 1994; Williamson 1994a). Even if the involvement of the IFIs bears the risk of backlash toward local politicians, who may be accused of "kowtowing to Washington," it also amounts to a proven mechanism of blame avoidance for unpopular policy measures (see Haggard and Webb 1993).[6]

A frequently raised argument for explaining radical change is a preceding crisis (see Sturzenegger and Tommasi 1998a, pp. 9–15).[7]

Although standard economic theory holds that welfare is maximized in a context of minimal distortions, some scholars of the political economy of policy reform have pointed to the "benefit of crises" (Drazen and Grilli 1993). Crises may put the economy on a welfare-superior path when situations of perceived emergency persuade opposing groups to agree on unpopular measures. A stalemate can be broken as crises may aid in the demolition of political coalitions that had previously blocked reform (see Williamson 1994a; Haggard and Kaufman 1995).[8] However, the "benefit of crises" hypothesis is not unanimously accepted.[9] It is difficult to quantify and has even been criticized as tautological: "That policy reform should follow crisis, then, is no more surprising than smoke following fire" (Rodrik 1996, p. 27). Other critics have noted that at times of economic crisis there usually are not enough resources to compensate reform losers. Although some scholars hold that crises may only amount to an opportunity to introduce ad hoc stabilization measures (see Haggard and Webb 1993; Nelson 1994; World Bank 1997), others have shown that crises may indeed bring about deep institutional reforms (see Wagener 1997).

The design of a reform strategy is more directly under reformers' control (see Haggard and Webb 1993; Rodrik 1993). There has been much discussion about the appropriate timing, speed, bundling, and tactical sequencing of fundamental reforms (see Sturzenegger and Tommasi 1998a; Lora 2000). The issue extends beyond the well-known "shock therapy versus gradualism" controversy (see Dewatripont and Roland 1998; Wei 1998). Big-bang strategies might render reforms irreversible before substantial opposition can build (see Sachs 1994), but there are also plausible arguments for strategic sequencing (see Martinelli and Tommasi 1998). When the most promising reforms are given priority, demonstration effects may be produced and political support created because benefits are visible early in the process (see Nelson 1994; World Bank 1997). Appropriate packaging and design, including compensation of adversely affected groups, are crucial for the feasibility of radical reforms because they might allow for bypassing vested interests and dividing the opposition. Reform design has a direct impact on the cost profile, or "redistributional calculus," of radical reforms (World Bank 1997, p. 146).

Even if the allocation of costs is relevant for the viability of reforms, high social costs will not necessarily obstruct radical reforms, particularly if those affected lack political voice and power (see Tommasi and Velasco 1996). Democratic regimes differ with regard to their capability for filtering discontent. Hence, many analyses of the political economy of policy reform consider the design of political institutions, such as the electoral and party system, and institutional veto points. A fragmented party system and dysfunctional intermediary institutions contribute to the "unfiltered" expression of political discontent. But the interpretation of reform costs and assignment of blame also matters (see Bönker 1995, pp. 189–190). In particular, distributional implications of large policy changes may be tolerated when a newly elected government succeeds in attributing them to the previous regime, a phenomenon called the "honeymoon effect" (see Williamson 1994a). This effect is reinforced when the previous regime has spent a long time in office and when the situation is perceived as being critical (Haggard and Webb 1993; Rodrik 1994). Conversely, radical reforms are less likely to succeed shortly before elections.

Obviously, not all of these stylized findings apply equally in all countries and for each area of economic reform. They can be expected, however, to provide useful insights regarding the political feasibility of radical pension reform in Latin America and Eastern Europe.

Privatizing Pensions in Latin America: The Cases of Argentina and Bolivia

Argentina—The Creation of the Mixed Model

The Argentine old-age security system was in considerable financial trouble in the 1980s and required substantial fiscal subsidies. It was not until Carlos Menem assumed the presidency in 1989, however, that pension reform gained momentum. Interestingly, this Peronist president discontinued the party's long-standing statist orientation and introduced a series of market-friendly reforms. In 1991, Domingo Cavallo, the new minister for economic affairs and architect of a bold economic reform program, put together a pension reform team that was dominated by economists rather than the traditional social security experts, that is, actuaries and lawyers with Bismarckian leanings. The team was headed by Walter Schulthess, a specialist in public finance and the newly appointed secretary of social security, who obtained financing from the United Nations Development Programme and the World Bank for a series of technical studies on pension reform. Inclined toward the "Chilean model," the reformers began a dialogue with political parties and social organizations in early 1992 to put the issue on the political agenda. At the same time, the Argentine government committed itself to structural pension reform in a standby agreement signed with the IMF. Pensioners' associations, distrusting the radical reform plans, mobilized their members against reform. The local business and finance community actively advocated pension privatization and welcomed it as a sign that market-friendly policies were to continue.

In June 1992, a draft law presented to congress proposed reducing the public system to the provision of a basic pension and the creation of a new individually fully funded scheme. The scheme was modeled on the Chilean precedent, albeit acquired rights would not be compensated for and all insured people under 45 years of age would be obliged to switch to the funded tier. Parliamentary commissions, trade unions, and pensioners' associations criticized various aspects of the project, including the loss of acquired rights for insured people below age 45, potential investment risks, high administrative costs, and the exclusively private administration of the fully funded scheme. The government soon realized that without the consent of the Peronist trade unionists—some of whom were members of congress—it would lack the parliamentary majority necessary to pass the pension law. Hence, numerous modifications were incorporated into successive versions of the proposed law. Most important, trade unions, public entities, mutual funds, and cooperatives were authorized to manage second-tier funds; all insured people would be frèe to choose between the public and the mixed scheme (and those who did not choose would be moved to the mixed scheme); a "compensatory benefit" was granted to those who switched to the mixed system, and an "additional benefit" was promised to those who stayed in the public system.[10] Eventually, the law passed in September 1993, and the new old-age security system came into force in July 1994. Since the reform, the public pension tier has been the recurrent target of fiscally motivated retrenchment, and the government even attempted unsuccessfully to abolish it in 2000.[11]

Bolivia—The Linking of Pension Privatization with Enterprise Capitalization

The financial problems of the public pension system in Bolivia date back to the 1970s and were aggravated by a severe recession and hyperinflation in the 1980s. Coverage amounted to only 12 percent of the labor force. With the assistance of José Piñera, the architect of the "Chilean model," and the financial support of the U.S. Agency for International Development (USAID), the ministry of finance proposed structural pension reform in Bolivia in the early 1990s. Because of the proximity of elections and opposition from the ministry of labor and the ministry of health—the portfolio responsible for social security—the proposal was shelved. In 1993, the newly elected President Gonzalo Sánchez de Lozada endorsed a series of "second-generation" structural reforms, including pension reform. For tactical reasons the new government decided to link pension privatization with enterprise capitalization, a program designed to inject fresh capital into formerly state-owned companies by partially privatizing their ownership. It is interesting to note that it was the political party (Movimiento Nacional-ista Revolucionario or MNR) represented by Sánchez de Lozada that led the 1952 revolution and the concomitant nationalization of Bolivia's largest firms, while embarking on a market-friendly course.

To end intragovernment conflicts on the direction pension reform should take, the ministries of labor and health were deprived of their authority over old-age security. Instead, Sánchez de Lozada created the National Pensions Office to lead the reform project, attaching it to the newly created ministry of enterprise capitalization. The Bolivian government was given financial and technical support by the World Bank and the Inter-American Development Bank (IADB) for its entire package of structural reforms, including pension reform. In 1995 a public relations campaign was started, but it failed to convince pensioners' associations and trade unions to support the reform. These organizations, however, had little political clout. The government coalition's strong parliamentary majority enabled it to enact the reform law in November 1996,without much plenary debate.

The Bolivian structural pension reform was very close to the Chilean prototype but it displayed some differences: all insured people, regardless of age, were moved immediately to the private system; there was no minimum pension or minimum investment yield; and because of the small market size, initially only two pension fund administrators were permitted. The insured population was divided between the two funds according to domicile and date of birth. This duopoly, which had been the result of an international bidding process, turned into a monopoly when the two Spanish banks that controlled the Bolivian pension funds merged in 1999.

Another important difference from the Chilean system is the link between pension reform and enterprise capitalization: roughly 50 percent of the shares of the capitalized state enterprises were credited to a "collective capitalization fund," run by the private pension funds. From May 1997 an *annual* pension of US$248 (called *"Bonosol"*) was paid from the dividends to all Bolivians above age 65, insured or not.[12] The *Bonosol* is thought to have greatly improved the political feasibility of both capitalization and pension reform because it created new stakeholders beyond the narrow boundaries of the old pension system. The incoming administration of Hugo Banzer stopped the payments for financial and political reasons, however, after only a few months. In June 1998 *Bonosol* was replaced with a less generous scheme called *"Bolivida,"* which did not begin to pay out benefits until December 2000.[13] Although important in gaining support for these two ambitious reform projects, the *Bonosol-Bolivida* scheme has not turned into a universal minimum pension and has proved extremely vulnerable to political manipulation.[14]

Privatizing Pensions in Eastern Europe: The Cases of Hungary and Poland

Hungary—The Mixed Precedent in Eastern Europe

By 1989 the need for fundamental reforms in Hungarian old-age security was widely acknowledged because the inherited PAYG system was seen as inequitable, inadequate, and unsustainable. The system's financial problems increased significantly during economic transformation. Early reforms introduced some changes to the organization, financing, and eligibility of the Hungarian pension scheme, but they were not sweeping enough to ensure its financial viability. Inadequate indexation practices added further distortions. Moreover, trade unions succeeded in delaying important reform measures. In contrast, the introduction of voluntary pension funds in 1994—the first move toward a diversification of the old-age provision—did not meet with political obstacles. Despite largely unsuccessful attempts to bring about thorough reform within the existing Hungarian old-age scheme, the ministry of welfare and the self-government of the pension fund stuck to the Bismarckian/Beveridgean traditions.

Meanwhile, the public PAYG system's dependence on budgetary subsidies gave the minister of finance an important stake in pension reform. Lájos Bokros, the author of a severe structural adjustment package, put pension privatization on the political agenda while serving as minister of finance, but it was up to his successor, Péter Medgyessy, to implement radical reform. The stalemate between the ministries of welfare and finance on the pension reform issue lasted almost two years until it was settled in spring 1996 when Medgyessy threatened to resign. The joint reform blueprint subsequently presented by both ministries strongly resembled the ministry of finance's earlier stance, but its mixed overall approach can be interpreted as satisfying both of the previously competing ministries. A pension reform committee led by István Györfi, a commissioner to the minister of finance, was set up to work on the planned reform, thereby bypassing the previously exclusive domain of the ministry of welfare. The reform team was actively supported by the World Bank's resident mission in Budapest and by USAID. In mid-July 1997, after only six weeks of debate, the government won legislative approval for the envisaged pension reform package well before the next elections that were scheduled for early 1998. The extraordinarily quick passage was not only the result of the governing coalition's strong parliamentary majority, but also of the government's strategy of prelegislative negotiations with relevant opponents over the pension reform draft. It should be noted, however, that Hungarian pension reformers were only willing to compromise on first-tier reforms; their basic paradigm choice was not put up for discussion with secondary pension reform actors, such as trade unions.

Hungary's new pension system, in force since 1998, combined a large mandatory public PAYG scheme with a partially mandatory IFF tier (three-quarters versus one-quarter of contributions). The Hungarian reform blueprint thus resembles the Argentine mixed approach to old-age security reform. Even if the lion's share of Hungarian old-age security will still be provided by the public PAYG tier, the reform involved a partial privatization of the existing public scheme, creating a precedent in the region: "Passage of the Hungarian pension reform by Parliament has demonstrated the political and economic feasibility of this type of reform in Central Europe" (Palacios and Rocha 1998, p. 213). It is interesting to note that this precedent in pension privatization was created by a Socialist-led government.[15]

Poland—Pension Privatization with Notional Defined Contribution

Although economic crisis and high inflation had afflicted Poland's public pension system (ZUS) since the 1980s, the financial strain was greatly aggravated by economic transformation. Policymakers had experienced strong resistance from the "grey lobby"—notably pensioners' associations and trade unions—when they tried to introduce relatively modest reform measures. The large number of pension reform drafts put forward since the early 1990s indicates the degree of disagreement about the path to reform. Although the ministry of labor and professors of social insurance law argued that a thorough reform of ZUS was sufficient and politically viable, the ministry of finance and social security experts with economic backgrounds advocated Latin American–style pension privatization. The finance portfolio's involvement in the pension reform issue was triggered by ZUS's financial dependence on sizable budgetary subsidies.

For a year and a half, pension reform was deadlocked by the conflict between the ministries of labor and finance. In early 1996, after a cabinet reshuffling, a new minister of labor was appointed (Andrzej Baczkowski) who quickly became the most important individual actor in Polish pension reform, moving his ministry considerably closer to the ministry of finance's position. A special task force for pension reform was set up, headed by Michal Rutkowski, an economist on leave from the World Bank. The plans for reform, published in October 1996, combined a reformed, downsized ZUS with a newly created, mandatory, fully funded tier. In terms of reform strategy, the initial idea was to get all pension reform laws passed before the September 1997 parliamentary elections, thereby defying conventional wisdom on political business cycles.

Baczkowski's sudden death delayed reform preparations, however, and Polish policymakers resorted to strategies of unbundling and deliberate sequencing of reform. The outgoing government, dominated by the post-socialist SLD (or "Left Democratic Alliance"), enacted the laws on the popular private pension fund tiers before the elections and presented itself to the electorate as the authors of a nearly completed pension reform. The more intricate part—ZUS reform, without which the private tier would not have come into force—was left to the incoming government, formed by the Solidarity party and the liberal UW (or "Freedom Union"), thus reflecting a cross-party consensus on pension privatization in Poland. Throughout the entire legislative process, the pension reform team negotiated with potential opponents of the envisaged reform, notably trade unions and pensioners' organizations, and agreed to some modifications of the first-pillar reforms that were finally enacted in late 1998.

Poland's new pension system, enacted in 1999, was a mixed type. The old ZUS scheme was fundamentally restructured, with the most important change being a shift toward the notional defined contribution principle.[16] The still dominant public scheme was combined with a newly created private pension fund tier (62.6 versus 37.4 percent of contributions). Although the system adopted major elements of the recent Latvian and Swedish reforms in the first tier, its mixed overall approach clearly was inspired by the Argentine reform precedent. The partial privatization of Polish old-age security amounts to a significant departure from local social insurance traditions, dating back to the end of the 19th century.[17]

Privatizing Pensions: Latin American and Eastern European Experiences

Since Huntington put forth his "third wave" hypothesis,[18] comparisons between Eastern European and Latin American transformations have lost their exotic feel. Classical cross-regional contributions on transition and consolidation include Karl and Schmitter (1991), Przeworski (1991b), and Przeworski and others (1995).[19] Obvious differences regarding the scope and sequence of transformations—paradigm change versus systemic transformation of the economy, asynchrony versus simultaneity of economic and political change—need not prevent fruitful comparison of the transitional regions (Schmitter and Karl 1994). The interdependence between economic and political change attracted much interest,[20] but there has been little comparative research on the political economy of individual policy areas. This is also true for the reform of old-age security: the similarity of approaches in Latin America and Eastern Europe has so far prompted no cross-regional analysis. This chapter analyzes pension privatization in both regions within the framework of the political economy of policy reform. Moreover, it discusses findings from previous comparative research regarding the political economy of pension reform in both regions. For Latin America, the research includes the published accounts of Kay (1998, 1999), Madrid (1999), Mesa-Lago (1999), Mora (1999), Busquets (2000), and Huber and Stephens (2000). Pension privatization in post-socialist countries has been analyzed by Müller (1999), Cain (2000), Orenstein (2000), and Nelson (2001), whereas Madrid (1998) and James and Brooks (2001) aim at designing a broader explanatory framework that extends beyond both regions.

The Transmission of Ideas in Old-Age Security Reform

Tables 2.1 and 2.2 indicate that, local details aside, the parallels in Latin American and Eastern European pension reforms are striking. The simultaneous adoption of similar blueprints across countries suggests that there is a common international transmission mechanism of ideas (Stallings 1994). In fact, policy transfer and the global diffusion of models affect an increasing array of contemporary policy change (Dolowitz and Marsh 2000; Weyland 2000). It is argued here that in the area of old-age security, a dominant epistemic community can be identified. Following the definition by Haas (1992, p. 3), an epistemic community is a network of professionals in a particular domain and with a common policy enterprise. The individuals may come from different professional backgrounds, but they share faith in specific truths, a set of normative and causal beliefs, patterns of reasoning, and discursive practices. This "new pension orthodoxy" (Lo Vuolo 1996) is a major factor behind pension privatization in Latin America and Eastern Europe.

Conservative critics of the welfare state had long prepared for a paradigm change in old-age security. Friedrich A. Hayek, Milton Friedman, Gordon Tullock, Martin Feldstein, Peter Ferrara, and others denounced the "perversity, futility and jeopardy" of providing public welfare (Hirschman 1991). In 1983 the Cato Institute even published a strategy of "guerrilla warfare against both the current U.S. social security system and the coalition that supports it" (Butler and Germanis 1983, p. 552). The past decades have witnessed an intensification and reframing of the debate on Social Security (Thompson 1983; Arnold, Graetz, and Munnell 1998). At the end of the cold war, the terms of the prevailing discourse in old-age protection shifted, in line with the rise of neoliberalism as the dominant paradigm. Today, mainstream economic scholarship argues in favor of replacing existing public pension systems with private funded schemes (Schmähl 1998).[21] The most frequently mentioned advantages expected of such a paradigm change is an increase in saving and efficiency improvements in both the financial and the labor markets, leading to an increase in long-term growth (see, for example, World Bank 1994; Corsetti and Schmidt-Hebbel 1997).

Although originally not contained in the so-called Washington consensus (Williamson 1990, 2000), systemic reform of old-age security schemes has become part of the neoliberal reform package. In Eastern Europe this paradigm shift coincided with the first post-socialist years, marked by a widespread move toward the market in economic policy. In Latin America, it concluded the era of the populist welfare state, which used to hand out social benefits to privileged interest groups in return for political support (Touraine 1989). In the wake of the debt crisis and the concomitant fiscal retrenchment, the majority of responsibility for social security was delegated to private institutions, while the state was assigned a subsidiary role with its tasks limited to poverty reduction and pension fund supervision (Nitsch and Schwarzer 1996). A World Bank research report (1994), intended to establish the guiding criteria of the organization's pension policy, attracted global attention and may be the best-known example of the new pension orthodoxy, as well as its major propagating mechanism.[22]

It is obvious that the Bank's report could not have influenced pension privatization in Chile (1980). On the contrary, it was the Chilean reform that had an impact on the World Bank's pension reform blueprint. In the case of those structural pension reforms that started in the 1990s, however, the impact of the pension orthodoxy has been significant. In practical terms, radical agenda-shifting was frequently shaped by World Bank advice and technical assistance. In recent years other IFIs and government agencies—such as the IMF, USAID, the IADB, and the Asian Development Bank (ADB)[23]—have followed suit. Although they have been involved in cross-conditionalities with the Bank that include pension privatization, as well as other forms of cooperation, overall they play a less significant role and sometimes appear to be less committed to orthodox thought than is the Bank.

It was only after the Chilean precedent that pension privatization turned from a theoretical concept into political reality. Its global impact as a role model notwithstanding, the demonstration effects from the Chilean model have been especially pronounced in Latin America itself, particularly after the end of the Pinochet regime. When policymakers in the region compared their countries' economic performances to the Chilean success story, they identified pension privatization as one of the ingredients of macroeconomic strength (Weyland 2000). Promotional activities of the Chilean pension funds and prominent reformers, such as José Piñera, also contributed to the diffusion of the precedent all over the subcontinent. In Latin America, autonomous policy learning by recipient countries tended to be more important than did direct influence of the IFIs as agenda-setters, although virtually all reform teams were effectively financed by the latter (Nelson 2000).

In the post-socialist pension reforms, Latin American role models were also influential, particularly the Chilean model and Argentine model (see table 2.2). "Latin American countries have become the world's laboratory for pension systems based upon individual retirement savings accounts" (Kay and Kritzer 2001, p. 51). Although Latin American reformers passed their experiences on to Eastern European policymakers, in person or through their writings,[24] the latter were more prone to look to the west than to the south in their search for models, given their European Union (EU) accession plans.[25] In their eyes, Latin America carried the stigma of being a less industrial region, and that rendered it inadequate as a role model (Orenstein 2000). Yet Chilean-style pension privatization was proposed as a major reform option by the IFIs (see, for example, World Bank 1994; Vittas 1997).[26] The World Bank and USAID also sponsored trips to Argentina and Chile for Polish members of parliament, social security experts, and journalists. Hence, in Eastern Europe where the connotations of the Chilean model were more likely to refer to the Pinochet regime than to a regional example of economic success, the IFIs played an important though low-key role as agents of transmission, helping enhance the low status of the Latin American precedents (Nelson 2000; Müller 2001a).

Political Actors and the Policy Context in Pension Reform

Pension privatization in Latin America and Eastern Europe was closely connected with the emergence of the new pension orthodoxy, but it was the domestic political process that eventually resulted in adoption of radical pension reform. The following analysis identifies the most important political actors in the pension reform arena and considers the policy context that shaped their room for maneuvering. This policy context was shaped by political factors, economic conditions, and policy legacies.

Scholars of the political economy of policy reform have stressed the importance of political leadership—courageous, committed individuals, often market-oriented economists—and their ability to communicate a coherent neoliberal vision. The case studies discussed above have shown that pension privatization amounts to a paradigm shift that may be helped greatly by such committed policymakers. Menem and Cavallo (Argentina), Sánchez de Lozada (Bolivia), and Bokros (Hungary) are famous for the radical, market-oriented reform packages they championed. In Argentina and Poland, there is unanimity that radical pension reform would have been impossible without Schulthess and Baczkowski, respectively, who set up these countries' reform teams. It should be noted that these country cases show another interesting similarity: in all four, the governing parties that implemented the neoliberal agenda had previously been known for their left-wing or populist leanings. This is true for the Peronists in Argentina, the MNR in Bolivia, and the post-socialist governments in Poland and Hungary who were the driving forces of pension privatization. Old-age security is not the only policy area in which radical reforms may be more successful when tackled by "unlikely" administrations. Cukierman and Tommasi (1998a, 1998b) refer to many cases where market-friendly reforms have not been carried out by conservative free marketeers, but rather by left-wing administrations. This phenomenon has been called the "Nixon-in-China syndrome" (Rodrik 1994; see also Ross 2000).

The case studies here have shown that radical paradigm change in old-age security was advocated mainly by ministries of finance and economy and staffed with neoliberal economists. Pension privatization perfectly matched these ministries' overall efforts to decrease the state's role in the economy, and they were supported by both local interest groups, such as business and financial organizations, and the IFIs. But there was also opposition to these radical plans, both within and outside government. More often than not, the ministries of labor, welfare, or health, responsible for the existing old-age security schemes, were reluctant to engage in structural pension reform, thus reflecting the existing Bismarckian traditions in both Latin America and Eastern Europe. In several countries, these ministries initially objected to the radical paradigm shift, but—given the predominance of the finance ministry in the cabinet—proved too weak to prevent it. Typically, the opposing portfolios' influence on reform design was limited by the establishment of small task forces, usually attached to the ministry of finance. These special pension reform committees worked out the draft legislation and clearly were designed to bypass the labor ministry's pension-related competencies. Other groups that opposed pension privatization included trade unions, social security employees, and—last but not least—pensioners' associations and special interest groups with privileged pension schemes. In some countries, left-wing parties also joined the opponents.

Specific features of the policy context also need to be considered, particularly those that provide reformers or reform opponents with significant action resources (Kay 1999). The executive branch's degree of control of the legislature was a relevant institutional variable, for example, in Bolivia and Hungary the large parliamentary majority of the governing coalitions allowed for swift passage of structural pension reform. In Argentina, Hungary, and Poland trade unions had traditional ties with the governing parties that they used to ease resistance, pointing to one of the ingredients of the Nixon-in-China syndrome. These ties meant that reform opponents were in a political position to force reformers to negotiate with them and to make concessions. In Argentina and Poland this even implied granting trade unions the right to run their own pension funds. A broader look at both regions shows that in some countries with an autocratic regime, a weak civil society (for example, Chile, Peru, and El Salvador), or both, there was very little or no public debate about the government's plans to privatize old-age security. In the first two cases, pension privatization was not even passed by congress; it was legislated by the executive branch via emergency decrees. By contrast, the Uruguayan and Latvian cases illustrate that elements of direct democracy (referenda, plebiscites) may even give reform opponents a chance to reverse pension reform laws that have already been passed.

The paradigm choice in Latin American and Eastern European old-age security appears to have been influenced substantially by economic factors and considerations. Pension privatization has been primarily proposed for macroeconomic motives as countries seek to embark on a virtuous circle leading to economic growth. Madrid (1998) and James and Brooks (2001) pointed to increased international capital mobility and the recent experiences of capital market crises that may have induced policymakers to seek to reduce vulnerability to capital outflows by boosting domestic savings and local capital markets. Contrary to these high hopes, however, the Chilean evidence suggests that pension privatization had a negative impact on national savings (Mesa-Lago 1998a). Moreover, given that the investment of funds abroad tends to be severely limited, it is surprising that the pre-reform situation of local capital markets, however poor, never seems to have been perceived as a constraint to pension privatization.

Scholars of the political economy of policy reform have highlighted that a preceding crisis may induce radical change—the so-called benefit of crises hypothesis mentioned earlier. Fiscal crises turn the ministry of finance into a potential actor in the pension reform arena. More specifically, when pension finances display a deficit, dependence on budget subsidies gives the ministry of finance (a likely advocate of the "new pension orthodoxy" in any case) an important stake in reforming old-age security (Müller 1999). Table 2.3 presents some relevant indicators of the budget deficit and public pension spending for the four case studies discussed here. It may come as no surprise that the finance or economics ministries played a key role in triggering the process of pension privatization in all four countries. Hence, the financial difficulties of the public PAYG schemes changed the relevant constellation of actors in such a way that the "privatization faction" was reinforced decisively. Furthermore, the enduring financial crises had severely eroded public confidence in the pre-reform pension systems, particularly in Latin America.

Another economic factor had an impact on the cases of pension reform reviewed above. When external debt is high (see table 2.3), governments tend to stress their general commitment to market-oriented reform.

Table 2.3   The Policy Context in Argentina, Bolivia, Hungary, and Poland: Some Relevant Indicators

	Argentina	Bolivia	Hungary	Poland
Overall deficit in government finance (prior to pension reform)[a]	–6.3	–5.7	–4.5	–2.4
Public pension spending as percentage of GDP (mid-1990s)[b]	4.9	2.5	9.7	14.4
Total external debt/GDP (1989)[c]	85.6	87.6	69.9	49.5
Population aged 20 to 59/population over 60 (1995)[d]	3.7	7.2	2.8	3.4
Estimated size of IPD:[e]				
• Age-based IPD/GDP	125	45	213	142
• Spending-based IPD/GDP	100	65	213	241

IPD = implicit pension debt.
a. World Bank (2000a, b, c, d). Argentina and Bolivia: 1989; Poland and Hungary: 1998.
b. World Bank (1999).
c. World Bank (2000a, b, c). Data for Poland are for 1986 (from World Bank 1998).
d. World Bank (1999).
e. James and Brooks (2001).

In this context the announcement of pension privatization can be interpreted as a signalling strategy (Rodrik 1998). Indeed, by the mid-1990s rating agencies had included radical pension reform as a favorable point in their country-risk assessments. Critical indebtedness also increases the likelihood of the IFIs' involvement in the local pension reform arena (Brooks 1998). The World Bank, with its prominent position in international old-age security reform, is a powerful external actor in a number of highly indebted Latin American and Eastern European countries because it "may signal that a developing country has embraced sound policies and hence boost its credibility" (Stiglitz 1998, p. 27). Together with other IFIs and government agencies, the Bank exerted its influence first and foremost as an agenda-setter in the local debate, engaging in expert-based knowledge transfer. Moreover, lending activities are central to the support of pension privatization in Latin America and Eastern Europe (Holzmann 2000). As noted by Kay (1999), policymakers were well aware that financial and technical support were available only for a pension reform that included a privatization component. Whereas in some countries, such as Hungary, the IFIs' involvement was kept low-key, in others, such as Argentina, local policymakers explicitly asked to include pension privatization in an IMF accord as a form of "blame avoidance" (Weaver 1986). In Poland, Michal Rutkowski's position as head of the special task force on old-age reform gave the Bank a pivotal channel to support local reform efforts, apart from its overall leverage in a context of high external debt (Müller 1999).

The importance of existing institutional arrangements for future reform paths—policy feedback or path dependence—has been stressed by earlier scholarship on welfare state development.[27] "Existing policies can set the agenda for change...by narrowing the range of feasible alternatives" (Pierson and Weaver 1993, p. 146).[28] Frequently, the success of reform strategies depends on earlier policy choices and the policy feedback resulting from them. In Bismarckian-style PAYG systems, lock-in effects and opportunity costs may result from the pension rights earned by the insured, thus engendering high transition costs. The size of these entitlements (frequently called "implicit pension debt") is determined by a number of factors, notably the percentage of the population covered and the maturity of the scheme (see table 2.3 for some estimates).

It has been argued elsewhere that the larger the implicit pension debt, the smaller the likelihood of radical pension privatization (Fox and Palmer 1999; James and Brooks 2001). The fact that most Eastern European countries—a region where coverage approached 100 percent—opted for the mixed reform path seems to support this hypothesis. Similar conclusions may be drawn from the cases of Argentina and Uruguay, where pre-reform coverage was high and reformers opted for a mixed scheme. Contrary to this, Bolivian reformers faced a much smaller implicit pension debt and a considerably younger population, and therefore believed that radical pension privatization was economically feasible. Estimates of the implicit pension debt should not be taken as a given, however, because this potential lock-in may be reduced by reform design.[29] Somewhat paradoxically, it was under the Pinochet dictatorship that recognition of acquired pension rights was most comprehensive (Mesa-Lago 2000). Yet a closer look at second-generation pension reforms shows that existing pension claims were rarely recognized completely, so as to reduce the fiscal costs of a shift to funding.[30] This reduction of total implicit pension debt is likely to entail welfare losses to retirees and older workers (Lindeman, Rutkowski, and Sluchynskyy 2000).

The Relevance of Reform Design

Our country cases have shown that in choosing pension privatization, Latin American and Eastern European policymakers reacted to failed attempts to make the existing PAYG schemes viable with parametric reforms, such as an increase in the retirement age and benefit cutbacks. From a conceptual point of view and, given the paradigmatic alternatives, these reform measures might be characterized as moderate. However, their drawback in political economy terms is the large blame-generating potential they entail, which makes them politically sensitive. These reforms easily allow the identification of individual losses, and are perceived as an attack on acquired entitlements—without anything in exchange (Müller 1999).

This reasoning highlights the strategic importance of reform design in old-age security reform. The relevance of tactical sequencing, strategic bundling, packaging, and compensation has been stressed by scholars of the political economy of policy reform (see Haggard and Webb 1993; Rodrik 1993; Sturzenegger and Tommasi 1998). The use of these devices is intended to lower political resistance to pension reform. Full or partial pension privatization even enables policymakers to hand out attractive stakes to potential opponents, thus creating constituencies for reform (Graham 1997). In Argentina, Poland, and Hungary, trade unions changed from opponents of pension privatization to entrepreneurs in the mandatory pension fund business. "Shifting to a funded scheme ... allows for arguments that all can win, thus abandoning intractable zero-sum games" (Holzmann 1997, p. 3).

The Bolivian case is an example of strategic bundling and indirect compensation.[31] Pension reform was linked with enterprise capitalization, thus facilitating both policy agendas. At the same time, the modest *Bonosol-Bolivida* scheme was aimed at creating new stakeholders, many of whom had never received a pension before—a particularly clever strategy in a country with extremely low coverage. It is instructive to compare Bolivia with the Polish case in which policymakers also intended to link privatization with systemic pension reform. However, Poland decided to use privatization proceeds to cover transition costs by supplying them to the state budget. Although this helped to solve the fiscal consequences of a partial shift to funding, it lacked any public visibility (Gesell-Schmidt, Müller and Süß 1999).

Hungarian and Polish reformers used tactical packaging when they distanced themselves from Latin American models and stressed the originality of local reform efforts (for example, Rutkowski 1998).[32] Despite the obvious conceptual parallels to Latin American models, policymakers decided to avoid all reference to these precedents as soon as they learned of their negative connotations among the East-Central European public (Müller 1999; Orenstein 2000).

As stressed by Pierson (1994), the political costs of reform can be lowered by increasing its complexity. In several Latin American and Eastern European countries, the reformers' strategy amounted to bundling some unavoidable, yet politically sensitive reforms of the public PAYG tier with the more visible introduction of individual pension fund accounts (Holzmann 2000; Lindeman, Rutkowski, and Sluchynskyy 2000). The bundling strategy increased the complexity of the planned reform, and at the same time lowered the visibility of retrenchment elements. This "obfuscation strategy" in Pierson's terms (1994, p. 21) entails the potential to mask cutbacks and to draw public attention to the granting of individualized ownership claims. The introduction of individual pension fund accounts tended to be perceived as the creation of a monitorable track record of individual property rights over time, rights that the political system would be less likely to take away.[33]

Contrary to this, Polish policymakers employed an unbundling approach based on strategic sequencing that was adapted to the political business cycle. Pension privatization was legislated before the elections, and the restructuring of the public tier was left to the new government. Although this move increased the visibility of retrenchment elements, making them more difficult to enact, the earlier passage of the second-tier laws may have created a path dependence in the sense that the subsequent enactment of the more difficult laws was made easier (Müller 1999).

In contrast to the unfavorable public perception of parametric reforms, the drawbacks related to pension privatization are easier to conceal. In most Latin American and Eastern European countries the scope and financing of transition costs—a major fiscal and distributional issue in a shift from PAYG to funded schemes—were successfully shielded from public debate. Hence, the public perception of the strengths and weaknesses of pension privatization was biased toward its advantages, and the concomitant fiscal burdens were ignored. This asymmetry of perception may explain why structural pension reform can be successfully pursued in a pre-electoral period (see, for example, Bolivia, Hungary, and Poland), contrary to the conventional notion that retrenchment and radical reforms are unlikely to be tackled when the hazards of accountability are high. Apparently the perceived attractiveness of pension privatization may outweigh its blame-generating potential, thereby differing greatly from the political-economic potential of PAYG-only reforms.

Concluding Remarks

A wave of pension privatizations in Latin America and Eastern Europe have occurred over the past decade. Each reform is unique in its features, as their architects rightly claim. Yet, intra- and cross-regional comparisons reveal that the basic design of each shows striking similarities to the others, as existing old-age security schemes are fully or partly substituted by privately run pension funds on a mandatory basis. Differences concern the size of the funded tier and thus the scope of the paradigm shift. So far, structural pension reform in Latin America predominantly has implied closing down or phasing out the public tier, while mixed and parallel reform paths have also been followed. Compared with this, there is only one post-socialist country (Kazakhstan) that replicated the Chilean model. The other transition countries that have embarked on pension privatization retained a downsized public pillar under a mixed reform strategy. Although half of Latin American countries have opted for some variant of pension privatization, most post-socialist transition countries still stick to PAYG-only reforms.

Latin American and Eastern European pension privatizations indicate that, contrary to conventional wisdom, radical reform can be accomplished in the area of old-age security. It has long been held that structural pension reform was possible only under an authoritarian regime, but recent trends have shown that a paradigm shift in social security can be feasible under democratic regimes. In this chapter, the making of pension reform in two Latin American and two Eastern European countries has been analyzed, drawing on the broader framework of the political economy of policy reform. By pointing to the emergence and the impact of the new pension orthodoxy, the importance of policy transfer in old-age security reform is explored. When examining the circumstances that enabled pension privatization in both regions, it turned out that the driving forces of pension privatization proved to be the neoliberally minded ministries of finance and economics, backed by the IFIs' policy advice and financial support. Many local pressure groups opposed structural pension reform. These groups' room for maneuvering was shaped by economic conditions, political and institutional factors, and earlier policy choices. The strategic importance of reform design was also discussed, pointing to cases of strategic bundling and unbundling, tactical packaging, and compensation. This analysis of the factors driving pension privatization points up the relevance of political economy considerations for understanding reform dynamics in the area of old-age security.

Notes

1. Similarly, Weaver (1986, p. 365): "It never pays to eliminate the [PAYG] system, regardless of how poor the return becomes."

2. On Latin American pension reforms, see Mesa-Lago (1998b), Queisser (1998), Müller (2000b), and Kay and Kritzer (2001).

3. On post-socialist pension reforms, see Palacios, Rutkowski, and Yu (1999), Fultz and Ruck (2000), and Müller (2000a).

4. For a comparative analysis of the Chilean and Argentine pension reforms, see Arenas de Mesa and Bertranou (1997) and Hujo (1999).

5. For a survey of existing contributions on the "dynamics of deterioration"—in absence of reforms—see Rodrik (1996, pp. 12–17, 21–25), and Tommasi and Velasco (1996, pp. 192–97).

6. See Rodrik (1994, pp. 30–31) for a critical view of the positive impact of foreign aid and conditionality on reform.

7. For an early discussion of "crisis as an ingredient of reform" see Hirschman (1963, pp. 260–64).

8. See Drazen and Grilli (1993) for a formalization of the argument that crises may improve welfare.

9. "Indeed, the objective identification of a crisis is no easier in the heady days of the Washington consensus than it was in the bad old days of those endless neo-Marxist debates about 'the crisis.'" (Toye 1994, p. 41)

10. Another important modification that helped win support for the reform law was the double state guarantee—in US$ and pesos—for contributions to the pension fund to be set up by Banco Nación, a public bank. However, the dollar-based guarantee was eliminated by presidential decree shortly after the passing of the pension reform law. See Torre and Gerchunoff (1999, p. 27).

11. On the politics of Argentine pension reform, see Isuani and San Martino (1995), Alonso (1998, 2000), Rossi (1999), and Torre and Gerchunoff (1999).

12. The idea was to pay the *Bonosol* only to those Bolivians who had attained majority on December 31, 1995, to reflect the contribution of the current working-age population to the state-owned enterprises.

13. The *Bolivida* scheme pays an annual pension of US$60 to those above age 50 (as of December 31, 1995), after they reach age 65. The Banzer government also promised "popular shares" to Bolivians between ages 21 and 50 (as of December 31, 1995), but this program has not been implemented.

14. On the politics of the Bolivian pension reform, see Gray-Molina, Pérez de Rada, and Yañez (1999), Pérez (2000), and Müller (2001b).

15. On the politics of Hungarian pension reform, see Ferge (1999), Müller (1999), and Orenstein (2000).

16. For a discussion of notional defined contribution plans, see Cichon (1999) and Disney (1999).

17. On the politics of Polish pension reform, see Müller (1999), Orenstein (2000), Hausner (2001), and Nelson (2001).

18. The "third wave of democratization" began in the mid-1970s in southern Europe and spread to Latin America and some Asian countries in the 1980s. In the late 1980s and early 1990s it eventually reached Eastern Europe (Huntington 1991). See also Merkel (1999).

19. Haggard and Kaufman (1995) compare Latin American and Asian transitions, and extend some of their findings to the transformation process in Eastern Europe (pp. 371–77).

20. See, for example, Przeworski (1991a), Bresser Pereira, Maravall, and Przeworski (1993), Linz and Stepan (1996), and Greskovits (1998).

21. Some "heterodoxy" remains, however. See Mesa-Lago (1996) and Ney (2000) for a comparative analysis of different policy prescriptions for old-age security.

22. "Over the last five years, the World Bank has established itself as a leader in pension reform issues in a world that is rapidly aging" (Holzmann 1999, p. 2). Holzmann (2000) provides an update on the World Bank's position on pension reform. For a recent critique, see Kotlikoff (1999) and Orszag and Stiglitz (1999).

23. The ADB was active in the Kazakh pension privatization.

24. An example of the latter is the Polish edition of José Piñera's prominent book (1991) with a Polish economist's preface titled, "Let's Learn from the Chileans!" (Wilczynski 1996). See also Piñera (2000).

25. It should be noted that in Western Europe no mainstream pension model has emerged. Rather, the region is characterized by a considerable heterogeneity in modes of old-age provision. Hence, EU accession negotiations do not entail a pension reform blueprint to be followed. However, the Swedish reform blueprint—a multipillar system combining notional defined contribution and full funding—has had an impact on some Eastern European countries (notably Latvia and Poland).

26. For similar recommendations, see also Holzmann (1994) and de Fougerolles (1996).

27. On the concept of policy feedback, see Esping-Andersen (1985) and Pierson (1993); for a recent discussion of the concept of path dependence, see Pierson (2000).

28. For existing legal constraints that have influenced pension reform outcomes, see the Peruvian and Colombian cases in which the constitution established social security as a responsibility of the state and private pension provision was permitted only on a supplementary basis. Consequently, policymakers opted for a parallel pension reform path (Mesa-Lago 1999).

29. Similarly Barr (2000): "The ability of governments to change the rules breaks the equivalence between implicit and explicit liabilities." p. 15.

30. Palacios, Rutkowski, and Yu (1999, p. 31) even claim that "[a]s part of its strategy, the government will *have to* renege on some pay-as-you-go commitments" [emphasis added by author].

31. For a discussion of different types of compensation, see James and Brooks (2001, pp. 159–63).

32. But compare Müller (1998).

33. Recent developments in Argentina make it clear, however, that political risk also may affect the private tier. In the midst of economic collapse, individual contribution rates were cut by more than half to stimulate consumption, while the AFJPs (or "Pension Fund Administrators") were forced into a massive debt restructuring and purchase of treasury bills. When government bonds surpassed 80 percent of the AFJPs' portfolio, the incoming Peronist administration suspended debt service, thereby threatening the future retirement benefits of 8.6 million affiliates.

References

The word *processed* indicates informally reproduced works that may not be commonly available through libraries.

Alonso, Guillermo V. 1998. "Democracia y reformas: Las tensiones entre decretismo y deliberación. El caso de la reforma previsional Argentina." *Desarrollo Económico* 38(150):595–626.

———. 2000. "Política y seguridad social en la Argentina de los '90." Madrid: Miño y Dávila Editores.

Arenas de Mesa, Alberto, and Fabio Bertranou. 1997. "Learning from Social Security Reforms: Two Different Cases, Chile and Argentina." *World Development* 25(3):329–48.

Arnold, R. Douglas, Michael J. Graetz, and Alicia H. Munnell, eds. 1998. *Framing the Social Security Debate. Values, Politics, and Economics.* Washington, D.C.: National Academy of Social Insurance.

Balcerowicz, Leszek. 1994. "Poland." In John Williamson, ed., *The Political Economy of Policy Reform.* Washington, D.C.: Institute for International Economics.

Barr, Nicholas. 2000. "Reforming Pensions: Myths, Truths, and Policy Choices." IMF Working Paper WP/007139. Washington, D.C.

Bery, Suman K. 1990. "Economic Policy Reform in Developing Countries: The Role and Management of Political Factors." *World Development* 18 (8):1123–131.

Bönker, Frank. 1995. "The Dog That Did Not Bark? Politische Restriktionen und ökonomische Reformen in den Visegrád-Ländern." In Hellmut Wollmann, Helmut Wiesenthal, and Frank Bönker, eds., *Transformation sozialistischer Gesellschaften: Am Ende des Anfangs.* Opladen, Germany: Westdeutscher Verlag.

———. 2002. *The Political Economy of Fiscal Reform in Eastern Europe.* Cheltenham, U.K.: Edward Elgar, forthcoming.

Börsch-Supan, Axel. 1998. "Germany: A Social Security System on the Verge of Collapse." In Horst Siebert, ed., *Redesigning Social Security.* Tübingen, Germany: Mohr.

Bresser Pereira, Luiz Carlos, José María Maravall, and Adam Przeworski. 1993. *Economic Reforms in New Democracies: A Social-Democratic Approach.* Cambridge, U.K.: Cambridge University Press.

Brooks, Sarah. 1998. "Social Protection in a Global Economy: The Case of Pension Reform in Latin America." Duke University. Processed.

Buchanan, James M. 1983. "Social Security Survival: A Public-Choice Perspective." *The Cato Journal* 3(2):339–53.

Busquets, José Miguel. 2000. "Las reformas de la Seguridad Social en Argentina, Bolivia, Chile y Uruguay (1981-1995)." Montevideo, Uruguay. Processed.

Butler, Stuart, and Peter Germanis. 1983. "Achieving a 'Leninist' Strategy." *The Cato Journal* 3(2):547–56.

Cain, Michael J. G. 2000. "Globalising Tendencies in Public Policy." *EMERGO* 7(2):6–19.

Cichon, Michael. 1999. "Notional Defined-Contribution Schemes: Old Wine in New Bottles?" *International Social Security Review* 52(4):87–105.

Corsetti, Giancarlo, and Klaus Schmidt-Hebbel. 1997. "Pension Reform and Growth." In Salvador Valdés-Prieto, ed., *The Economics of Pensions. Principles, Policies, and International Experience.* Cambridge, U.K.: Cambridge University Press.

Cukierman, Alex, and Mariano Tommasi. 1998a. "Credibility of Policymakers and of Economic Reforms." In Federico Sturzenegger and Mariano Tommasi, eds., *The Political Economy of Reform.* Cambridge, Mass.: MIT Press.

———. 1998b. "When Does It Take a Nixon to Go to China?" *American Economic Review* 88(1):180–97.

Dewatripont, Mathias, and Gérard Roland. 1998. "The Design of Reform Packages under Uncertainty." In Federico Sturzenegger and Mariano Tommasi, eds., *The Political Economy of Reform.* Cambridge, Mass.: MIT Press.

Disney, Richard. 1999. "Notional Accounts As a Pension Reform Strategy: An Evaluation." *World Bank Pension Reform Primer.* Washington, D.C.

Dolowitz, David P., and David Marsh. 2000. "Learning from Abroad: The Role of Policy Transfer in Contemporary Policy-Making." *Governance: An International Journal of Policy and Administration* 13(1):5–24.

Drazen, Allan, and Vittorio Grilli. 1993. "The Benefit of Crises for Economic Reforms." *American Economic Review* 83(3):598–607.

Esping-Andersen, Gøsta. 1985. *Politics Against Markets: The Social Democratic Road to Power.* Princeton, N.J.: Princeton University Press.

Ferge, Zsuzsa. 1999. "The Politics of the Hungarian Pension Reform." In Katharina Müller, Andreas Ryll, and Hans-Jürgen Wagener, eds., *Transformation of Social Security: Pensions in Central-Eastern Europe.* Heidelberg: Physica.

de Fougerolles, Jean. 1996. "Pension Privatization in Latin America—Lessons for Central and Eastern Europe." *Russian and East-European Finance and Trade* 3(32):86–104.

Fox, Louise, and Edward Palmer. 1999. "New Approaches to Multi-Pillar Pension Systems: What in the World Is Going On?" Washington, D.C. Processed.

Fultz, Elaine, and Markus Ruck. 2000. "Pension Reform in Central and Eastern Europe: An Update on the Restructuring of National Pension Schemes in Selected Countries." ILO-CEET Report No. 25. Budapest.

Gesell-Schmidt, Rainer, Katharina Müller, and Dirck Süß. 1999. "Social Security Reform and Privatisation in Poland: Parallel Projects or Integrated Agenda?" *Osteuropa-Wirtschaft* 44(4):428–50.

Götting, Ulrike. 1998. *Transformation der Wohlfahrtsstaaten in Mittelund Osteuropa. Eine Zwischenbilanz.* Opladen, Germany: Leske + Budrich.

Graham, Carol. 1997. "From Safety Nets to Social Policy: Lessons for the Transition Economies from the Developing Countries." In Joan Nelson, Charles Tilly, and Lee Walker, eds., *Transforming Post-Communist Political Economies.* Washington, D.C.: National Academies Press.

Gray-Molina, George, Ernesto Pérez de Rada, and Ernesto Yañez. 1999. "La economía política de reformas institucionales en Bolivia." Red de Centros de Investigación, Documento de Trabajo R-350. Washington, D.C.: Inter-American Development Bank.

Greskovits, Béla. 1998. *The Political Economy of Protest and Patience: East European and Latin American Transformations Compared.* Budapest: CEU Press.

Haas, Peter M. 1992. "Introduction: Epistemic Communities and International Policy Coordination." *International Organization* 46(1):1–35.

Haggard, Stephan, and Robert R. Kaufman. 1995. *The Political Economy of Democratic Transitions.* Princeton, N.J.: Princeton University Press.

Haggard, Stephan, and Steven B. Webb. 1993. "What Do We Know about the Political Economy of Economic Policy Reform?" *The World Bank Research Observer* 8(2):143–68.

Harberger, Arnold C. 1993. "Secrets of Success: A Handful of Heroes." *American Economic Review—Papers and Proceedings* 83(2):342–50.

Hausner, Jerzy. 2001. "Security through Diversity: Conditions for Successful Reform of the Pension System in Poland." In János Kornai, Stephan Haggard, and Robert R. Kaufman, eds., *Reforming the State: Fiscal and*

Welfare Reform in Post-Socialist Countries. Cambridge, U.K.: Cambridge University Press.

Hirschman, Albert O. 1963. *Journeys Toward Progress: Studies of Economic Policy-Making in Latin America.* New York: The Twentieth Century Fund.

———. 1991. *The Rhetoric of Reaction: Perversity, Futility, Jeopardy.* Cambridge, Mass.: Harvard University Press.

Holzmann, Robert. 1994. "Funded and Private Pensions for Eastern European Countries in Transition" *Revista de Análisis Económico* 9(1):183–210.

———. 1997. "On Economic Benefits and Fiscal Requirements of Moving from Unfunded to Funded Pensions." Forschungsbericht 9702. Saarbrücken, Germany: University of Saarland.

———. 1999. "The World Bank and Global Pension Reform—Realities not Myths." Washington, D.C. Processed.

———. 2000. "The World Bank Approach to Pension Reform." *International Social Security Review* 53(1):11–34.

Huber, Evelyne, and John D. Stephens. 2000. "The Political Economy of Pension Reform: Latin America in Comparative Perspective." United Nations Research Institute for Social Development (UNRISD) Occasional Paper 7, Geneva.

Hujo, Katja. 1999. "Paradigmatic Change in Old Age Security: Latin American Cases." In Katharina Müller, Andreas Ryll, and Hans-Jürgen Wagener, eds., *Transformation of Social Security: Pensions in Central-Eastern Europe.* Heidelberg: Physica.

Huntington, Samuel. 1991. *The Third Wave: Democratization in the Late Twentieth Century.* Norman, Okla.: University of Oklahoma Press.

Isuani, Ernesto Aldo, and Jorge A. San Martino. 1995. "El nuevo sistema previsional Argentino ¿Punto final a una larga crisis?" Primera parte: *Boletín Informativo Techint* 281:41–56; Segunda parte: *Boletín Informativo Techint* 282:43–67.

James, Estelle, and Sarah Brooks. 2001. "The Political Economy of Structural Pension Reform." In R. Holzmann and J. Stiglitz, eds., *New Ideas about Old-Age Security: Toward Sustainable Pension Systems in the 21st Century.* Washington, D.C.: World Bank.

Karl, Terry Lynn, and Philippe C. Schmitter. 1991. "Modes of Transition in Latin America, Southern and Eastern Europe." *International Social Science Journal* 128:268–84.

Kay, Stephen J. 1998. "Politics and Social Security Reform in the Southern Cone and Brazil." Ph.D. diss., University of California at Los Angeles. Processed.

———. 1999. "Unexpected Privatizations: Politics and Social Security Reforms in the Southern Cone." *Comparative Politics* 31(4):403–22.

Kay, Stephen J., and Barbara E. Kritzer. 2001. "Social Security in Latin America: Recent Reforms and Challenges." *Economic Review* first quarter:41–52.

Kotlikoff, Laurence J. 1999. "The World Bank's Approach and the Right Approach to Pension Reform." Boston. Processed.

Krueger, Anne O. 1993. "Virtuous and Vicious Circles in Economic Development." *American Economic Review—Papers and Proceedings* 83(2):351–55.

Lindeman, David, Michal Rutkowski, and Oleksiy Sluchynskyy. 2000. *The Evolution of Pension Systems in Eastern Europe and Central Asia: Opportunities,*

Constraints, Dilemmas and Emerging Practices. Washington, D.C.: World Bank.

Linz, Juan J., and Alfred Stepan. 1996. *Problems of Democratic Transition and Consolidation. Southern Europe, South America, and Post-Communist Europe.* Baltimore: The John Hopkins University Press.

Lo Vuolo, Rubén M. 1996. "Reformas previsionales en América Latina: el caso Argentino." *Comercio Exterior* 46(9):692–702.

Lora, Eduardo. 2000. "What Makes Reform Likely? Timing and Sequencing of Structural Reforms in Latin America." IADB Research Department Working Paper 424. Washington, D.C.

Madrid, Raúl. 1998. "The Determinants of Pension Reform Around the World, 1992–97." Processed.

———. 1999. "The New Logic of Social Security Reform: Politics and Pension Privatization in Latin America." Ph.D. diss., Stanford University, Stanford, Calif.

Martinelli, César, and Mariano Tommasi. 1998. "Sequencing of Economic Reforms in the Presence of Political Constraints." In Federico Sturzenegger and Mariano Tommasi, eds., *The Political Economy of Reform.* Cambridge, Mass.: MIT Press.

Merkel, Wolfgang. 1999. "Systemtransformation: Eine Einführung in die Theorie und Empirie der Transformationsforschung." Opladen: Leske + Budrich.

Merton, Robert K. 1948. "Discussion." *American Sociological Review* 14(1):164–68.

Mesa-Lago, Carmelo. 1996. "Pension system reforms in Latin America: the position of the international organizations." *CEPAL Review* 60:73–98.

———. 1998a. "La reforma de pensiones en América Latina: Tipología, comprobación de presupuestos y enseñanzas." In Alejandro Bonilla García and Alfredo H. Conte-Grand, eds., *Pensiones en América Latina: Dos Décadas de Reforma.* Geneva: International Labour Organisation.

———. 1998b. "The Reform of Social Security Pensions in Latin America: Public, Private, Mixed and Parallel Systems." In Franz Ruland, ed., *Verfassung, Theorie und Praxis des Sozialstaats: Festschrift für Hans F. Zacher zum 70. Geburtstag.* Heidelberg: Müller.

———. 1999. "Política y reforma de la seguridad social en América Latina." *Nueva Sociedad* 160:133–50.

———. 2000. "Estudio comparativo de los costos fiscales en la transicion de ocho reformas de pensiones en América Latina." Serie Financiamiento del Desarrollo 93. Santiago de Chile: CEPAL.

Mora, Marek. 1999. "The Political Economy of Pension Reforms: The Case of Latin America." Washington, D.C. Processed.

Müller, Katharina. 1998. "Shall We Forget the Latin American Precedents?" *Transition* 9(5):29.

———. 1999. *The Political Economy of Pension Reform in Central-Eastern Europe.* Cheltenham, U.K.: Edward Elgar.

———. 2000a. "Die Reform der Alterssicherung in den östlichen Transformationsländern: Eine Zwischenbilanz." *Deutsche Rentenversicherung* 5:139–52.

———. 2000b. "Pension Privatization in Latin America." *Journal of International Development* 12:507–18.

———. 2001a. "Conquistando el Este—Los modelos previsionales latinoamericanos en los países ex socialistas." *Socialis. Revista Latinoamericana de Políticas Sociales* March:39–52.

———. 2001b. "Die Privatisierung der bolivianischen Alterssicherung: Eine Zwischenbilanz." In Rafael Sevilla and Ariel Benavides, eds., *Bolivien—das verkannte Land?* Bad Honnef, Germany: Horlemann.

Nelson, Joan M. 1994. "Panel Discussion." In John Williamson, ed., *The Political Economy of Policy Reform.* Washington, D.C.: Institute for International Economics.

———. 2000. "External Models, International Influence, and the Politics of Social Sector Reforms." Washington, D.C. Processed.

———. 2001. "The Politics of Pension and Health-Care Reforms in Hungary and Poland." In János Kornai, Stephan Haggard, and Robert R. Kaufman, eds., *Reforming the State: Fiscal and Welfare Reform in Post-Socialist Countries.* Cambridge, U.K.: Cambridge University Press.

Ney, Steven. 2000. "Are You Sitting Comfortably...Then We'll Begin: Three Gripping Policy Stories about Pension Reform." *Innovation: The European Journal of Social Sciences* 13(4):341–71.

Nitsch, Manfred, and Helmut Schwarzer. 1996. "Recent Developments in Financing Social Security in Latin America." *Issues in Social Protection* 1, Geneva: International Labour Organisation.

Orenstein, Mitchell. 2000. "How Politics and Institutions Affect Pension Reform in Three Postcommunist Countries." World Bank Policy Research Working Paper 2310, Washington, D.C.

Orszag, Peter R., and Joseph E. Stiglitz. 1999. "Rethinking Pension Reform: Ten Myths About Social Security Systems." Washington, D.C. Processed.

Palacios, Robert, and Roberto Rocha. 1998. "The Hungarian Pension System in Transition." In Lajos Bokros and Jean-Jacques Dethier, eds., *Public Finance Reform during the Transition: The Experience of Hungary.* Washington, D.C.: World Bank.

Palacios, Robert, Michal Rutkowski, and Xiaoqing Yu. 1999. "Pension Reforms in Transition Economies." Washington, D.C. Processed.

Pérez B., Martín. 2000. "Circuito político de una política pública: reforma al sistema de pensiones en Bolivia." La Paz, Bolivia. Processed.

Pierson, Paul. 1993. "When Effect Becomes Cause: 'Policy Feedback' and Political Change." *World Politics* 45(4):595–628.

———. 1994. *Dismantling the Welfare State? Reagan, Thatcher, and the Politics of Retrenchment.* Cambridge, U.K.: Cambridge University Press.

———. 1996. "The New Politics of the Welfare State." *World Politics* 48(January):143–79.

———. 1998. "Irresistible Forces, Immovable Objects: Post-Industrial Welfare States Confront Permanent Austerity." *Journal of European Public Policy* 5(4):639–60.

———. 2000. "Increasing Returns, Path Dependence, and the Study of Politics." *American Political Science Review* 94(2):251–67.

Pierson, Paul, and R. Kent Weaver. 1993. "Imposing Losses in Pension Policy." In R. Kent Weaver and Bert A. Rockman, eds., *Do Institutions Matter? Government Capabilities in the United States and Abroad.* Washington, D.C.: Brookings Institution.

Piñera, José. 1991. *El cascabel al gato. La batalla por la Reforma Previsional.* Santiago de Chile: Zig-Zag.

———. 1996. *Bez obawy o przyszlosc.* Warsaw: Centrum im. Adama Smitha & Fundacja im. Hugona Kollątaja.

———. 2000. "A Chilean Model for Russia." *Foreign Affairs* 79(5):62–73.

Przeworski, Adam. 1991a. *Democracy and the Market: Political and Economic Reforms in Eastern Europe and Latin America.* Cambridge, U.K.: Cambridge University Press.

———. 1991b. "Spiel mit Einsatz: Demokratisierungsprozesse in Lateinamerika, Osteuropa und anderswo." *Transit* 1:190–211.

Przeworski, Adam, and 20 others. 1995. *Sustainable Democracy.* Cambridge, U.K.: Cambridge University Press.

Queisser, Monika. 1998. *The Second-Generation Pension Reforms in Latin America.* Paris: Organisation for Economic Co-operation and Development.

Rodrik, Dani. 1993. "The Positive Economics of Policy Reform." *American Economic Review—Papers and Proceedings* 83(2):356–61.

———. 1994. "Comment." In John Williamson, ed., *The Political Economy of Policy Reform.* Washington, D.C.: Institute for International Economics.

———. 1996. "Understanding Economic Policy Reform." *Journal of Economic Literature* 34(March):9–41.

———. 1998. "Promises, Promises: Credible Policy Reform via Signalling." In Federico Sturzenegger and Mariano Tommasi, eds., *The Political Economy of Reform.* Cambridge, Mass.: MIT Press.

Ross, Fiona. 2000. "Beyond Left and Right: The New Partisan Politics of Welfare." *Governance: An International Journal of Policy and Administration.* 13(2):155–83.

Rossi, Alejandro. 1999. "Reforma previsional ¿cómo y porqué?" Buenos Aires. Processed.

Rutkowski, Michal. 1998. "A New Generation of Pension Reforms Conquers the East—A Taxonomy in Transition Economies." *Transition* 9(4):16–19.

Sachs, Jeffrey. 1994. "Life in the Economic Emergency Room." In John Williamson, ed., *The Political Economy of Policy Reform.* Washington, D.C.: Institute for International Economics.

Schmähl, Winfried. 1998. "Comment on the Papers by Axel Börsch-Supan, Edward M. Gramlich, and Mats Persson." In Horst Siebert, ed., *Redesigning Social Security.* Tübingen, Germany: Mohr.

Schmitter, Philippe C., and Terry Lynn Karl. 1994. "The Conceptual Travels of Transitologists and Consolidologists: How Far to the East Should They Attempt to Go?" *Slavic Review* 53(1):173–85.

Stallings, Barbara. 1994. "Discussion." In John Williamson, ed., *The Political Economy of Policy Reform.* Washington, D.C.: Institute for International Economics.

Stiglitz, Joseph E. 1998. "An Agenda for Development in the Twenty-First Century." In Boris Pleskovic and Joseph E. Stiglitz, eds., *Annual World Bank Conference on Development Economics 1997.* Washington, D.C.: World Bank.

Sturzenegger, Federico, and Mariano Tommasi. 1998a. "Introduction." In Federico Sturzenegger and Mariano Tommasi, eds., *The Political Economy of Reform.* Cambridge, Mass.: MIT Press.

————, eds. 1998b. *The Political Economy of Reform*. Cambridge, Mass.: MIT Press.

Thompson, Lawrence H. 1983. "The Social Security Reform Debate." *Journal of Economic Literature* 21(December):1425–467.

Tommasi, Mariano, and Andrés Velasco. 1996. "Where Are We in the Political Economy of Reform?" *Journal of Policy Reform* 1:187–238.

Torre, Juan Carlos, and Pablo Gerchunoff. 1999. "La economía política de las reformas institucionales en Argentina: Los casos de la política de privatización de Entel, la reforma de la seguridad social y la reforma laboral." Red de Centros de Investigación, Documento de Trabajo R-349. Washington, D.C.: Inter-American Development Bank.

Touraine, Alain. 1989. *América Latina—Política y sociedad*. Madrid: Espasa-Calpe.

Toye, John. 1994. "Comment." In John Williamson, ed., *The Political Economy of Policy Reform*. Washington, D.C.: Institute for International Economics.

Vittas, Dimitri. 1997. "The Argentine Pension Reform and Its Relevance for Eastern Europe." World Bank, Financial Sector Development Department. Policy Research Working Paper 1819. Washington, D.C.

Wagener, Hans-Jürgen. 1997. "Transformation als historisches Phänomen." *Jahrbuch für Wirtschaftsgeschichte* 2:179–91.

Weaver, R. Kent. 1986. "The Politics of Blame Avoidance." *Journal of Public Policy* 6(October–December):371–98.

Wei, Shang-Jin. 1998. "Gradualism versus Big-Bang: Speed and Sustainability of Reforms." In Federico Sturzenegger and Mariano Tommasi, eds., *The Political Economy of Reform*. Cambridge, Mass.: MIT Press.

Weyland, Kurt. 2000. "Learning from Foreign Models in Latin American Policy Reform." Nashville, Tenn. Processed.

Whitehead, Laurence. 1990. "Political Explanations of Macroeconomic Management: A Survey." *World Development* 18(8):1133–146.

Wilczyński, Waclaw. 1996. "Uczymy się od Chilijczyków!" In José Piñera, *Bez obawy o przyszlosc*. Warsaw: Centrumim. Adama Smitha & Fundacja im. Hugona Kollątaja.

Williamson, John, ed. 1990. "Latin American Adjustment: How Much Has Happened?" Washington, D.C.: Institute for International Economics.

————. 1994a. "In Search of a Manual for Technopols." In John Williamson, ed., *The Political Economy of Policy Reform*. Washington, D.C.: Institute for International Economics.

————, ed. 1994b. *The Political Economy of Policy Reform*. Washington, D.C.: Institute for International Economics.

————. 2000. "What Should the World Bank Think about the Washington Consensus?" *The World Bank Research Observer* 15(2):251–64.

Williamson, John, and Stephan Haggard. 1994. "The Political Conditions for Economic Reform." In John Williamson, ed., *The Political Economy of Policy Reform*. Washington, D.C.: Institute for International Economics.

World Bank. 1994. *Averting the Old Age Crisis: Policies to Protect the Old and Promote Growth*. London: Oxford University Press.

———. 1997. *The State in a Changing World: World Development Report 1997.* London: Oxford University Press.

———. 1998. "Poland at a Glance." Washington, D.C. Processed.

———. 1999. "Labor and Social Protection. Thematic Sites: Pensions." Washington, D.C.: World Bank. http://wbln0018.worldbank.org/HDNet/HD.nsf/SectorPages/SP?Opendocument

———. 2000a. "Argentina at a Glance." Washington, D.C. Processed.

———. 2000b. "Bolivia at a Glance." Washington, D.C. Processed.

———. 2000c. "Hungary at a Glance." Washington, D.C. Processed.

———. 2000d. "Poland at a Glance." Washington, D.C. Processed.

3

The Rediscovery of Politics: Democracy and Structural Pension Reform in Continental Europe

Steven Ney

When reflecting on pension reform experiences, scholars and policymakers alike tend to dwell on the difficulties of reform, the irrationality of policymaking, and the barriers to structural change. To learn why structural pension reform is so difficult, some scholars concentrate on the fiscal and economic contexts of reform efforts (James and Brooks 1999), others analyze individual political behavior (Disney 1996), and still others look at the interaction of political constraints at different levels of governance (Pierson 1994, 1996; Pierson and Weaver 1993; Hinrichs 2000, 2001). Despite this variety in methods and approaches, the general and somewhat disturbing implication running through most studies is that democracies create nearly insurmountable barriers to structural pension reform. Not only do democratic polities provide few electoral incentives for embarking on pension reform, but pluralist politics also create ample opportunities for adversaries to hobble reform efforts. The common wisdom emerging from this line of argument is that the best that would-be reformers can hope for is an iterative process of incremental and piecemeal change. Because radical or structural pension reform is politically costly, any attempt to restructure pension systems fundamentally is tantamount to political suicide and, for all intents and purposes, impossible.

Based on empirical evidence from four continental European countries (Austria, France, Germany, and Italy),[1] this chapter suggests that democracies and democratic practices actually have enabled rather than constrained structural pension reform in Europe. Rather than look to macropolitical variables to explain pension reform processes (as do the political scientists reviewed in the first section below), this chapter will look very closely at the subpolitics of European pension policy networks. An analysis of European pension policy communities reveals that the reluctance to reform has more to do with the dominance of expert-oriented policy networks than with democratic politics. As explained in the second section below, these ideologically cohesive and organizationally integrated corporatist policy communities were successful at insulating policy networks from both parliamentary and public scrutiny. As a result, much of pension policymaking prior to the 1990s was incremental and piecemeal, geared toward maintaining the institutional status quo.

From about 1990 onward, however, new types of policy actors successfully challenged the ideological and political dominance of established pension policy networks in continental Europe. As these actors introduced new ideas and concepts into European pension reform debates (many of them critical of established pension systems), they broadened the scope of political conflict: European pension debates now feature competing accounts of the pension issue rather than one pension orthodoxy. Consequently, pension policymaking has become more contentious and conflictual because a far more volatile "garbage can" policy process is replacing the predictability of corporatist bargaining. In short, European pension policymaking has rediscovered pluralist politics. This rediscovery of principled policy conflict has coincided with structural reform measures in continental Europe.

The Politics of Pension Reform

Most commentators and observers agree that social policymaking is not as much fun as it used to be. Perpetual crises of social security budgets caused by increasingly competitive global markets, persistent unemployment, and demographic aging remind us that the heady days of welfare state expansion are most definitely over. Nowadays, social policy seems to be about adapting welfare states, including pension systems, to harsher economic climates. In practice, this has meant retrenching and reducing the generosity of welfare state provisions.

Under these new circumstances, pension reform in democratic polities has become a thorny, politically risky, and inherently divisive policy issue. Despite what seems to be overwhelming evidence in favor of incisive structural reforms, pension systems have proven remarkably immune to fundamental change. Finding that theories of welfare state expansion have not explained welfare state retrenchment[2] (Pierson 1994, 1996), political scientists have suggested that the observed resilience of welfare states may be related to the ways that contemporary democracies and their institutions are structured.

The Institutional Limits to Welfare State Retrenchment in Democracies

The political process of retrenching welfare states is not the mirror image of the process of expanding them. In fact, Paul Pierson (1994, 1996) argues that retrenchment is an altogether more treacherous exercise for two reasons. First, current retrenchment policies have dramatically different electoral implications than did the expansionary efforts of the past. Retrenchment involves imposing concrete losses on a specific group within the electorate. Because this is not likely to be popular with voters,[3] policymakers anxious about reelection will find that a "...simple 'redistributive' transfer of resources from program beneficiaries to taxpayers, engineered through cuts in social programs, is generally a losing proposition" (Pierson 1996, p. 146). Second, welfare state retrenchment takes place in different institutional contexts than did welfare state expansion. Over the past decades, social policymaking has given rise to networks of professional bodies and advocacy groups that design, administer, implement, and evaluate social policy. Not only may these interest groups be in a position to mobilize a substantial part of the electorate (for example, the "grey lobby" in the United States or unions in continental Europe), but they also may be able to obstruct policy implementation where they have a role in the administration of welfare state programs. As a result, rather than policymakers attempting to claim credit for expansive welfare state reforms, the "new politics of the welfare state" (Pierson 1996) is about shunting and avoiding the blame for unpopular benefit cuts to escape punishment at the hands of voters.

As a result of the institutional structures of contemporary democracies themselves, pension retrenchment is bound to be a thorny and precarious political project. Political scientists such as Paul Pierson (1994), Kent Weaver (Pierson and Weaver 1993), and Giuliano Bonoli (2000) have analyzed how patterns of formal and informal political institutions shape pension reform *strategies*. Democratic institutions regulate political participation and contestation by defining so-called veto points at which the political opposition may intervene in the policy process (Bonoli 2000; Ebbinghaus and Hassel 2000; Müller 1999). Bonoli (2000) argues that pension reform will be more difficult, require more complex governmental strategies, and lead to qualitatively different reform pathways in polities with many veto points (such as Switzerland or the United States) than in polities that concentrate political power in the hands of the government (such as the United Kingdom). Yet, political institutions do not determine pension reforms in any mechanical sense. Pierson and Weaver (1993) argue that political systems that concentrate power also focus accountability. With few institutional mechanisms for avoiding blame, begrudged voters will know exactly who is responsible and whom to punish at the ballot box (Pierson 1994, 1996). The fate of any particular reform, Pierson argues, will depend on whether the concentration of power outweighs the concentration of accountability. Formal political institutions, then, are important in the sense that they frame policy processes, regulate political contestation, and define feasible pension reform pathways (Pierson 1994). Their direct impact on pension reforms, however, remains ambiguous and complex.

In addition to formal political institutions, the design and structure of pension systems themselves create barriers for retrenchment. Here political scientists point to path dependency and institutional lock-in as crucial determinants of pension reform *options*. Whether a pension system operates along the lines of the social insurance model or of Beveridge's vision of social security makes a substantial difference to available policy alternatives and policy tools. For example, Bismarckian systems allow policymakers to manipulate contribution rates and noncontributory elements, whereas policymakers in Beveridgean systems can work with means-tested benefits and eligibility criteria (Bonoli 2000). More fundamentally, long-term financial commitments encoded in the institutional design of pension systems may lock policymakers into a specific reform trajectory. The most prominent example of institutional lock-in is the pay-as-you-go (PAYG) system. The accrued pension claims of present generations, observers argue, give rise to prohibitively high transition costs that prevent a wholesale shift to fully funded pensions (Hinrichs 2001; Pierson 1994). Beyond financing mechanisms, pension system designs also designate who is involved in running the pension systems and who has an interest in maintaining or changing the status quo. For instance, in continental European countries pension systems are located in a social space shared by governments, labor unions, and employers' associations (Ebbinghaus and Hassel 2000). Bi- and tripartite management regimes, such as in France, Germany, or Italy not only introduce veto points into the decisionmaking process; they also define stakeholders and their interests in the pension system.

In sum, the literature tells us that welfare state retrenchment and pension reform in democracies is difficult because

- they are likely to be unpopular with the electorate
- democratic polities provide ample opportunities for contesting unpopular policy (via veto points) or for punishing policymakers (via elections)
- the structures of welfare state institutions and pension schemes themselves rule out certain policy options from the outset, thereby narrowing the feasible set of policy alternatives.

How have policymakers dealt with these institutional constraints? As a rule, Pierson (1994, 1996) argues, policymakers have tried to mitigate the electoral impact of imposing losses by either maximizing electoral margins or minimizing political opposition to the reform. Basing his argument on evidence from four countries,[4] he maintains that policymakers have applied any or all of three blame-avoidance strategies. First, policymakers and politicians have played off different groups in the policy community. Second, policymakers have pursued strategies of compensation by providing financial benefits to potential losers in retrenchment policies. Third, and most important, would-be reformers have lowered the public visibility of benefit cuts. For example, according to Pierson, policymakers can obfuscate retrenchment by formulating highly complicated reforms and burying the potential policy outcomes in technical jargon. Another strategy for blurring political responsibility, Pierson points out, is to delegate decisions to ad hoc commissions or to associate political opposition with retrenchment in consensus-based policymaking (Pierson 1994).

In Europe, Bonoli (2000) maintains, institutional contexts seem to imply specific political strategies. Unitary systems that centralize power, such as the United Kingdom, imply a bold political strategy of imposing unpopular pension reforms and absorbing the electoral impacts.[5] Conversely, governments in polities with many veto points, such as France or Switzerland, have to adopt more circumspect and inclusive approaches. Here, successful pension reform strategies are likely to diffuse blame by including political adversaries (such as labor unions or pro-welfare interest groups) in policy formulation and by featuring bargained outcomes among contending policy actors. This process, which Ebbinghaus and Hassel (2000) call "concertation," occurs when social partners trade quid pro quos (Bonoli 2000). Concertation reduces potential opposition to a reform by implicating political adversaries in the reform itself.

The institutional barriers to pension reform have not prevented it from occurring. However, changes to pension systems have come only after protracted, cumbersome, and iterative reform processes. Policymakers' need to avoid blame for unpopular pension reforms has made the adaptation of welfare states a slow and incremental process (Pierson 1996; Bonoli 2000; Hinrichs 2001). Moreover, until very recently (see below) reforms have moved well within the institutional logic of existing pension provision.

Democracies and Pension Reform

The most significant aspect of the "new politics of the welfare state" (Pierson 1996) is that successful pension reform requires the suspension of democratic mechanisms. Evidence from many European countries[6]

seems to suggest that policymakers have used blame-avoidance strategies to pursue unpopular reform agendas. Obfuscation strategies have
kept voters and opposing policy actors uninformed about the effects of
reform proposals. Compensation, in turn, has bought acquiescence from
powerful groups of voters at the cost of less concentrated interests. Concertation effectively has banished choice from the political system: consensual policymaking has implied that voters have been left with few
real alternatives to governmental reform agendas (Nullmeier and Rüb
1993). As Pierson (1994) points out, retrenchment is an exercise in avoiding or even suppressing policy conflict. If, however, we understand
democracy to be a system of political contestation (Dahl 1971), then
blame avoidance amounts to circumventing the democratic policy
process.

If this is true, the implication that democracies and pluralist politics
rule out structural pension reform would be ominous. Reform-minded
policymakers, it would seem, are stuck between a rock and a hard place.
On one hand, pluralist politics condemns them to the "pension misery-
go-round" of frustrating, never-ending reforms unless they can find
ways around the democratic policy process. On the other hand, alternatives to pluralist democracies are even less appealing than is the pension
misery-go-round (Pierson 1996).

This bleak conclusion, however, emerges from the way the literature
emphasizes the point of decision in pension reform processes. This focus
on decisionmaking is problematic for two reasons. First, pluralist democracies are specifically designed to diffuse political power at the point of
decision. Institutional features, such as parliaments, the separation of
powers, cyclical and frequent elections, or an independent judiciary,
ensure that political power in democracies diffuses across many policy
actors (Dahl 1961; Polsby 1981). Perhaps, then, it should not come as
much of a surprise that imposing unpopular retrenchments at this point
in the policy process is likely to be difficult. Second, and more significant, the point of decision in real policy processes may be more difficult
to identify than the literature will have us believe. As Pierson (1994)
points out, blame avoidance is also about breaking down one transparent point of decision into many less transparent decisions scattered
across the policy process. Significantly, policy actors can affect outcomes
by defining pension policy problems to suit their preferred solutions,
thereby controlling pension reform agendas. Applying political power
at the earlier stages of policymaking is a far more subtle activity.

A related weakness is the focus on behavioral aspects of pension
reform. Pension policymaking is not only about maximizing individual
or organizational utility functions. Political conflicts over the welfare
state are also conflicts over fundamental ideas and values. The institutions from which pension reforms emerge give rise to specific norms,

practices, and worldviews. When institutions and their members clash, so do the constitutive values and practices. Yet reforming pension systems is also a communicative process (Rein and Schön 1994). Parties to pension reform will rely on rhetoric and argument to persuade, cajole, and mobilize other policy actors (Fischer and Forester 1993; Rein and Schön 1993).[7] How different policy actors frame pension reform issues and the extent to which political adversaries can successfully challenge them will have a profound effect on policy outcomes.

The Subpolitics of Pension Reform

The previous section outlined how the general characteristics of pluralist democracies impose constraints on pension reforms, but that only tells part of the story. As Pierson (1994) points out, analyzing welfare state reforms means thinking about the consequences of big government. Another development associated with big government is the so-called differentiated polity (Rhodes 1997). Increasingly, policymaking in advanced industrial states has become specialized and fragmented. In almost all countries, states have taken on regulative responsibilities for an ever increasing spectrum of social activities. As these responsibilities have grown in number and in size, so too has the demand for specialized knowledge, technical advice, and policy delivery capabilities. This development has given rise to functionally segregated networks of institutions and policy actors that focus on particular social problems. In these networks and communities, policy actors define issues, set agendas, formulate proposals, and implement decisions. In the differentiated polity, policy (including pension reform) is made in policy communities.

Assessing the impact of pluralist democracies on pension reform implies that we examine these subcutaneous policy processes. As in other specialized policy arenas, pension reforms in Europe have emerged from relatively stable networks of experts, politicians, interest groups, and state agencies. What, then, has been going on in these policy networks to make pension reform so difficult? Moreover, to what extent have these policy networks enabled political contestation and participation in policymaking?

Pension Policymaking Prior to the 1990s: Consensus, Exclusion, and Nondecisions

European pension policy communities developed in the "golden age of the welfare state" (Pierson 1994). In the three decades following the end of World War II, expansion of European welfare states gave rise to specific structures and styles of social policymaking.

Although the particular institutional setups differed from country to country, many of these decisionmaking systems have been exclusive institutional networks insulated from both public scrutiny and other policy networks.

Institutional Actors, Network Structures, and Agenda-Setting. In Europe, pension system design has determined who participates in pension policymaking. In general, the more a pension system resembles the social insurance model, the more pronounced are the corporatist decisionmaking structures. Whether in the German and Austrian pension carriers (*Rentenversicherungsträger*), in the French supplementary pension schemes, or in the governing bodies of the Italian pension system, administration of pension schemes in continental Europe features some form of bi- or tripartite management regime (Linnerooth-Bayer 2001; Ney 2001; Bonoli 2000; Bozec and Mays 2001; Cioccia 2001; Antichi and Pizzuti 2000). As a result, continental European pension policy communities before the 1990s broadly conformed to the corporatist model of interest intermediation (Schmitter and Lehmbruch 1979). The institutional policy actors within pension policy networks reflected corporatist cleavages: as a rule, pension policy formulation and decisionmaking was a bargaining process limited to representatives from state, capital, and labor.[8]

A feature common to all European pension policy communities is their strong reliance on expertise. Apart from political elites, the pension policy issue has been the sovereign province of experts. In corporatist systems, pension expertise traditionally has emerged from the legal profession and, to a lesser but increasing degree, the economists' guild. In the United Kingdom and in Nordic countries, expertise relies more on economic theory and actuarial sciences than on law. In either case, requirements of technical expertise have erected high barriers to entry for would-be reformers. Consequently, the number of players has been rather limited: in most countries, the wider pension policy community consists of 20 to 30 policy-relevant institutions. When considering institutional actors who seriously impinge on pension reforms, this number falls to 10 to 15 (Ney 2001 and Mayhew 2001).

How did these institutional actors relate to one another? Following Rhodes (1990, 1997) we can think of policy networks as systems of exchange and dependence between institutions. To fulfill policy goals, institutions depend on the resources of other organizations. In pursuing these goals, institutions interact, exchange, and bargain. The stronger these interorganizational resource dependencies, Rhodes argues, the more integrated and cohesive a policy network is likely to be.

In continental Europe, corporatist policy communities featured strong organizational interdependencies between institutional actors.

A key resource in pension policymaking was (and continues to be) credible pension knowledge (Reynaud 2000). Before the 1990s state actors and pension bureaucracies (such as the pension carriers in Austria and Germany or the state in France) operated and controlled all sites that produced legitimate pension knowledge. Whether it was pension expenditure statistics, demographic and financial projections, or forecasts about future developments in benefits and contributions, the source of credible knowledge resided within corporatist policy communities. In that way state bureaucracies could tie the corporatist partners into the bargaining process: Impact on pension policy required "credible pension data," which was available from a limited number of controlled sources (Nullmeier and Rüb 1993; Bozec and Mays 2001). In return, social partners provided political cooperation and compliance. A legitimate claim to governance thus strongly coincided with the control of superior access to pension knowledge.

These interorganizational resource dependencies gave rise to tightly organized, institutionally interdependent pension policy communities. Frequent interaction among individual policy actors with shared epistemic commitments led to the emergence of a highly selective, ideologically coherent, and institutionally interdependent group of policymakers (see also Nullmeier and Rüb 1993). By effectively insulating the issue area from other policy spheres and from other policy actors, pension policy communities managed to control problem definition, agenda-setting, and policy formulation.

Policy change occurred within narrowly delimited and carefully defined boundaries, if it took place at all. The close correspondence between pension provision and political decisionmaking implied that each attempt to reform pension schemes also tested the political viability of the corporatist bargaining system. So as not to upset the fragile balance of power between policy actors and to substantiate to external contenders the claim to superior knowledge, policymaking in continental Europe included extensive consensus-seeking (Ney 2001; Bozec and Mays 2001; Nullmeier and Rüb 1993). One way of achieving consensus was to control the emergence of conflict. By limiting the pension reform agenda to relatively innocuous issues, pension policy communities curtailed political conflict by either excluding or co-opting dissenting voices. Policy communities defined pension problems so that the solutions fell exclusively *within* the institutional logic of existing pension provision. The policy community a priori defined pension issues as technical ones amenable to managerial solutions. Typically, pension reforms in these countries emerged from an intricate bargaining process aimed at achieving consensus across every conceivable political cleavage in the pension policy community.[9]

Policy Processes and Democratic Institutions. Unlike what public choice models and concepts of blame avoidance would have us believe, democratic institutions have played a marginal role in European pension reform. In most European countries (with the exception of Norway), pension policymaking was thoroughly depoliticized and deparliamentarized, even during times of welfare state expansion.

In corporatist policy communities, such as the British pension policy network, pension reforms emerged from a myriad of ad hoc committees and commissions. These committees and commissions were set up by corporatist policy actors and served three basic political purposes. First, they allowed policy network participants to define the pension issue, set pension reform agendas, and control participation. Second, this "ad hocracy" provided venues for "partisan mutual adjustment" (Lindblom 1958) between corporatist policy actors. Third, and most important, these policy venues created a policy space institutionally remote from formal democratic institutions and public scrutiny.

On one hand, the sheer number of committees and commissions with varying degrees of importance made for an opaque policy process. Unless they were situated on the inside of the policy community, it was difficult for policy actors to reconstruct the origin and evolution of a particular pension reform.[10] On the other hand, because ad hoc committees and commissions were not subject to the same rules of public disclosure and access as were parliamentary committees, for example, corporatist policy communities could keep the public at arm's length. In countries such as Austria, Germany, and the United Kingdom,[11] there was more than a little truth to the popular image of decisionmaking in smoke-filled backrooms. Moreover, members of political parties within the corporatist policy communities (usually depicted as "social policy experts") acted as ideological and organizational gatekeepers. Rather than carrying new ideas into pension policy communities, these politicians often were more effective in keeping new concepts and approaches out of pension policymaking (Nullmeier and Rüb 1993).

By the time that a particular pension reform reached parliament, there was little left for parliamentarians to decide. Corporatist partners had closed the deals in the relatively safe confines of the ad hocracy and senior politicians relied on party discipline to avoid any embarrassment in parliament. Rather than exerting political control, parliament merely rubber-stamped pension reforms drafted in corporatist policy communities. For example, the passage of the German Pension Reform (PRA) Act of 1992 shows how the policy community outmaneuvered the *Bundestag*.[12] Not only did parliament have little time to process the PRA 1992 bill;[13] the ad hocracy continued to work on details of pension reform after its passage (Pabst 1999). Similar patterns emerged in the Austrian pension reform of 1985 when the social partnership decided upon the substantive content of the reform and relegated parliamentary ratification to a mere formality (Linnerooth-Bayer 2001).

Corporatist Policy Communities, Incremental Pension Reform, and Democracy. A closer look at the subpolitics of pension reform in Europe prior to the 1990s reveals that there may be a less robust relationship than previously thought between democratic institutions and incremental pension reform. Pension policy communities in Europe, the locus of pension policy formulation, have been anything but democratic. In continental European countries and to a lesser extent in the United Kingdom, policy communities have been small, selective, and highly cohesive policy networks based on specialized expertise. These networks dominated pension policymaking until (and in some case well into) the 1990s. By monopolizing credible expertise and technical knowledge as well as excluding potential contenders, these institutional networks effectively controlled policy conflict. Moreover, these tightly integrated policy communities insulated themselves from other policy networks, parliament, and public scrutiny. Despite functioning blame-avoidance mechanisms,[14] however, European pension reforms before the mid-1990s consisted of cautious and incremental retrenchments to existing pension systems. On the whole, reforms prior to the 1990s were parametric adjustments of existing institutional arrangements that did not seriously challenge the underlying organizational structure of public pension provision.

The reason why continental European polities in the past have eschewed structural pension reforms is related not to the structure of pluralist democracies but to the configuration of pension policy communities. As we have seen, pension systems in corporatist polities imply specific decisionmaking structures. These structures empower certain social groups at the cost of other groups. In this sense pension systems are more than a technical device for transferring income across generations. Rather, pension systems represent both a modus operandi and specific distribution of political power within the pension policy network. Any change to the pension system that moves outside the prevalent institutional logic of pension provision also challenges the decisionmaking system and the distribution of power, which in turn encodes a particular set of beliefs, enabling a fundamental policy conflict. The subpolitics of pension policymaking suggest, therefore, that pre-1990 reform efforts aimed at securing existing pension systems and their accompanying distribution of political power in the face of financial pressures. To defend pension systems, continental pension policy communities simply recalibrated existing institutional mechanisms (consensus policymaking, monopoly of knowledge, expert-driven policymaking, and so forth) to suit more austere social policy goals. If we are to believe the sociological systems theory that political power is the "currency" of political systems, then there is no rational basis for any political organization to relinquish it.[15] For this reason, it is in the most fundamental interest of pension policy community participants to limit pension reform to problems amenable to systemic palliatives. This maintains and reproduces the corporatist decisionmaking system in which all participants have a stake. In sum, it is not democratic institutions but rather the lack of democratic practices within pension policy communities that explains the absence of structural pension reforms in continental Europe prior to the 1990s.

Pension Policymaking in the 1990s: Expanding the Scope of Political Conflict

By the end of the 1990s, the picture had changed completely. Not only had the governments made decisive cuts to pension benefits, but nearly all countries had sought solutions outside established PAYG, defined-benefit pension systems.

The leaders of this process have been Poland, Italy, the United Kingdom, and Norway.[16] The Polish pension reform of 1997 effectively terminated the Bismarckian-style pension system (Góra 2001). Under the new system, workers under the age of 40 will make contributions into both a notional defined contribution public pillar and a fully funded pension scheme (Perek-Bialas, Chlon-Dominczak, and Ruzik 2001). Similarly, Italian policymakers have established fully funded pension schemes at firm level (Cioccia 2001; Reynaud 2000). In the United Kingdom, the cuts to the State Earnings-Related Pension Scheme (SERPS) in the mid-1980s and the tax incentives for private pensions have led to a considerable shift toward private pension provisions (Mayhew 2001). In Norway, despite expansion of the universalist elements of the pension system, there has been considerable growth in private pensions: between 1982 and 1996 the proportion of old-age income from private pensions increased from 16.4 percent to 21.6 percent (Ervik 2001).

Even in continental European countries, policymakers have implemented alternatives to established social insurance systems. In Germany, the most recent reforms have created a voluntary pension pillar based on credit reserve (CR) funding and located in the private sector (Rehfeld 2001). Similarly, the Thomas Law of 1997 in France created the legal and organizational framework for private sector pension provision. Only Austrian policymakers have not moved outside the institutional logic of the social insurance system (Linnerooth-Bayer 2001).

What has triggered these reforms? If the form and practices of policy communities constrained structural pension reform prior to the 1990s, we should look for and expect to find changes at the level of European pension policy communities. Indeed, throughout the 1990s European pension policy communities became less cohesive and more diverse in terms of membership, structure, and practices.

New Policy Actors and Old Interorganizational Ties. In the last decade there has been an influx of new institutional actors into most European pension policy communities. These new actors have challenged dominant ways of thinking about pension reform, and the institutional ties characteristic of European pension policy communities have begun to loosen.

The most prominent new interest groups to enter the European pension policy communities have come from the banking and insurance industries. This trend is most visible in the United Kingdom and in Poland where pension reform created a formal space for increased industry involvement in policymaking. To a lesser extent, the same is also true in continental Europe. In France, Germany, and Italy, the private financial sector has increased its attempts to influence pension reform outcomes by adopting more proactive policy strategies and circumventing established corporatist channels of policy interaction (Ney 2001; Bozec and Mays 2001; Ervik 2001). Even in Austria, where corporatist interest mediation remains strong, the private sector is becoming increasingly active in providing pension-related products (Linnerooth-Bayer 2001).

Another significant addition to pension policy communities in many European countries is the media. Throughout the last decade, all countries have revealed a change in both the frequency and content of articles about pension reform issues. Media coverage tends to describe the issue as an impending financial crisis: The emphasis is on the inequitable distribution of burdens across generations. Metaphors such as "the tidal wave of old age" (Norway), the "struggle of the generations" (Germany), and the "demographic time-bomb" (ubiquitous) underline the alleged urgency of policy action. In general, the media are quick to criticize policymakers for inaction. In continental countries, the media equate parametric reforms with governmental weakness, agency capture, and electoral cynicism: The failure to reform pension systems radically (such as a shift to a fully funded financing mechanism) reflects the inability of policymakers to rid themselves of old-fashioned corporatist dogmas, and their unwillingness to jeopardize the grey vote" (Bozec and Mays 2001; Ney 2001).[17]

At the level of political elites, the 1990s have brought about a reshuffling of political allegiances. Political parties no longer mirror corporatist cleavages. Rather, many major political parties in Europe are split internally among competing approaches to pension reform. Moreover, in continental European polities, supporters of conventional social policymaking rapidly are disappearing from the political map. In Germany the purge of old-style social policy experts from both major parties (most important, from the German Social Democratic Party) has been particularly noticeable. Similarly, an entire generation of politicians in Italy was wiped out by the *Mani Pulite* inquiries. The same process has occurred to a lesser degree in Austria and France. In those countries, traditional social democratic values weathered the ideological upheavals of the 1990s far better than in Germany or the United Kingdom. The shift of the union's traditional allies toward the center of the political spectrum has meant that the unionized labor movement can no longer count on uncompromising political support from socialist or social democratic parties.

The new policy actors have come replete with innovative ideas and approaches to pension policymaking. In many cases, new actors in the policy communities have established competing sites of knowledge production. For example, the significance of think-tanks increased throughout the 1990s. The independence of think-tanks varies, but most are close to a particular policy position or political party. For example, Demos in the United Kingdom is (somewhat unfairly) said to be close to "New Labor," the Copernic Foundation in France leads the intellectual charge on the neo-liberal "culture of *Bercy*," and the ZeS in Germany is close to a conventional German social policy approach. Other think-tanks have more concrete institutional ties to policy actors: the *Deutsches Institut für Altersvorsorge* is nominally independent but receives funding from the Deutsche Bank Group, and Deutsche Bank Research is a department of the banking corporation whose mission is to inform the Deutsche Bank's board of directors (Ney 2001).

How have these changes affected pension policy communities? The diversification of participants has helped loosen formerly cohesive interorganizational ties at two levels. First, the new entrants have challenged the cognitive monopoly of conventional pension knowledge. Not only are they in a position to interpret pension data within the conventional pension paradigms,[18] but they have also brought novel approaches to the pension issue. In many European countries, generational accounting and internal rate of return comparisons have questioned conventional pension policy lore (Ervik 2001; Ney 2001; Bozec and Mays 2001). There is no longer one dominant pension truth but several alternative and competing ones. In a real sense, the transformation of pension policy communities has created scientific uncertainty.[19] More methodological pluralism implies that policy actors will come to different conclusions about the efficacy and effects of pension reform. Increasingly then what policy actors choose to believe depends on where they stand in the pension policy community. The growing plurality of ideas has (re)politicized pension knowledge.

Second, both the additions to the pension policy community and the changing socioeconomic conditions of the 1990s have fractured corporatist interaction. Increasing international competition and changing forms of accumulation and employment have transformed the political outlook of pension policy actors. In general, employers and employer organizations have become decidedly indifferent toward national social policymaking (Ney 2001). Tight labor markets, perceived global competitive pressures, and access to global markets imply that employers and enterprises no longer rely as strongly on cooperation and compliance from other social partners, specifically unions. Consequently, private sector policy actors throughout the 1990s have become increasingly assertive in terms of their own perceived interests and increasingly recalcitrant relative to union demands. This tendency is most marked in Germany, and less so in France and Italy. In Austria, however, employers are still relatively cooperative but have become far more proactive (Linnerooth-Bayer 2001).

Common Challenges, Conflicting Solutions: Advocacy Coalitions, Policy Stories, and Agenda-Setting. The influx of new members and ideas into European policy communities has widened the scope of political conflict for pension policymaking. As a result, pension policy debates have become more polarized and divisive. Formerly cohesive pension policy communities have split into conflicting "advocacy coalitions" (Sabatier and Jenkins-Smith 1993). These coalitions consist of institutional and individual policy actors who rally around distinctive sets of beliefs about a particular issue area. In general, at least three different sets of beliefs have guided European policy actors in constructing conflicting "policy stories" about pension reform.

Policy stories are rhetorical devices designed to convince, cajole, and persuade opposing policy actors and provide a rhetorical rallying point for allies (Stone 1988; Fischer and Forester 1993). This, however, does not mean that policy stories are mere fiction or conjecture (as protagonists of opposing policy stories will claim). Rather, policy stories allow policy actors to be *selectively* objective: the stories provide a narrative, framed by fundamental normative beliefs about social organization, that selectively highlights certain aspects of a policy issue while de-emphasizing other aspects (Douglas 1982; Thompson, Ellis, and Wildavsky 1990; Rayner 1991; Thompson, Rayner, and Ney 1998). The aim of a policy story is to construct a plausible, credible, and legitimate argument in

favor of a particular course of action. Contending policy stories start
from differing initial assumptions, provide specific interpretations of
pension policy problems, and offer particular policy solutions. In this
way, policy actors arrive at very different solutions for common policy
problems.

Common Challenges. Despite ideational diversity within and across
national pension policy communities, policymakers in most European
countries perceive general policy challenges similarly.[20] First, policym
akers and experts in all countries understand demographic aging and the
unfavorable future development of dependency ratios to be the root
cause of the pension problem. Policymakers in all countries point out that
demographic imbalances will place considerable financial strain on
existing pension systems in the future. Second, policymakers in all
countries point to the social, economic, and political developments
commonly referred to as globalization. Increasingly, economic agents—
enterprises or individual workers—compete in global markets. For many
policymakers this implies that future societal wealth will depend on costs
and competitiveness. Moreover, European policymakers point to changes
in household structures and employment patterns. Increasingly, the male-
breadwinner model and lifelong employment are becoming the
exceptions rather than the rule. In the future, pension systems will have
to cope with such issues as discontinuous employment histories (whether
for spells of unemployment, training, or maternity/paternity leave).

Although there is rough agreement about general problems, the interpretation of policy challenges has given rise to conflicting policy stories.
Differing constructions of the pension issue have divided national pension communities in similar ways.

The Crisis Story: Intergenerational Fairness and Efficiency. In
general, advocacy coalitions emphasizing intergenerational equity seek
to expand the scope of political conflict. The fundamental problem,
advocates argue, is that defined-benefit PAYG systems are in dire
financial straits.

The socioeconomic and demographic developments of the last 20
years have squeezed public PAYG pension systems in three ways. The
first financial pressure emerged from demographic aging. Increasing
longevity and falling fertility rates mean that the dependency ratio in
most European countries will increase sharply after about 2010 (OECD
1998). Proponents of the crisis story contend that this will lead invari-
ably to a steep and unsustainable increase in social security costs for
workers and firms. Globalization of goods and financial markets creates
a second squeeze on pension systems. In the future, global markets will
reward those economies with low production costs. However, current

public PAYG systems, replete with generous pension benefits, are likely to drive production costs to unsustainable levels. Crisis story proponents maintain that this inevitably leads to unemployment, contribution evasion by younger workers, and a loss of international competitiveness. In all cases, pension systems will lose revenue. The third squeeze originates in the fundamental flaws of existing European public pension systems. Almost all European countries feature generous provisions for early retirement. Falling labor market participation rates show that European workers are eager to take advantage of early retirement provisions (Gruber and Wise 1997). Given increasing longevity and demographic aging, however, early retirement adds to the already daunting financial burdens of public PAYG systems. Advocates emphatically conclude that the crisis is upon us now and the need for decisive policy action is acute.

What should policymakers do? Advocates of the crisis story favor pension reforms that reduce social insurance costs and urge policymakers to look for alternatives to public PAYG systems. Policy actors have suggested diverse ways for reducing the expenditure of public PAYG schemes, including increasing the retirement age, abolishing early retirement, reducing replacement rates, and cutting redistributive elements within pension systems. It is significant that advocates of this policy story suggest that pension provision be made more transparent by erecting institutionally distinct pension pillars that would fulfill different functions of old-age protection (that is, poverty alleviation, long-term savings, and coinsurance). In ideal circumstances, pension pillars should be located in institutions best suited to fulfill assigned functions; redistribution would be a public task whereas long-term savings would best be managed by the private sector (World Bank 1994). Advocates of the crisis story maintain that pension reform should aim to diversify old-age income provision.

The institutional location of this advocacy coalition differs among European countries. The most obvious raconteurs of the crisis story are "Washington consensus" economists, the banking and insurance industries, and market-oriented politicians (such as Silvio Berlusconi in Italy or Guido Westerwelle in Germany). Less obvious but far more politically significant is the growing support for the crisis story in social-democratic parties across Europe. Arguably, one of the defining features of "New Labor" in Britain, France, and Germany is that left-wing politicians are taking the crisis story seriously. Moreover, throughout Europe the media have been particularly receptive to arguments about intergenerational equity. This trend is probably most pronounced in Germany and Italy where the media have more or less subscribed to the crisis scenario (Cioccia 2001; Ney 2001). Yet, even in Austria and France, the media have reported on the crisis story, albeit somewhat more cautiously.

The Social Stability Story: Social Peace and Intergenerational Solidarity. Advocacy coalitions focusing on social stability generally limit the pension issue to technical problems. Here the issue is how best to adapt and fine-tune existing systems to meet demographic and socioeconomic challenges. As the argument goes, demographic aging and socioeconomic change require judicious and measured social management by competent experts. Given the central role and proven track record of existing pension systems in securing social stability and intergenerational solidarity, the main challenge is to keep those institutional mechanisms intact. Doing so, advocates argue, includes securing the public's trust in the pension system by providing stable and reasonable replacement rates. Proponents of the stability story suggest that the real problem is that particular policy actors systematically have undermined trust in existing pension systems.

The advocacy coalitions arguing for social stability emphasize the need for judiciously balanced fine-tuning and adaptation to secure the long-term viability of existing pension systems. The catalog of proposed reform measures is extensive and differs widely among and even within countries at different points in time. The leitmotiv is to rely on the organizational resources of established PAYG systems without changing the basic institutional identity of the pension system. In general, reform proposals have suggested increases in contributions, retrenchment of benefits, and reductions of redistributive elements in public PAYG pension schemes. Unlike among advocates of the crisis story, the aim of reform options here is to obviate the need for substantial private sector involvement in pension provision. Private pension provision should be no more than a supplement to public provisions.

In continental countries advocates for the stability story still represent the pension policy establishment. Typically located in key positions within the administrative structure of the PAYG pension system, proponents of the rational management approach still command considerable influence over pension policy debates. But in several continental European countries the cognitive and policymaking authority of the pension "expertocracy" has become shaky. Particularly in Italy and, to a lesser extent, in France and Germany more market-oriented discourses have undermined the cognitive and policymaking status of the established pension policy communities, which have not been able to avert partial or total shifts toward private sector provision. In Austria, where ideas of rational management still dominate pension reform debate, the debate concerns the rational management of pension cuts rather than pension system expansion.

The Social Justice and Equality Story. The advocacy coalition stressing social justice and equality applies a holistic view to expand the pension issue beyond economic or technical considerations. In this arena pension schemes are part of a socioeconomic system that, in general, is highly inequitable. By relying on standard, male-dominated patterns of employment, existing public and emergent private sector pension schemes penalize marginal and vulnerable social groups, including the working poor, families, women, foreigners, people with special needs, and people living alternative lifestyles. Demographic aging and globalization are likely to exacerbate existing social problems of inequality. Pension reforms need to be a part of a general societal reform agenda.

The policy options proposed by advocates of social justice and equality aim at leveling inherent social inequities. Pension reforms, they argue, need to recalibrate old-age income provision to enable individuals to fully determine their own destinies. This means that pension benefits should free the aged from both patriarchal state intervention and the vagaries of capital markets. To realize this degree of individual self-determination, pension benefits should provide an adequate level of old-age income to all citizens, regardless of labor market participation or nationality. Advocates propose to increase redistribution among different social groups: higher pensions need to fall so that lower pensions can increase. Moreover, proponents of this policy story urge policymakers to harmonize different pension systems (and thereby abolish occupational privileges) and to increase coverage of the pension scheme to all citizens, regardless of national or labor market status.

The social justice and equality policy story languishes at the margins of most European pension policy debates. In continental countries, its most vociferous proponents are the German and Austrian Green Parties. Despite the German Green Party's government participation, however, proponents of this discourse have had only a limited impact on current German pension reform plans. In Austria the Greens are consigned to an opposition role at both governmental and policy community level: their impact on pension reform has been negligible. In France, Italy, and Poland policy arguments about social justice barely exist.[21]

Policy Stories and Policy Conflict. The policy stories outlined above provide principled narratives that help policy actors make sense of the pension issue. By providing policy actors with cognitive and normative maps, the conflicting policy stories define and delimit a discursive sphere in which policy debate takes place. This space outlines the borders of legitimate argument in the policy community: policy stories determine what counts as a fact and what types of arguments are out of bounds. We can visualize this in terms of a triangular policy space (see figure 3.1).

The relationship between contending advocacy coalitions is one of inherent conflict (Sabatier and Jenkins-Smith 1993; Rayner 1991).

Figure 3.1   The Triangular Policy Space

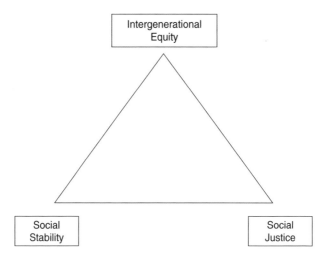

Within this discursive policy space, advocacy coalitions will clash over correct definitions of the pension issue, appropriate policy responses, and suitable policy instruments. Their members will beseech other policy actors and the public. Agenda-setting then becomes an argumentative process refracted through such institutional factors as the distribution of power and resources in policy communities.

How has policy conflict developed in continental European pension debates? The main fault line in most systems runs between the proponents of the crisis and the social stability stories. Policymakers and experts in these countries stylize the conflict as a struggle of economic policy against social policy; a clash among CR, defined contribution and PAYG, and defined benefits; and a battle between the ideals of liberal markets and rational social management. In continental Europe dominant policy actors have either co-opted the social justice policy story (as in Austria and Germany) or have stonewalled it completely (France and Italy).

Moreover, the degree and level of conflict between the warring factions on the continent differ from country to country. In France and Germany, the level of conflict is extremely high because the pension reform debate has become a proxy for more fundamental governance issues. In Sabatier and Jenkins-Smith's (1993) words, the clash between advocacy coalitions concerns "deep core" and "policy core" beliefs—that is, the fundamental structures of social insurance pension schemes and the corporatist decisionmaking system. With decision stakes so high, the current debate in these countries has deteriorated into a "dialogue of the deaf" (Sabatier and Jenkins-Smith 1993) or an "intractable policy controversy" (Rein and Schön 1994). Pension knowledge has become a rhetorical resource. Policy actors no longer can solve disagreements by recourse to facts because the facts have become an integral part of an advocacy coalition's rhetorical strategy. This is the "repoliticization" of pension knowledge. What seemed to be an objective fact a decade ago now reveals a fundamental political bias. Indeed, the form of political interaction has become less than genteel because policy debates are characterized by mutual recriminations and accusations. Each side accuses the other of irresponsibility and dubious ulterior motives. On one side, policy actors claim that unions and governments merely want to save their own political necks by burdening young workers (see Ney 2001; Cioccia 2001; Bozec and Mays 2001; Linnerooth-Bayer 2001). On the other side, contending policymakers conjure up images of destitute pensioners and class warfare for the sake of short-term profits that line fat-cat employers' pockets. In short, agreement—let alone consensus—is unlikely.

In Italy and Austria, in turn, political conflict over pensions is at a more moderate level. In Italy financial crisis helped policymakers convey the necessity and urgency of reforms (Cioccia 2001; Ebbinghaus and Hassel 2000). In Austria pension policy debates do not yet concern fundamental issues of old-age income provision (Linnerooth-Bayer 2001).

Policy Processes and Policy Outputs: Garbage Cans and Structural Reforms. The 1990s have witnessed the partial break-up of corporatist pension policy communities. Shifts at political levels and more general socioeconomic changes have made pension policy communities more diverse both in membership and ideas. As a result, pension policymaking in Europe has become a more contentious, conflictual, and pluralist activity. Although pension reform is a national legislative issue and policy communities have become more open, parliaments still play a relatively minor role in decisionmaking. Pension policymaking, now as in the 1980s, takes place in a gray and informal area located in the anteroom, or front yard of the formal parliamentary process. This gray area consists of a multitude of informal, ad hoc commissions, committees, hearings, policy advisory groups, and expert round tables whose membership and policy relevance reflect the political power constellations within the pension policy community.

Given the informal and ad hoc nature of the pension policy process, recent changes have introduced political uncertainty into pension policymaking. Conflict in pension policy communities not used to political confrontation has made reform a precarious affair. Whereas the corporatist system of interest mediation carefully regulated who interacted with whom, where, when, and—most important—about what, policy interaction in the last decade has occurred in increasingly unpredictable ways.

Pension policy communities, particularly in continental European polities, have not kept pace with the shifting and uncertain alliances at the policy elite level. In Austria and Germany present government coalitions (conservatives and ultra-rightists in Austria, Social Democrats and Greens in Germany) would have been unthinkable only a few years ago. In both polities governments have circumvented corporatist decision-making structures. In Germany the present government has kept the traditional pension policy establishment at arm's length (Ney 2001). In Austria policymakers simply invented new policy venues to keep pension reform from the sway of the powerful Austrian social partnership (Linnerooth-Bayer 2001). In Italy the replacement of the entire post-war party system has given rise to vulnerable and volatile new political alliances on both the right and left of the political spectrum (Cioccia 2001; Antichi and Pizzuti 2000). The result of these developments has been the emergence of a structural disparity between political elites and the pension policy community: in the former we find a more fluid configuration that rapidly adjusts to changes, whereas the latter features relatively inflexible structures geared toward securing continuity.

The expanding scope of political and ideational conflict has suspended the implicit rules of policy engagement in pension policy communities. Policy conflict and competition on "knowledge markets" successively have eroded those policy norms that secured consensual decisionmaking in policy communities, and policy actors in continental European countries have not agreed on a new set of rules that could regulate the more conflictual policy sphere. Indeed, in countries such as Austria, France, and Germany these rules are an integral part of heated policy conflict.

Rather than conforming to rational models of policymaking, pension policy processes are becoming more similar to "garbage cans" (Cohen, March, and Olsen 1972; Kingdon 1984).[22] Whereas corporatist policy communities tightly regulated policy streams, the influx of new members and new ideas allowed the streams to drift. As a result European pension policymaking has become far more vulnerable to forces beyond the immediate control of policy communities. For example, although overall pension reforms in the 1990s generally have moved systems away from unitary provision and toward diversity, during the decade there were spectacular failures. In Austria the failure of the 1995 pension reform led to the collapse of the coalition government. The German Pension Reform Act of 1999 (*Rentenreformgesetz 1999*) arguably hastened the demise of the Kohl era and then was overturned by the incoming coalition government between the German Social Democrats, the SPD, and the German Green party only a year after it was adopted. In Italy the Berlusconi government failed to implement planned reforms because of the defection of the ultra-right-wing coalition partner, the *Lega Nord*. The pension policy process in Europe, it would seem, has become more volatile.

In continental European countries the development toward a more unpredictable policy process has culminated in a spate of reforms that have moved beyond the institutional logic of social insurance pension provision. In all social insurance countries except Austria, reforms have created the legal and organizational basis for fully funded private sector old-age income provision. Although these fully funded pillars are relatively modest compared with private provision in, say, Norway, Poland, or the United Kingdom, they nonetheless mark a departure from established pension reform policy patterns.

Arguably, the widening of pension policy communities and the expansion of the scope of political conflict have provided the discursive and institutional space for placing structural reform proposals on European policy agendas. Moreover, these types of changes, which Pierson (1994, 1996) calls "systemic retrenchments," are likely to have a significant effect on future pension reforms. If institutional path dependency structures pension reform options, then the changes to policy networks and policy communities in the 1990s are likely to influence pension policymaking in the future. Pluralization of pension policy communities has created a new type of playing field for European social policymaking. It is significant that structural pension reform is an integral part of this new field.

Conclusion: Democracy and Structural Pension Reform

Pension reform in the last decade and a half has introduced diversity to both pension systems and policymaking. In terms of reforming actual pension systems, differing initial conditions and institutional path dependency have led to a host of different pension reform measures across Europe. However, two general reform trends emerge in almost all European countries:

- reform has streamlined public pension systems by tying benefits closer to contributions
- reform has provided space for the development of private sector forms of old-age income provision.

These trends imply a shift in responsibility for old-age security. Increasingly, European states are divesting themselves of pension provision obligations. Private sector providers enthusiastically have agreed to help with the responsibility for old-age income. In a very real sense, pension reforms are creating a viable role for private sector pension provisions by lowering expectations about the level of future public pension benefits.

These developments should come as a bit of a surprise. Analyses of pension reform politics generally point out that structural and radical pension reforms in mature democracies are improbable to impossible. The structures and practices of democratic institutions inherently militate against departures from the status quo. Because the electorate fears losses (the negativity bias) and politicians seek reelection (the vote motive), any form of welfare state retrenchment, let alone structural pension reform, is an unattractive political proposition. To cut welfare state benefits, democratic structures and practices (that is, majority voting) force policymakers to avoid political responsibility by diffusing blame. Whether through obfuscation, compensation, or concertation, pension reforms imply suspending democratic practices in one way or another. The best would-be reformers can hope for are incremental, piecemeal, and iterative reforms of the pension misery-go-round. As Katharina Müller (1999) points out, analysts who

> "...*do* focus on the political viability of cutbacks, consider only cautious retrenchment: when Pierson and Weaver (1993) explore how moderate cutbacks of public pension schemes can be made politically feasible...a radical reform of old-age security is ruled out" (p. 44, original emphasis).

A closer look at the subpolitics of functional pension policy domains, however, tells a somewhat different story. Particularly in continental European countries, social insurance–type pension systems gave rise to ideologically coherent, tightly integrated, and highly cohesive corporatist policy networks. Based on claims to superior expert knowledge, these policy communities successfully insulated themselves from democratic institutions such as parliaments and from public scrutiny. Within the model of corporatist intermediation, the social insurance institutions implied specific governance structures, created policymaking capabilities, and distributed political power among policy actors. As a result, pension systems became synonymous with a specific mode of decisionmaking: Any reform of pension systems also implied a potential redistribution of power and policymaking capabilities. For this reason reform efforts necessarily remained well within the social insurance paradigm.

Throughout the 1990s corporatist models of interest intermediation were replaced by a more complex and more conflictual policy process. In Europe, pension policy communities have become less integrated and more populous. New policy actors, such as those from the banking and insurance sectors, as well as personnel changes at the level of political elites have introduced new ideas and concepts. Increasing ideational diversity, however, has been synonymous with greater scientific uncertainty and policy conflict. Whereas pension policymaking before the

1990s was based on consensus across corporatist and political cleavages, pension reform in the 1990s was characterized by increasingly hostile political conflict. In many countries, pension reform debates have become intractable policy controversies in which knowledge and credible pension data are merely rhetorical resources.

Significantly, however, the breakdown of corporatist decisionmaking structures has created space for alternative pension reform ideas. By the end of the 1990s, almost every continental European country had taken its first steps along the road to fully funded private sector pension provision. The pluralization of political contestation, the expansion of the scope of political conflict, and widening policy participation have enabled, not constrained, structural pension reforms.

It would seem, therefore, that the general argument that democracies tend to rule out structural pension reforms requires some qualification. Although it is undoubtedly true that welfare state retrenchment is unpopular with some policy actors and that democratic polities provide ample opportunity to contest unpopular policy, it would be rash to conclude that democratic institutions and practices per se impede pension reform. And although thinkers like Paul Pierson (1994, 1996) and Giuliano Bonoli (2000) provide us with compelling accounts of how democratic institutions shape policy outcomes, the politics of welfare state retrenchment are decided not only in the very public arenas of parliaments and elections. Rather, because advanced democratic polities are what Rod Rhodes (1997) calls "differentiated polities," policy processes and policy debates in functional policy domains are crucial for any pension reform. In the past in continental Europe these policy subsystems have been neither particularly pluralistic nor democratic: as we have seen, relatively small networks of experts successfully dominated agenda-setting by excluding rival pension reform proposals. Only when the grip of these networks over pension policymaking loosened in the 1990s did structural pension reform enter the policy debate in many European countries.

This does not mean that imposing welfare state retrenchments has become easier for European policymakers. In fact, proposals for structural reforms of European pension systems continue to cause quite vociferous and acrimonious policy conflict as well as the mobilization of political opposition. The only difference now is that structural reform proposals are receiving more serious attention from policymakers than such proposals did even a decade ago. What this does mean, however, is that the macrolevel characteristics of democratic polities, such as the cognitive biases of European electorates, majority voting, or the structures of formal political institutions, may be less important in determining policy outputs than theorists like Pierson or Bonoli wish to believe. The institutional and cognitive resources for defining and framing pension issues within pension policy communities may enable policy actors to exert an unduly restrictive influence over the policy process as a whole.

Does this mean that European pension policymaking is now happily democratic? Not necessarily. At present, European pension policy communities and processes are in flux. It is unclear what the new equilibrium will look like or, indeed, whether there will be a new equilibrium. Although European pension policy communities have moved toward polyarchy in terms of political contestation and inclusion (Dahl 1971), there is still a considerable democratic deficit.

First, the beneficiaries of changes in policymaking structures and styles have been governments and state bureaucracies. In a very real sense, increasing the diversity of actors and ideas has increased the strategic options open to governments. The breakdown of corporate-style consensual policymaking has emancipated governments from the strictures of epistemically uniform pension policy experts. Rather than one pension truth, policymakers now have the choice of several plausible policy stories. Because credible pension knowledge no longer resides solely within the corporatist pension policy community, there are far more scientifically sound pension policy options among which to choose. For governments with vague and broad ideological commitments (such as those of most major European parties), more ideational and institutional diversity means an increase in potential strategic alliances. This, in turn, means more governmental leverage on potential partners because governments are less constrained (ideologically and in terms of credible pension knowledge) by policy actors' demands. Increasing governmental autonomy in agenda-setting and policy formulation is not necessarily the same thing as increasing popular control over pension policymaking.

Second, pension experts (who now tend to disagree more than they agree) still execute pension policymaking predominantly in the front yard of the parliamentary process by pension experts. Although an increase in diversity and conflict is desirable from a democratic perspective, democracy also implies the existence of institutional mechanisms for peacefully resolving policy conflict. As evidence shows, the parliamentary front yard is far more suitable to corporatist consensus-seeking than to the resolution of intense and fundamental policy conflicts. If the pension policy process in Europe is to be democratically accountable, policymakers will have to design suitable political venues equipped with the institutional means for resolving fundamental policy conflict.

Third, the high level of divisive policy conflict now evident in many continental European countries is probably not conducive to pension policymaking. The risk is creating policy deadlock (wherein policy conflict gets in the way of necessary reform) or vicious policy cycles (in which successive new governments overturn the pension reforms of their predecessors). Moreover, deadlock at the level of the policy community empowers state bureaucracies and central government by suspending the regulatory function of policy communities.

In essence, policymakers face two general options:

- They can *remove the pension issue from the public sphere*. Policymakers can institutionally insulate the pension issue from policy conflict and thus create an independent pension institution that stands above the political fray (for example, the Polish Office of the Plenipotentiary). This strategy is problematic, however, for several reasons. First, the credibility of the institution will depend on finding a common problem definition on which all actors can agree. The 1990s, however, have seen a dismantling of common and consensual definitions of the pension issue. Second, this strategy implies a return to exclusionary and democratically unaccountable pension policymaking. Apart from being undesirable from a democratic point of view, the strategy assumes that actors can agree on whom to exclude from policymaking. Again, recent developments provide no indication that such a consensus is emerging. Another way to remove pension reform from political conflict is to privatize the issue. By shifting the management of pensions into the private sector, commercial secrecy would replace public accountability. This strategy is likely to prove difficult because the transition is likely to be the subject of heated political conflict causing policy deadlock. In short, policymakers may never reach their goal. And given that private sector pension providers are not interested in providing redistributive benefits, even the most sweeping privatization (see, for example, proposals by the U.S.-based Cato Institute) would leave a residual element in the public sphere.

- They can *further expand the scope of conflict*. An alternative strategy for policymakers is to shift the pension issue from the informal expert-dominated gray area it now inhabits into the full glare of public scrutiny. This would imply expanding access to pension policymaking and pension policy deliberation to an increasing number of sociopolitical influences. Although this would enhance democratic decisionmaking, inevitably it would decelerate the pension policy process. Moreover, creating a more open and therefore more conflictual policy sphere requires an institutional framework that constructively channels ideological policy conflict. Parliaments traditionally have provided the institutional framework for peacefully resolving policy conflicts in democracies, but given the current suspicion many citizens in Europe harbor toward the parliamentary process, this strategy may need to include citizens directly in the pension reform policy process.

Whatever policymakers choose to do, pension reform in continental countries is unlikely to fade from the agenda in the near or even medium future. Neither, I suspect, is policy conflict likely to disappear. Policymakers' current methods of reform are likely to alienate citizens from pension policymaking and, by extension, from politics in general. Avoiding the breakdown of trust in policymaking will mean thinking about reforms to the pension policy *process* as much as to the actual reform. In short, policymakers need to look for ways to further democratize pension reform.

Notes

1. The empirical evidence was collected during the first phase of the PEN-REF project. The project actually analyzed pension reform processes in seven European countries (Austria, France, Germany, Italy, Norway, Poland, and the United Kingdom). Although the main emphasis here will be on the four continental European social insurance systems, the analysis will point out interesting differences to the other countries.

2. Williamson and Pampel (1993) identify five different approaches to explaining welfare state expansion. These include the industrialism perspective, the social democratic perspective, the neo-Marxist perspective, and the state-centered explanations (for a brief overview, see also Müller 1999).

3. Voters may "suffer" from Prospect Theory's negativity bias, which makes them fear losses more than they value gains (Pierson 1994, 1996; see also Kahnemann and Tversky 1981) or, as Hinrichs (2001) points out, the electorate may more readily empathize with pensioners than with the unemployed or the disabled. Moreover, in many countries of continental Europe workers perceive accrued pension claims as earned rights (Hinrichs 2000); in many cases, pension claims have the legal status of quasi-property.

4. Germany, Sweden, the United Kingdom, and the United States (Pierson 1996).

5. This, Bonoli argues, is indeed how the Thatcher government introduced the 1986 Social Security Act, although Paul Pierson (1994) would probably take issue with this finding. The Thatcher government, he argues, was not nearly as successful in "rolling back the boundaries of the state" as it had claimed to be. Pierson recounts several instances in which the conservative government shied away from incisive welfare state cuts for fear of the electoral backlash. Part of the success of British pension reform in the 1980s, both Bonoli and Pierson agree, occurred because the decision to introduce private pensions went with the grain of the overall structure of British old-age pension provision.

6. This is both empirical evidence to which the different theorists refer (Pierson 1994, 1996; Bonoli 2000; Bonoli and Palier 2001; Hinrichs 2000) and evidence from the PEN-REF project (http://www. iccr-international.org/penref).

7. Pierson (1994) himself hints at these less tangible but nonetheless important aspects of pension reform: "Far more than in an era of welfare state expansion, struggles over social policy become struggles over information about causes and consequences of policy change" (p. 8).

8. The more universalist systems in Norway and the United Kingdom, in turn, produced different kinds of policy communities. In these two countries central government administers

pension provision. Unlike in social insurance countries, unions and employers' representatives do not have a favored status in policymaking: in effect, they are ordinary interest groups. Although the (atypically) strong role of the Norwegian parliament in pension policymaking provides an access point for unions in Norway, British unions have had little influence on pension reform (Ervik 2001; Mayhew 2001). Furthermore, given sizeable private sector pension provision in the United Kingdom, the pension industry was also an important policy actor. Consequently, universalist systems have given rise to less rigid decisionmaking structures.

9.   In fairness, this tendency was less pronounced in different continental European countries. Whereas consensus politics featured most strongly in German-speaking countries, pension policymaking in France and Italy was more divisive and aggressive.

10.   Which, of course, diffuses and avoids blame.

11.   Albeit for different reasons. British bureaucracy is notoriously secretive (Rhodes 1997).

12.   For a more detailed account, see Nullmeier and Rüb (1993) or Pabst (1999).

13.   The bill was introduced to the *Bundestag* in October 1989 with a view to passing the bill well before Christmas. Incidentally, the *Bundestag* passed the bill on the ninth of November, about an hour before the German Democratic Republic authorities announced the opening of the inner-German border.

14.   Functioning with differing degrees of efficiency in different continental European countries. If pressed, one could rank continental European countries from most efficient to least as follows: Austria, Germany, Italy, France.

15.   Moreover, contrary to what public choice theories assume, there is also no reason to assume that organizations and individual policy actors seek political power for sinister reasons. Power is a means of getting things done in politics as money is a means of getting things done in the market. It is a systematic prerequisite for meaningful action.

16.   Roughly in that order.

17.   In Austria media attention has been less sustained and has concentrated more on particular reform issues.

18.   A simple explanation here may be the increased accessibility of computing power. Nullmeier and Rüb (1993) point out that in the 1980s, the Federal Republic of Germany's labor ministry was the only location with sufficient computing power to crunch credible numbers. In the 1980s, the ministry performed all calculations of alternative pension reform plans. Although this nominally remains the case (see Ney 2001), credible if not necessarily legitimate projections now emerge from a number of different sources.

19.   In a social constructivist rather than engineering sense.

20.   One explanation may be that the definitions of current pension problems emerged from cohesive policy communities in the past. This also would dispel the idea that current reforms are problem-driven in any way. The problems for which recent reforms are supposedly the solution have been known in pension policy communities for a long time (see Nullmeier and Rüb 1993).

21.   The Norwegian and British pension systems, however, institutionalize egalitarian principles, albeit to considerably different degrees. In Great Britain the basic state pension provides equal benefits to all contributors at comparatively low rates of wage replacement. In Norway the basic universal pension benefits are more generous and eligibility is independent of labor market participation. Consequently, policy arguments in the social justice and

equality vein have more of an impact on policy debates than in continental countries. Whereas, however, the British debate is about ameliorating old age poverty in an essentially market-oriented context, the Norwegian debate is about granting fundamental social rights.

22. Briefly, the "garbage can" or "multiple streams" approach claims that policymaking emerges from a highly complex and chaotic process. At any one time, so the argument goes, three independent streams run through the political system. The first stream contains all of the potential policy problems that rattle around in a polity. The second stream consists of policy solutions to a host of existing and putative policy problems. The last stream, the political stream, determines the status of a policy issue. Its components are the national mood, the constellation of organized political forces, the composition of government, and the drive for consensus-building (bandwagoning, bargaining, and so forth). The upshot of the argument is that an issue can only reach the policy agenda when all three streams meet. That depends not only on the activity of policy entrepreneurs who try to link solutions to problems (or vice versa) but also on a host of unpredictable factors (such as catastrophes, crises, swings in public opinion, and so forth). When the streams meet, a policy window opens for a limited amount of time through which policy actors can launch a particular policy (see Kingdon 1984).

References

Antichi, Massimo, and Felice Roberto Pizzuti. 2000. "The Public Pension System in Italy: Observations on Recent Reforms, Methods of Control and their Application." In Emmanuel Reynaud, ed., *Social Dialogue and Pension Reform*. Geneva: International Labour Organisation.

Bonoli, Giuliano. 2000. *The Politics of Pension Reform: Institutions and Policy Change in Western Europe*. Cambridge, U.K.: Cambridge University Press.

Bonoli, Giuliano, and Bruno Palier. 2001. "How do Welfare States Change? Institutions and their impact on the Politics of Welfare State Reform in Western Europe."In Stephen Leibfried's (ed.) *Welfare State Futures*. Cambridge, U.K.: Cambridge University Press.

Bozec, Géraldine, and Claire Mays. 2001. "Pension Reform in France." *PEN-REF Project Deliverable D2*. Vienna: The Interdisciplinary Centre for the Comparative Research in the Social Sciences (ICCR).

Cioccia, Antonella. 2001. "Italian Case Study—The Italian Pension System and Pension Reform Pathways." *PEN-REF Project Deliverable D2*. Vienna: ICCR.

Cohen, Michael, James March, and Johan Olsen. 1972. "A Garbage Can Model of Organisational Choice." *Administrative Science Quarterly* 17:1–25.

Dahl, Robert. 1961. *Who Governs? Democracy and Power in an American City?* New Haven, Conn.: Yale University Press.

———. 1971. *Polyarchy: Participation and Opposition*. New Haven, Conn.: Yale University Press.

Disney, Richard. 1996. *Can We Afford to Grow Older? A Perspective on the Economics of Ageing*. Cambridge, Mass.: MIT Press.

Douglas, Mary, ed. 1982. *Essays in the Sociology of Perception*. London: Routledge and Keegan Paul.

Ebbinghaus, Bernhard, and Anke Hassel. 2000. "Striking Deals: Concertation in the Reform of Continental European Welfare States." *Journal of European Public Policy* 7(1):44–62.

Ervik, Rune. 2001. "The Norwegian Case Study." *PEN-REF Project Deliverable D2*. Vienna: ICCR.

Fischer, Frank and John Forester, eds. 1993. *The Argumentative Turn in Policy Analysis and Planning*. London: Duke University Press/UCL Press.

Góra, Marek. 2001. "Beyond the Opposition of PAYGO and Funding." Paper presented at the PEN-REF Workshop, "Setting European Pension Reform Agendas," June, International Institute for Applied System Analysis, Laxenburg, Austria.

Gruber, Jonathan, and David Wise. 1997. "Social Security Reform Programs and Retirement Income around the World." Working Paper 6134, National Bureau of Economic Research (NBER) Working Paper Series.

Hinrichs, Karl. 2000. "Von der Rentenversicherungs-zur Altersversicherungs-politik: Reformen und Reformprobleme." In Karl Hinrichs, Herbert Kitschelt, and Helmut Wiesenthal, eds., *Kontingenz und Krise: Institutionenpolitik in kapitalistischen und postsozialistischen Gesellschaften. Claus Offe zu seinem 60ten Geburtstag*. Frankfurt am Main: Campus.

———. 2001. "Ageing and Public Pension Reforms in Western Europe and North America: Patterns and Politics." In Jochen Clasen, ed., *What Future for Social Security? Debates and Reforms in National and Cross-National Perspective*. The Hague, The Netherlands: Kluwer Law International.

James, Estelle, and Sarah Brooks. 1999. "The Political Economy of Pension Reform." Revision of paper presented at the World Bank Research Conference, September 14–15, Washington, D.C.

Kahnemann, Daniel, and Amos Tversky. 1981. "The Framing of Decision and the Psychology of Choice." *Science* 211:453–58.

Kingdon, John W. 1984. *Agendas, Alternatives and Public Policies*. Boston: Little Brown.

Lindblom, Charles. 1958. "Policy Analysis." *American Economic Review* 19:78–88.

Linnerooth-Bayer. 2001. "The Austrian Case Study." *PEN-REF Project Deliverable D2*. Vienna: ICCR.

Mayhew, Les. 2001. "A Comparative Analysis of the UK Pension System Including the Views of Ten Pension Experts." *PEN-REF Project Deliverable D2*. Vienna: ICCR.

Müller, Katharina. 1999. *The Political Economy of Pension Reform in Central-Eastern Europe*. Cheltenham, U.K.: Edward Elgar.

Ney, Steven. 2001. "Country Report Germany." *PEN-REF Project Deliverable D2*. Vienna: ICCR.

Nullmeier, Frank, and Friedbert Rüb. 1993. *Die Transformation der Sozialpolitik: Vom Sozialstaat zum Sicherungsstaat*. Frankfurt am Main: Campus.

OECD (Organisation for Economic Co-operation and Development). 1998. *Maintaining Prosperity in an Ageing Society*. Paris.

Pabst, Stefan. 1999. "Sozialpolitische Entscheidungsprozesse in der Bundesrepublik Deutschland zwischen 1982 unf 1989: Eine Literaturübersicht." *ZeS Arbietspapier Nr. 8/99*. Bremen: ZeS.

Perek-Bialas, Jolanta, Agniezska Chlon-Dominczak, and Anna Ruzik. 2001. "Country Report for Poland." *PEN-REF Project Deliverable D2*. Vienna:ICCR.

Pierson, Paul. 1994. *Dismantling the Welfare State? Reagan, Thatcher, and the Politics of Retrenchment*. Cambridge, U.K.: Cambridge University Press.

———. 1996. "The New Politics of the Welfare State." *World Politics* 48 (January): 143–79.

Pierson, Paul D., and R. Kent Weaver. 1993. "Imposing Losses in Pension Policy." In R. Kent Weaver and Bert A. Rockman, eds., *Do Institutions Matter? Government Capabilities in the United States and Abroad.* Washington, D.C.: Brookings Institution.

Polsby, Nelson. 1981. *Community Power and Political Theory.* 4th ed. New Haven, Conn.: Yale University Press.

Rayner, Steve. 1991. "A Cultural Perspective on the Structure and Implementation of Global Environmental Agreements." *Evaluation Review* 15(1):75–102.

Rehfeld, Uwe. 2001. "The German Pension Reform 2001." Paper presented at the PEN-REF Workshop, "Setting European Pension Reform Agendas," June, International Institute for Applied System Analysis, Laxenburg, Austria.

Rein, Martin, and Donald Schön. 1993. "Reframing Policy Discourse." In Frank Fischer and John Forester, eds., *The Argumentative Turn in Policy Analysis and Planning.* London: Duke University Press/UCL Press.

———. 1994. *Frame Reflection: Towards the Resolution of Intractable Policy Controversies.* New York: Basic Books.

Reynaud, Emmanuel, ed. 2000. *Social Dialogue and Pension Reform.* Geneva: International Organisation of Labour.

Rhodes, R.A.W. 1990. "Policy Networks: A British Perspective." *Journal of Theoretical Politics,* 2(3):293–317.

———. 1997. *Understanding Governance: Policy Networks, Governance, Reflexivity and Accountability.* Buckingham, U.K.: Open University Press.

Sabatier, Paul, and Hank Jenkins-Smith, eds. 1993. *Policy Change and Learning: An Advocacy Coalition Approach.* Boulder, Colo.: Westview Press.

Schmitter, Philippe C., and G. Lehmbruch, eds. 1979. *Trends towards Corporatist Intermediation.* Beverly Hills, Calif.: Sage.

Stone, Deborah. 1988. *Policy Paradox and Political Reason.* Glenview, Ill: Scott Foresman.

Thompson, Michael, Richard Ellis, and Aaron Wildavsky. 1990. *Cultural Theory.* Boulder, Colo.: Westview Press.

Thompson, Michael, Steve Rayner, and Steven Ney. 1998. "Risk and Governance Part II." *Government and Opposition* 33(3):139–66.

Williamson, John B., and Fred C. Pampel. 1993. *Old-Age Security in Comparative Perspective.* Oxford, U.K.: Oxford University Press.

World Bank. 1994. *Averting the Old Age Crisis: Policies to Protect the Old and Promote Growth.* Oxford, U.K.: Oxford University Press.

4
Population Aging, Electoral Behavior, and Early Retirement

Florence Legros

In many countries, rising pension spending has become a major feature of contemporary public finance. This has led to tax increases that much of the public believes to be too large. Although pension systems were balanced for a long time, demographic and economic trends lately have reduced tax bases while the number of beneficiaries has increased. This situation cannot be sustained. The schemes' deficits are now obvious; furthermore, the development of intergenerational accounting has shown that the tax burden will be heavy on future generations. The solidarity principle that undergirded the schemes is no longer respected and beneficiaries often appear to be better off than those who pay.

As shown by Casamatta, Cremer, and Pestieau (2000) and Cremer and Pestieau (2000), pension schemes, particularly in Western Europe, have shifted from meeting justifiable claims to supporting entrenched interests.

Many modifications have yet to be implemented, of course—most of them minor parametric reforms with the explicit or implicit aim of retrenching the generosity of the schemes. But because of the projected doubling of dependency ratios in most countries, long-term coherent solutions have to be applied to ensure a socially balanced distribution of burdens.

One of these solutions—one that seems most adequate to strengthen the pay-as-you-go (PAYG) pension schemes—is to raise the rights vesting period to keep the pensions-to-wages ratio constant and to limit the contribution rate increase. Raising the retirement age appears to be the best way to balance pension schemes so as to share the burden across generations. The huge deterioration of the PAYG returns, as the contribution period increases, is then balanced by better returns for future generations who have to support lower contribution rates (Hamayon, Legros, and Sylvain 2000 for the French case).

This policy raises some issues that could explain the strong opposition of the public to such reform:

- An increase in the retirement age may appear to be unrealistic in a period of high unemployment, especially for older workers.
- For that reason, this solution generally is associated with a decline of expected replacement rates.

The predicted labor force decline in most Organisation for Economic Co-operation and Development (OECD) countries is expected to induce a return to low unemployment, which would invalidate such criticisms. Dissent in this case does not concern the feasibility of the policy, but the policy itself. This is why a reactivation of immigration, for instance, appears to be a successful plan, although it is known that this option is neither efficient nor realistic.

Why then does the pension age remain so low? One of the reasons may be that pension reforms find their justification in the very long run, far beyond the horizon of the next elections and too far in the future for a government to realize their benefits (Hinrichs 2000). Another explanation is provided by Casamatta, Cremer, and Pestieau (2000) and Cremer and Pestieau (2000). They argue that majority voting may favor the entrenched interests of the elderly. They show that if the authorities can implement two types of reforms (an economic one, such as pension reform, and a noneconomic one, such as the passage of a civil rights law) implicit coalitions between the elderly (pension reform opponents) and part of the younger generation (favorable to the noneconomic reform) can lead to an excessive PAYG contribution rate. Assimilating pension reform opponents into the oldest part of the population is an interesting idea because it is obvious that retired people have a direct and short-term interest in generous pension schemes and, by implication, in high contribution rates.

The pension reform debate reveals that retiree lobbies have displayed strong opposition to reforms aimed at retrenching PAYG pensions. For instance, the American Association of Retired Persons (AARP), a powerful lobby with 35 million members, defends American seniors' interests. In the Netherlands, the General Alliance of Aging Persons (AOV) and Union 55+ surprisingly won seven seats in parliament in 1994. Similarly, the French Retirees Confederation displays strong opposition to any reform aimed at diminishing PAYG generosity.

In some countries, such as Germany, it has been argued that the fact that one-third of the current population is over 55 years old has not been an obstacle to change. Simulations show that these retirees will not suffer from pension reform, which will affect only future generations. That may explain why retiree lobbies in Germany did not react too strongly to reform and why trade unions did.

Active retiree lobbies, however, will be stronger in the future. The number of people aged 60 or older will double between now and 2040 in most OECD countries. In addition, the electoral activity of the elderly is generally more dynamic than that of the young. In France, 95 percent of retirees are registered to vote (compared with 86 percent for the young generation), and among registered voters, 85 percent of the elderly do vote (compared with 78 percent for the whole population). Furthermore, retirees—and especially the youngest among them—are well represented within the trade unions, as is the case in southern European countries.

In this chapter, retirees (or near-retirees, as in Browning [1975] where the key generation is the older working generation whose members have an incentive to favor high tax rates to obtain a generous pension) are assumed to have the political weight now and in the future to alter governments' political choices, as discussed in Casamatta, Cremer, and Pestieau and Cremer and Pestieau. The main differences between our model and theirs is that we study

- the impact of such choices on the design of pension schemes and especially how these schemes will differ from the optimal scheme (in their mix between PAYG and funded schemes on the one hand and pensionable age on the other)
- the design of the pension scheme when the older generation is the electoral majority and when it is not altruistic.

The aim of this chapter is not to measure the distributive impact of one scheme compared with another; we already know that these measures often rely on specific assumptions. Instead, this discussion tries to marry the usual literature about the desirability of various pension schemes and different problems of macroeconomic linkage (effect on wages, interest rates, and so forth) with the literature on political economy that explains how economic policy choices are made and how macroeconomic efficiency is affected by those choices. For instance, Hanson and Stuart (1989) show how the younger generation may choose to save less in order to force the older generation to transfer more. This logic is quite similar to that in Alesina and Tabellini (1990), who study how future generations' welfare can be altered by some economic policy choices, considering that there are important links among these choices, income distribution, and future economic growth. For example, one can show that if the majority (the median voter of a specific election) has a low wage, it will prefer an income redistribution policy that relies on strong capital taxation, which will offset economic growth (Alesina and Rodrik 1991; Bertola 1991; Person and Tabellini 1992), or a taxation of highest incomes, which will discourage labor supply (Krugman 1993).

In this chapter we will study these conflicts between retired (and nearly retired) people and workers in a general equilibrium model with overlapping generations in which the variable to be chosen by the authorities is the contribution rate and the variable to be chosen by households in response is the retirement age.

The chapter is organized as follows: The first section presents the model. The second section presents the different voting configurations according to the majority. That section focuses on the following three cases:

- When the social planner maximizes the whole population's welfare; in this case, it is meaningful to distinguish whether the government overemphasizes the older generation
- When the younger generation has the electoral majority (there is a demographic increase)
- When the older generation has the electoral majority. This can result from a coalition of current and soon-to-be retirees; depending on the profile of the age pyramid, this coalition has important weight.

The third section presents two extensions: first, the effect of a demographic shift—a situation occurring when a self-interested older generation has the electoral majority—and, second, the specific impact of increasing life expectancy compared with the usual simple case of negative population growth.

An Overlapping Generation Model with a Flexible Retirement Age

The model developed here is a simple overlapping generations model. As usual, it considers two generations—the young (the y index) and the elderly (the o index)—and two periods. These periods are long enough to represent the whole life cycle (except childhood) when both the periods are considered.

The active population is M_t. It is the sum of the youngest part of the working population N_t (the size of the generation born in t) plus part h of the older generation. As the life cycle is divided into two periods, h is the working part of the older generation and the share of time during which the older generation works. The elderly receive a retirement pension during a part $(1 - h)$ of their old age when they do not work, h being the retirement age chosen by consumers. Workers receive a real wage, w.

The mandatory pension scheme is a PAYG scheme. Its equilibrium can be written as follows: $\tau w_t M_t = \lambda w_t (1 - h_t) N_{t-1}$ with $M_t = N_t + h_t N_{t-1}$ and $N_t = (1 + n) N_{t-1}$ where n is the population growth rate λ is the replacement rate of the pension scheme, and τ is the contribution rate. In each period t, the total amount of contributions balances the total amount of benefits.

The PAYG pension scheme equilibrium can be rewritten in the following way to account for the previous relationships:

$$\lambda_t = \tau \frac{1 + n + h_t}{1 - h_t}$$

Consumers' Behavior and Their Retirement Age Choice

The budgetary constraints of consumers can be written as follows (with the first equation referring to the first period when people are young, working, consuming, and saving; the second equation referring to the second period, $t + 1$, during which the older generation lives with a retirement pension, the savings accumulated previously, and a wage received during the working part of the period):

$$\begin{cases} C_t^y + s_t = w_t(1 - \tau) \\ C_{t+1}^o = s_t(1 + r_t) + w_{t+1}h_{t+1}(1 - \tau) + w_{t+1}\tau(1 + n + h_{t+1}) \end{cases} \tag{1}$$

where C_t is the consumption of the period t, s is savings, w is the real wage, and r is the real interest rate. As mentioned, the y index indicates the young and the o index indicates the elderly.

The utility function is assumed to have the following form:

$$U = \ln C_t^y + \frac{1}{1 + \rho} \ln C_{t+1}^o + \frac{\alpha}{1 + \rho} \ln(1 - h_{t+1}) \tag{2}$$

where ρ is the time preference and α measures the degree of preference for leisure.

Maximizing the utility function as shown in (2) with respect to the intertemporal constraint drawn from (1) provides consumption and labor supply behavior:

$$\begin{cases} C_{t+1}^o = \frac{1 + r_t}{1 + \rho} C_t^y \\ \frac{w_{t+1}}{C_{t+1}^o} - \frac{\alpha}{1 - h_t} = 0 \end{cases} \tag{3}$$

A brief conclusion can be drawn from (3). An increase of h (if consumers postpone their retirement) will increase the marginal utility of the consumption. There will be a negative relationship between the retirement age and the real wage.

Saving behavior can be written as

$$s_t = \frac{w_t(1 - \tau)}{2 + \rho} - \frac{1 + \rho}{2 + \rho} \frac{w_{t+1}(h_{t+1} + \tau + \tau n)}{1 + r_t} \tag{4}$$

As usual, savings increase when current income increases and decrease with future income—to a greater extent if the PAYG pension is generous (τ is large) or if the retirement age is high. (Pestieau and Michel [2000] argue that in some cases a government that wants to increase the macroeconomic savings rate has to maintain a flexible retirement age and a low replacement rate.) We have to note that in that family of models, there is an underlying hypothesis of perfect information. People are able to link the contribution rate to the generosity of the scheme (that is, the replacement rate) and to know the exact mechanisms that lead to a given pension level.

In the long run, as $w_t = w_{t-1} = w$,

$$
\begin{cases}
s_t = \dfrac{w(1-\tau)}{2+\rho} - \dfrac{1+\rho}{2+\rho}\,\dfrac{w(h+\tau+\tau n)}{1+r} \\[2ex]
C^o = \dfrac{1+r}{2+\rho}\,w(1-\tau) + \dfrac{1}{2+\rho}\,w(h+\tau+\tau n) \\[2ex]
h(\alpha+2+\rho) = 2+\rho-\alpha[1+r-\tau(r-n)]
\end{cases}
\tag{5}
$$

The relationship depicted in (5) is rather usual. The last equation shows that the retirement age is increasing with τ if $r > n$ (that is, if there is a lack of capital in the economy) and is diminished by the preference for leisure α.

If $r > n$, the PAYG pension scheme is inefficient—that is, savings are more attractive than the PAYG system—and an increase in τ lowers the discounted income over the life cycle and, incidentally, lowers the consumption. The marginal utility of consumption increases, and that raises the retirement age.

In addition, an increase of α (that induces a decrease of h) leads to a higher savings (s) and lower aggregate consumption.

In most of the following developments, we will study the situation in which $r > n$, which is the usual depicted case (higher yields of savings compared with those provided by the PAYG scheme). We will not address the case of a transition toward a fully funded scheme.

The Firms

In order to have a complete frame for the economy, we now have to look at the firms' behavior via their production function. The production function adopted here has constant returns on capital and labor:

$$ Y_t = M_t^a K_t^{1-a} $$

where Y is output, K is capital, and M is the active population.

The per capita aggregates of a young, active agent can be expressed as $y = Y/N$ and $k = K/N$. The production per capita is given by

$$y_t = \left[\frac{h_t}{(1+n)} + 1\right]^a k_t^{1-a} \tag{6}$$

If the retirement age (h) increases, the quantity of work is higher and the production will be increased as well. The real equilibrium wage and interest rate are given by

$$\begin{cases} w_t = a\left[1 + \dfrac{h_t}{1+n}\right]^{a-1} k_t^{1-a} \\[2ex] r_t = \left[1 + \dfrac{h_t}{1+n}\right]^a (1-a)k_t^{-a} \end{cases} \tag{7}$$

which says that if h increases, the total active population increases with respect to the size of a generation and the marginal productivity of work because the real wage is lower. On the other hand, the marginal productivity of capital is higher, so r is higher.

Equilibrium

The amount of savings in t, of the young generation, finances the capital available in $t + 1$:

$$N_t s_t = N_{t+1} k_{t+1} \tag{8}$$

The long-run savings equilibrium can be written (from [8], [5] and [7]) as

$$a\left[1 + \frac{h}{1+n}\right]^{a-1} \frac{1}{2+\rho}\left[1 - \tau\left(1 - \frac{1+\rho}{1+r}(1+n)\right) - \frac{1+\rho}{1+r}\frac{2+\rho-\alpha(1+r)}{2+\rho+\alpha}\right.$$

$$\left. + \frac{1+\rho}{1+r}\frac{\alpha\tau(r-n)}{2+\rho+\alpha}\right] = (1+n)k^a \tag{9}$$

If the agents postpone their retirement (if h increases), per capita capital will be diminished through two channels:

1. The real wage will decrease and so will consumers' ability to save.
2. The retirement pensions level will increase and contributions will be paid over a longer period.

Voting Configurations

Here we consider the following three situations corresponding to different policy options.

1. The authorities maximize social welfare (U) with results from the weighted sum of each category utility. Each category, for young and older agents, is weighted by its share in the whole population. If the size of the young population is considered equal to 1, then collective welfare is given by the following formula:

$$U^C = \ln C_t^y + \frac{1}{1+n} \ln\left(C_t^o\right) + \frac{\alpha}{1+n} \ln(1 - h_t). \tag{10}$$

2. The young agents represent the majority of the voters (they are more numerous than the old voters in a situation of demographic growth—that is, $n > 0$). The vote leads the authorities to maximize the intertemporal utility of the young agents:

$$U^Y = \ln C_t^y + \frac{1}{1+\rho} \ln\left(C_{t+1}^o\right) + \frac{\alpha}{1+\rho} \ln(1 - h_{t+1}) \tag{11}$$

The impact of a variation of τ on the young generation's welfare is obtained by a simple transformation of (10) in (11): the weight $(1 + n)$ is changed into $(1 + \rho)$ to account for the present value of the forthcoming retirees' future income (that is, the income of those who are young now).

3. The old agents are more numerous than the younger ones ($n < 0$) in a situation of demographic decrease. The old agents' welfare is maximized by $U^O = \ln C_t^o + \alpha \ln(1 - h_t)$, where the weight of the young generation becomes 0.

The Effect of a Contribution Rate Variation

The main problem here is that the authorities will choose τ accounting for the indirect effect on h (chosen by the consumers) that results from the variations of τ (chosen by the authorities according to the majority they want to satisfy). As shown by the expressions of the three types of welfare (see the appendix), the relationship between the variables is not obvious because different channels are working in different directions. The following effects are certain:

- $\partial w / \partial \tau < 0$: when the contribution rate increases, the equilibrium wage decreases mainly because savings—and per capita capital—decrease, as does the economic growth rate. This effect is intensified if $r > n$; in this case, the PAYG is inefficient with regard to savings and an increase in τ increases h ($\partial h/\partial \tau < 0$): agents work longer to boost their present income and such an increase in the retirement age diminishes the equilibrium wage.

- $\partial r/\partial \tau > 0$: for the opposite reason, particularly because the increase in τ slows the capital accumulation and the interest rate is increased. If there is a lack of capital, $r > n$, the effects are stronger; in this case, the increase in the interest rate is more important.

Unfortunately, the global effects are more problematic. On the one hand, if $r > n$ (if the economy suffers from a lack of capital) and if the PAYG pension scheme becomes more generous (if τ increases), the retirement age increases (h) because an increase in τ reduces the current income. The agents will choose a high retirement age. So there is a positive relationship between τ and h.

On the other hand, if τ increases, the per capita stock of capital falls (because savings are reduced), the real wages fall (because of the increase in h), and the interest rate increases (because of the additional lack of per capita capital).

In addition, based on (5): $\partial h/\partial r = (-\alpha + \tau\alpha)/(\alpha + 2 + \rho) < 0$, which means that a rising interest rate (r) will diminish h (the retirement age) because it reduces the present value of additional, intertemporal potential income that would be due to a higher h. The optimal value of h is then diminished.

To summarize, it is very difficult to draw a clear conclusion unless we compare the three policies focusing on two particular cases.

A Comparison of the Three Policies

To compare the effects on the retirement age of an increased contribution rate—fixed by the authorities to satisfy either the whole community, the youngest, or the oldest—we have to compare $\partial U^C/\partial \tau$, $\partial U^Y/\partial \tau$, $\partial U^O/\partial \tau$, focusing on the terms in $1/(2 + \rho + \alpha)$ that represent the response of the retirement age in front of a variation in τ. Two cases can be discussed.

First, it is assumed that $r \approx n$, which indicates a nearly optimal capitalization of the economy. This implies that

- $\frac{\partial \partial h}{\partial \tau} = 0$ (an increase in τ does not change the present income value)

- $\frac{\partial r}{\partial \tau} > 0$ and $\frac{\partial h}{\partial r} < 0$ (from [5])

- $\frac{\partial w}{\partial \tau} < 0$

- $\frac{\partial r}{\partial \tau}$ and $\frac{\partial w}{\partial \tau}$ are not linked with h (from [11]).

On the other hand, it was shown in (3) that

$$\frac{w_{t+1}}{C_{t+1}^{o}} = \frac{\alpha}{1 - h_{t+1}} \quad \text{or, in the long run,} \quad \frac{w}{C^{o}} = \frac{\alpha}{1 - h}.$$

The effect of the retirement age on the different expressions of the welfare, when $\partial h / \partial \tau = 0$ and when $\partial w / \partial \tau = 0$ and $\partial r / \partial \tau = 0$, are not linked with h (this is the case when $\partial h / \partial \tau = 0$) has the sign of

- $\frac{2 + n}{2 + \rho} \frac{w}{C^{o}} - \frac{\alpha}{1 - h}$ for $\frac{\partial U^{C}}{\partial \tau}$, the impact of a variation of the contribution rate on social welfare

- $\frac{w}{C^{o}} - \frac{\alpha}{1 - h}$ for $\frac{\partial U^{Y}}{\partial \tau}$; note that this is equal to 0 and denotes the optimal consumption behavior

- $\frac{1}{2 + \rho} \frac{w}{C^{o}} - \frac{\alpha}{1 - h}$ for $\frac{\partial U^{O}}{\partial \tau}$.

The signs of $\partial U^{Y} / \partial \tau$ and $\partial U^{O} / \partial \tau$, the effect of the contribution rate on the young and older generations' welfare, are no longer linked with the relative values of n and ρ, but if $\rho > n$ (a situation that will be discussed later), then the three policies can be classified as follows:

$$\frac{\partial U^{O}}{\partial \tau} < \frac{\partial U^{C}}{\partial \tau} < \frac{\partial U^{Y}}{\partial \tau} = 0$$

If the government overemphasizes the interest of today's older generation, the retirement age will be lower than the age toward which consumers' choice would have led. If the elderly have an electoral majority, the retirement age will be lower than the one toward which social welfare maximization would have led.

If $\rho > n$, which is the case if the authorities overweight the older generation relative to the weight the young generation gives itself once it has aged, $\partial U^{C} / \partial h < 0$, that is, the authorities want a lower retirement age than the consumers would want. This is because they overweight the loss of leisure that the elderly would suffer if they were to postpone their retirement.

Because in this model the retirement age is a response to the contribution rate, and because $\partial r / \partial \tau > 0$ and $\partial h / \partial \tau < 0$, the authorities will increase the contribution rate until the retirement age is at the level desired by the majority (whether the whole population or the elderly). This contribution rate will be higher than the one desired by consumers and the younger generation. In this configuration, the dominant effect is the effect of r, the interest rate. An increase in h will diminish w and increase r; this will decrease the present value of the additional income due to an increase in h, and h will decrease.

In this configuration, the majority, if it is held by the elderly, will induce the authorities to increase the contribution rate, τ, and this will decrease the retirement age, h. The main result will be a higher equilibrium wage that will induce increased pensions. Of course, if the social planner underweights the older generation, the results have to be changed: the retirement age is then higher than expected by individuals and much higher than expected by the older generation.

Next to be considered is $r \gg n$. In such a case, another channel is at work. There is a direct impact of τ on h. If τ increases and if the PAYG pension scheme is not efficient ($r \gg n$), an increase in τ will "impoverish" the consumers (diminish their discounted income), which will increase h. People will have to work more if they want to take advantage of the high rate of return on the higher savings accumulated during a longer career.

It is easy to see that $\partial U^C / \partial \tau$ will take the sign of

$$\left[\frac{2+n}{2+\rho} \frac{w}{C^o} - \frac{\alpha}{1-h} \right] \frac{\partial h}{\partial \tau} \quad \text{with} \quad \frac{\partial h}{\partial \tau} > 0 \quad \text{if } r > n$$

If $\rho > n$ (for the reasons discussed above), $\partial U^C / \partial \tau < 0$. An increase in τ reduces the welfare because it increases h and

$$\frac{\partial U^O}{\partial \tau} < \frac{\partial U^C}{\partial \tau} < \frac{\partial U^Y}{\partial \tau} = 0$$

The authorities are led to diminish τ below the individuals' choice and this will decrease h (and avoid a decrease in w). If the elderly have the electoral majority, the decreases of τ and of h will be stronger. To provide a higher pension level, the authorities who design the pension scheme to satisfy the old generation prefer a low retirement age (which maintains high wages). If they were designing the pension scheme to satisfy the young generation, they would prefer a high retirement age to allow the young generation to profit from the high interest rate. Because of the positive correlation between τ and h in this case, the contribution chosen is lower if authorities want to satisfy the elderly.

On the other hand, if $\rho < n$ (if there is a demographic increase and a large lack of capital accumulation) the results are different: the elderly want a higher contribution rate τ than the rate to which the individual choices would have led.

Note that when $r \gg n > \rho$, ρ is weak and this reflects the fact that the young generation has a weak weight in the collective utility. In this case, the increase of h induces a rather small decrease of w (large demographic growth allows for an increase in the retirement age). In this case, the impact of h on the wage and further on the pension level is what is important. This leads to a situation in which an increase in h causes the response of τ to be linked with wages. Note that when $r > n$ (there is not such a great difference between the PAYG rate of return and the savings rate of return), the increasing effect on h of a higher τ depends on the relative weight of the income effect and substitution effect. Blake (2001) suggests a superiority of the substitution effect in the British case.

Two Extensions

Demographic Shift and an Egoistic Older Generation

In the above discussion, growth is regular whether the young or the old generation held an electoral majority. We now turn to a dramatically different case: the old generation has the electoral majority but does not take into account what happens to subsequent generations. The problem becomes a question of maximizing the older generation's own welfare. The older generation maximizes only its welfare (at time t): it chooses a contribution rate τ that will be applied to subsequent generations (the younger generation's vote does not account for this choice because of a demographic shift). This behavior is termed here "egoism."

It is assumed that the interest rate is exogenous (as in a small, open economy; this simplifies the reasoning but does not change the results); it is represented as $\bar{r}$. The older generation's income (and consumption) is $C_t^o = s_{t-1}(1 + \bar{r}) + w_t(h_t + \tau(1 + n))$. As s_t was determined earlier, it is considered exogenous.

The older egoistic generation must find an optimal pair (τ, h_t) to maximize its welfare. It seems clear that this optimum will rely on a high contribution rate and a low level of h (which implies high wages and therefore high PAYG pensions).

The old generation maximizes its pension in this way: *Max:* $\tau[(1 + h) + h_t]w_t$. This implies that *Max:* $\tau h_t w_t$. The main problem is that we have to account for the indirect effects on h and w.

Accounting for (7), the firms' profit maximization condition, this leads to *Max*$_\tau$: τh_t^a and $\partial h_t/\partial \tau = -h_t/\tau a < 0$, and when τ increases $\partial h_t/\partial \tau$ decreases. This leads us to consider that an optimal value of τ can be found.

Which are the decisive variables? Accounting for (3), the labor supply condition, we have to consider that

$$\frac{\partial h_t}{\partial \tau} = -\alpha\left[\frac{\partial h_t}{\partial \tau} + (1 + n)\right] - \alpha \bar{s}(1 + \bar{r})\frac{1}{a}(1 - a)\left[1 + \frac{h_t}{1 + n}\right]^{-a}\frac{\partial h_t}{\partial \tau}\frac{1}{1 + n}\bar{k}^{a-1}$$

where all of the predetermined variables x are denoted $\bar{x}$. Note that the equilibrium condition (savings = capital) disappears (we are in an open economy and the difference is equal to the current account balance) and by implication capital is predetermined.

The optimal value of τ is high if

- the preexisting capital level ($\bar{k}$) is high because in this case the wages are increased
- the exogenous interest rate $\bar{r}$ is low (and n is negative because of the demographic shift), and $\bar{s}$ is low so that the older generation is less sensitive to the interest rate level and will continue to choose a generous PAYG pension scheme.

If the older generation takes only its own interests into account, it can choose a high contribution rate compatible with a low retirement age. This is because it is possible to find the point where the elasticity of the oldest workers' labor supply to the contribution rate is very weak.

Specific Effects of Increasing Life Expectancy

Usually, when the life expectancy increases between two generations, even with constant fertility rates, each age cohort is more numerous than the previous one because life expectancy improvement comes from lower death probabilities at each age, (figure 4.1). But in the recent past,

Figure 4.1   Probabilities According to Life Expectancies

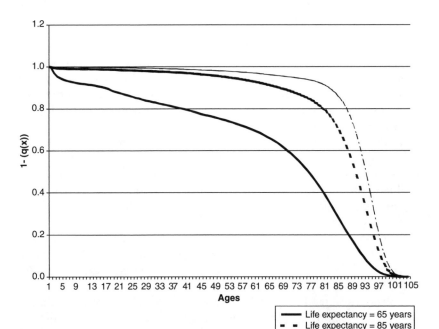

longer life expectancies have been attributed mainly to a large decrease in death probabilities among older people.

A simple way to represent such an increase in life expectancy is to consider that it mainly concerns the older generation. Notwithstanding the simplicity of such an hypothesis, a constant increase in the size of the population at all ages can be summarized by n, the natural population growth rate, while a varying increase in the size of the population according to age would require a more complicated model.

If we consider that a rise in life expectancies can be summarized by the death rate, q, which affects individuals only when they are old, some of the previous equations must be changed. The PAYG pension scheme equilibrium becomes $\tau w_t [N_t + h_t(1-q)N_{t-1}] = \lambda w_t(1-h_t)(1-q)N_{t-1}$ while $N_t = (1+n)N_{t-1}$ remains identical. The PAYG pension scheme equilibrium can be rewritten this way:

$$\lambda_t = \tau \frac{[1 + n + h_t(1-q)]}{(1-h_t)(1-q)}$$

The budgetary constraint of the older consumers will be changed according to this marginal modification:

$$C_{t+1}^o = s_t(1+r_t) + w_{t+1}h_{t+1}(1-\tau) + w_{t+1}\tau\left(\frac{1+n}{1-q} + h_{t+1}\right)$$

The PAYG yield is now $(1 + n)/(1 - q)$ instead of $1 + n$. This means that when life expectancy increases by way of a lower mortality rate (q decreases), the PAYG yield is decreased if any other parameter changes. That is because the same number of contributors have to pay pensions for a greater number of retired people.

In our model, these lower yields will induce a stronger substitution effect. Because the PAYG yield is diminished, the PAYG scheme will be less efficient (it becomes easier to have $r \gg n$) and the substitution effect will be more obvious, lowering both the retirement age (increasing the equilibrium wage) and the contribution rate to give a more important role to savings.

If the increase in life expectancy relies on a longer retirement period as well, the yields change. To simplify the problem and avoid a complete rewriting of the model with a new "very old" generation, only the PAYG rate of return is amended.

It is now assumed that P cohorts of retirees are alive (a cohort is the set of individuals born during the same year); their size N remains constant. If T is the contributing period length (that is, T cohorts are contributing) and P is the pensionable period length (P cohorts of retirees are living), the contributions = pensions balance can be written as $T_t \tau N w_t = P_t \lambda N w_t$, while τ and λ are still the contribution and the replacement rates, respectively. The replacement rate can be expressed as $\lambda = \tau(T_t/P_t)$ and decreases if the retirement period P increases.

Let us now compute the PAYG yield for individuals, σ. It is given by equating the present value of contribution flows sum with the present value (discounted by the PAYG rate of return) of pension flows sum; in the long run:

$$\sum_{i=0}^{T-1} \tau w (1+r)^i = \sum_{i=1}^{P} \frac{\lambda w}{(1+\sigma)^i}.$$

After calculation, simplification, differentiation, and approximation,

$$d\sigma = -\sigma \frac{dP}{P+1}.$$

This shows that $d\sigma$ is small. The reason is that the increase in life expectancy raises the PAYG yield because people will receive their pensions for a longer period while the replacement rate decreases with a constant contribution rate. As a result of these two opposite effects, and if the increase in life expectancy results both from smaller mortality rates and longer retirement periods, then the PAYG yield will not be changed. In that case, the first conclusions presented here will not be altered.

Concluding Remarks

When the PAYG pension scheme is not perceived as inefficient (that is, it provides the same yields as savings), the major channel by which the contribution rate has an impact on welfare is the interest rate. In this configuration, there are two types of reasons why the retirement age is lower than it would be if the individual were perfectly free to choose:

1. The authorities underweight the younger generation; the older generation is powerful and demands a low retirement age, which is obtained with a high contribution rate.
2. Retired people have an electoral majority.

On the other hand, if the economy suffers from a significant lack of capital accumulation, if the interest rate is much higher that the PAYG pension scheme rate of return, and if people perceive that the PAYG scheme is not efficient, then the younger generation of wage earners will choose a higher retirement age than the authorities would choose. This results from their ignoring the impact of such an increase on the real wage. The authorities are led to diminish the contribution rate to create incentives for people to save more and retire earlier (the discounted income is not reduced any more if the PAYG represents a smaller share of this income). The older generation wants to diminish the contribution rate and the retirement age at the same time—in this case, a conclusion that is not really consistent with observation.

Whether old people do or do not retire sooner because they perceive no difference between the interest rate and the PAYG rate of return, it should be concluded that the egoistic case is relevant. In an extreme configuration of this case, if a demographic shift gives the electoral majority to the elderly and if the older generation does not care about the other generations (including the forthcoming older generations), the older generation can select a high contribution rate linked with a low retirement age. The intermediate configuration, in which the elderly only take care of old generations (including subsequent ones), can be interpreted as myopic: the old generation does not want any rolling back of the welfare state, despite the unknown effects on younger generations (as suggested by Pestieau 2001).

References

Alesina, A., and D. Rodrik. 1991. "Distributive Politics and Economic Growth." Working Paper 3668. National Bureau of Economic Research (NEBR) Working Paper Series. Cambridge University Press.

Alesina, A., and G. Tabellini. 1990. "A Positive Theory of Fiscal Deficits and Government Debt in a Democracy." *Review of Economic Studies* 57:403–14.

Bertola, G. 1991. "Factor Shares and Savings in Endogenous Growth?" Working Paper 3851. National Bureau of Economic Research (NBER) Working Paper Series. Cambridge University Press.

Blake, D. 2001. "The Impact of Wealth on Consumption and Retirement Behavior in the U.K." Paper presented at the meeting, "Epargne et retraite," Lyon I University, March 13–14.

Browning, E. 1975. "Why the Social Insurance Budget Is Too Large in a Democracy." *Economic Inquiry* 13(September): 373–88.

Casamatta, G., H. Cremer, and P. Pestieau. 2000. "Political Sustainability and the Design of Social Insurance." *Journal of Public Economics* 75(3):341–364.

Cremer, H., and P. Pestieau. 2000. "Reforming Our Pension System: Is It a Demographic, Financial or Political Problem?" *European Economic Review* 44:974–83.

Hamayon, S., F. Legros, and A. Sylvain. 2000. "Incidence d'un fond de réserve des retraites dans une maquette démo-économique." Paper presented at the meeting, "Epargne et retraite," Lyon I University, March 13–14.

Hanson I., and C. Stuart. 1989. "Social Security as Trade among Living Generations." *American Economic Review* December:1182–195.

Hinrichs, K. 2000. "Elephants on the Move. Patterns of Public Pension Reform in OECD Countries." *European Review* 8(3):353–78.

Krugman, P. 1993. "Inequality and the Political Economy of Eurosclerosis." Center for Economic Policy Research (CEPR) Discussion Paper 867. November.

Person T., and G. Tabellini. 1992. "Growth, Distribution and Politics." *European Economic Review* April:593–602.

Pestieau, P. 2001. "Are We Retiring So Early?" Paper presented at the CESifo conference, Munich, May 2–3.

Pestieau, P., and P. Michel. 2000. "Retraite par répartition et âge de la retraite." *Revue économique* 51(HS; February):15–30.

Appendix

Maximization of the Social Welfare (Collective Utility)

The authorities maximize the social welfare in the long run by the following formula:

$$U^C = \ln C_t^y + \frac{1}{1+n}\ln\left(C_t^o\right) + \frac{\alpha}{1+n}\ln(1 - h_t). \qquad (10)$$

Consumers have chosen h and

- $h = \dfrac{2 + \rho - \alpha(1 + r - \tau(r - n))}{2 + \rho + \alpha}$

- $C^y = \dfrac{w(1+\rho)}{2+\rho}\left[1 - \tau\left(1 - \dfrac{1+n}{1+r}\right) + \dfrac{1}{1+r}\left(\dfrac{2+\rho-\alpha(1+r)}{2+\rho+\alpha}\right) + \dfrac{1}{1+r}\alpha\tau\dfrac{r-n}{2+\rho+\alpha}\right]$

The authorities choose τ, taking into account the indirect effect on h that results from an increase in τ (whose interpretation is not obvious):

$$\frac{\partial U^C}{\partial \tau} = \left(1 + \frac{1}{1+n}\right)\frac{1}{C^y}\left(\frac{C^y}{w}\frac{\partial w}{\partial \tau} - w\frac{1+\rho}{2+\rho}\left(1 - \frac{1+n}{1+r}\right)\right)$$

$$+ w\frac{1+\rho}{2+\rho}\frac{\alpha(r-n)}{\alpha+2+\rho}\frac{1}{1+r}\right) + \frac{1}{1+n}\frac{1}{1+r}\frac{\partial r}{\partial \tau} + \left(1 + \frac{1}{1+n}\right)\frac{1}{C^y}$$

$$\times\left(-\tau\frac{1+n}{(1+r)^2} - \frac{2+\rho}{(1+r)^2}\frac{1}{\alpha+2+\rho} - \frac{\alpha\tau(r-n)}{(1+r)^2}\frac{1}{\alpha+2+\rho}\right)$$

$$+ \frac{1}{1+r}\frac{\alpha\tau}{\alpha+2+\rho}\right)\frac{\partial r}{\partial \tau} - \frac{\alpha}{1+n}\frac{1}{1-h}\frac{\alpha(r-n)}{\alpha+2+\rho}$$

$$+ \frac{\alpha}{1+n}\frac{1}{1-h}\frac{\alpha}{\alpha+2+\rho}\frac{\partial r}{\partial \tau} \qquad (10')$$

It is specified that attention first has to be paid to the terms that link the retirement age and the contribution rate; take into account the expressions of w and r given by the firms' equilibrium conditions (7), it comes out that

$$\begin{cases} \dfrac{\partial w}{\partial \tau} = -a(1-a)\left(1+\dfrac{h}{1+n}\right)^{a-2}\dfrac{1}{1+n}\dfrac{\partial h}{\partial \tau} + a\left(1+\dfrac{h}{1+n}\right)^{a-1}(1-a)k^{-a}\dfrac{\partial k}{\partial \tau} < 0 \\[4mm] \dfrac{\partial r}{\partial \tau} = a(1-a)\left(1+\dfrac{h}{1+n}\right)^{a-1}\dfrac{1}{1+n}\dfrac{\partial h}{\partial \tau} - a(1-a)\left(1+\dfrac{h}{1+n}\right)^{a}k^{-a-1}\dfrac{\partial k}{\partial \tau} > 0 \end{cases}$$

$$(12)$$

and

- $\dfrac{\partial h}{\partial \tau} = \dfrac{-\alpha(1-\tau(r-n))}{\alpha+2+\rho} < 0$ or > 0 according to the relative values of r and n (and is positive as soon as $r > n$).
- $\dfrac{\partial w}{\partial \tau} < 0$

Based on that equation set we know that on one hand, if $r > n$ (if the economy suffers from a lack of capital) and if the PAYG pension scheme becomes more generous (if τ increases), the retirement age (h) increases because an increase in τ reduces the actual income. So, there is a positive relationship between τ and h. On the other hand, if τ increases, the per capita stock of capital drops (because the saving is reduced), the real wages drop (because of the increase in h), and the interest rate increases (because of the additional lack of k).

In addition, from (5):

$$\frac{\partial h}{\partial r} = \frac{-\alpha+\tau\alpha}{\alpha+2+\rho} < 0$$

Furthermore, a rising interest rate (r) will lower h because it reduces the present value of the additional, intertemporal income due to a higher h; the optimal value of h is then diminished.

In addition, if $r > n$, the effects of τ on w and r are strengthened:

- $\dfrac{\partial h}{\partial \tau} > 0$, that is, $\tau \uparrow$, $h \uparrow$, $w \downarrow$ intensifies $\dfrac{\partial w}{\partial \tau} < 0$.
- $\dfrac{\partial k}{\partial \tau} > 0$, that is, $\tau \uparrow$, $k \downarrow$, $r \uparrow$ intensifies $\dfrac{\partial r}{\partial \tau} > 0$.

This implies that, in (10'), when τ raises h increases (and the leisure utility is reduced); $\partial w/\partial \tau$ becomes more negative and w decreases, while $\partial r/\partial \tau$ becomes more positive and r increases. This last point lowers h (and the leisure utility is increased). The global effect of an increase in τ is ambiguous.

Maximization of the Younger Generation's Welfare

The authorities have to maximize

$$U^Y = \ln C_t^y + \frac{1}{1+\rho}\ln\left(C_{t+1}^o\right) + \frac{\alpha}{1+\rho}\ln(1-h_{t+1}) \tag{11}$$

or

$$U^Y = \ln C_t^y + \frac{1}{1+\rho}\ln\left(C_t^y \frac{1+r}{1+\rho}\right) + \frac{\alpha}{1+\rho}\ln(1-h_{t+1})$$

With regular economic growth, in the long run

$$U^Y = \left(1 + \frac{1}{1+\rho}\right)\ln C^y + \frac{1}{1+\rho}\ln\left(\frac{1+r}{1+\rho}\right) + \frac{\alpha}{1+\rho}\ln(1-h)$$

The impact of a variation of τ on the young generation's welfare is obtained by a simple transformation of $(10')$ in (11): the weight $(1 + n)$ is changed into $(1 + \rho)$ to account for the present value of the forthcoming retirees' future income. The expression to be analyzed is quite similar to $(10')$:

$$\frac{\partial U^Y}{\partial \tau} = \left(1 + \frac{1}{1+\rho}\right)\frac{1}{C^y}\left(\frac{C^y}{w}\frac{\partial w}{\partial \tau} - w\frac{1+\rho}{2+\rho}\left(1 - \frac{1+n}{1+r}\right)\right.$$

$$+ w\frac{1+\rho}{2+\rho}\frac{\alpha(r-n)}{\alpha+2+\rho} - \frac{1}{1+r}\right)$$

$$+ \frac{1}{1+\rho}\frac{1}{1+r}\frac{\partial r}{\partial \tau} + \left(1 + \frac{1}{1+\rho}\right)\frac{1}{C^y}$$

$$\times\left(-\tau\frac{1+n}{(1+r)^2} - \frac{2+\rho}{(1+r)^2}\frac{1}{\alpha+2+\rho} - \frac{\alpha\tau(r-n)}{(1-r)^2}\frac{1}{\alpha+2+\rho}\right.$$

$$\left. + \frac{1}{1+r}\frac{\alpha\tau}{\alpha+2+\rho}\right)\frac{\partial r}{\partial \tau}$$

$$- \frac{\alpha}{1+\rho}\frac{1}{1-h}\frac{\alpha(r-n)}{\alpha+2+\rho} + \frac{\alpha}{1+\rho}\frac{1}{1-h}\frac{\alpha}{\alpha+2+\rho}\frac{\partial r}{\partial \tau}$$

Maximization of the Older Generation's Welfare

The authorities now have to maximize

$$U^O = \ln C_t^o + \alpha \ln(1 - h_t)$$

(13)

which implies (13')

$$\frac{\partial U^O}{\partial \tau} = \frac{1}{C^y}\left(\frac{C^y}{w}\frac{\partial w}{\partial \tau} - w\frac{1+\rho}{2+\rho}\left(1 - \frac{1+n}{1+r}\right) + w\frac{1+\rho}{2+\rho}\frac{\alpha(r-n)}{\alpha+2+\rho} - \frac{1}{1+r}\right)$$

$$+ \frac{1}{1+r}\frac{\partial r}{\partial \tau} + \frac{1}{C^y}\left(-\tau\frac{1+n}{(1+r)^2} - \frac{2+\rho}{(1+r)^2}\frac{1}{\alpha+2+\rho}\right.$$

$$\left. -\frac{\alpha\tau(r-n)}{(1+r)^2}\frac{1}{\alpha+2+\rho} + \frac{1}{1+r}\frac{\alpha\tau}{\alpha+2+\rho}\right)\frac{\partial r}{\partial \tau}$$

$$-\frac{\alpha}{1-h}\frac{1}{\alpha+2+\rho}\left[r - n - \frac{\partial r}{\partial \tau}\right]$$

In these equations the weight of the young generation, which was 1 in the previous expressions, is 0.

5

Commitment and Consensus in Pension Reform

Agnieszka Chlon-Dominczak and Marek Mora

At the end of the 20th century and at the beginning of the 21st century, most European countries have placed pension reform high on their agendas. In the European Union (EU), the majority of countries undertook some parametric changes in their pay-as-you-go (PAYG) public pension schemes, aiming to reduce the level of implicit pension debt. Radical reforms, focusing on the introduction of a mandatory, capital-funded pillar of support, were introduced only in the Netherlands and in the United Kingdom in the 1980s. In the 1990s Italy and Sweden reshaped their PAYG pillar with a notional defined contribution (NDC) system. Sweden also introduced a funded second pillar and began to shift its third pillar, quasi-mandatory occupational schemes, in the direction of advanced funding.

Also in the 1990s Hungary, Latvia, and Poland introduced pension reforms based on the multipillar principle, with a mandatory funded element.[1] Other countries are considering this option, including Bulgaria, Croatia, Estonia, Lithuania, the former Yugoslav Republic of Macedonia, and Romania. Poland and Latvia significantly reshaped their PAYG systems following the NDC concept. After initial discussion, several countries, such as the Czech Republic and Slovenia decided not to follow the multipillar path, but rather to rationalize their PAYG systems to stabilize the long-run financial balance.

Pension reform is an ongoing process that has several phases. Orenstein (2000) divides the process into three steps: commitment building, coalition building, and implementation. Commitment building begins when a government takes official action toward developing a reform proposal. This stage can be characterized by extensive bargaining, debate,

We are grateful to Robert Holzmann and Michal Rutkowski for their support and help, and to Edward Palmer and other participants in the International Institute for Applied System Analysis/World Bank conference, "Learning from the Partners" (Part I, "Political Economy of Pension Reform") for their comments on the earlier draft of this chapter.

and negotiations. The commitment of politicians and agreement among experts are crucial for this process to succeed. At the coalition building stage, the reform concept is presented to a wide spectrum of leading players, including political parties, trade unions, and the public, to gain their acceptance. Key steps are concept presentation; its dissemination, feedback and consensus building; work on new legislation; and, finally, enactment of laws. At the implementation stage, new institutions are built and existing ones are reformed. Most important, social security institutions have to adapt to the new environment. This is a stage at which new players appear and take part in the discussion. Amendments and changes to the initial proposal often are made. Implementation is also usually the longest-lasting stage of the reform, taking at least a few years.

Despite the fact that radical pension reforms have been discussed in almost every country, they have been implemented in only a few. The following questions arise: What is necessary for a reform proposal to be officially presented by the government, and what factors are necessary for successful implementation? In this chapter we attempt to analyze issues related to the first two stages of the reform process. We ask

1. What factors have an impact on pension reform commitment, that is, what triggers pension reform and what are the motives behind it?
2. What is necessary for pension reform preparation to be successfully finalized and the coalition building stage completed?

So far the most commonly used method to study political economy questions has been qualitative country-by-country or comparative analysis. Most of the studies have focused on Latin American and Central and Eastern European (CEE) countries.[2] Another more quantitative econometric approach was used by James and Brooks (1999), who tried to answer the question of how political economy influenced the probability of achieving pension reform and its nature. The methodology used in our study is based on a survey of experts and decisionmakers involved in the pension reform process in several countries. We constructed a questionnaire including both qualitative and quantitative questions that enable us to investigate the factors that influence reform actions from the perspective of the pension system and institutions involved in the reform process.

We used two surveys: the first for countries with pension reform, the second for countries without pension reform. We defined a reform country as one that adopted or implemented a law introducing a mandatory capital-funded pillar or an NDC system (so-called systemic pension reform). A nonreform country is one that did not attempt to change its pension system at all or that introduced only parametric changes. The first survey contained 20 questions and was addressed to both policymakers and pension experts.[3] The second contained 14 questions and was addressed only to pension experts.[4] The main motivation for using the survey of decision-makers and experts was to get a larger set of data on the decisionmaking process than that available from studies of particular countries.

The survey was disseminated in two rounds. In the first round, we used World Bank channels; in the second round we approached the participants of the "Learning from the Partners" conference who did not reply in the first round.[5] The main focus of the survey was on Central and Eastern European countries with some examples from EU countries and Latin America. We received 34 answers from 25 countries (table 5.1). Of the countries responding, 13 countries reformed their pension systems and 12 did not. Most of the answers were received from countries

Table 5.1   Respondents to the Questionnaire

Country	Number of answers	Experts	Decisionmakers	Both
Reformer				
Argentina	2			2
Bulgaria	2	2		
Croatia	2	1		1
Hungary	2	2		
Latvia	1		1	
Macedonia, FYR	1		1	
Mexico	1			1
Moldova	1	1		
Poland	1		1	
Romania	1	1		
Switzerland	1	1		
United Kingdom	2	2		
Uruguay	1			1
Reforming country total	18	10	3	5
Nonreformer				
Azerbaijan	1	1		
Brazil	1	1		
Czech Republic	1	1		
Finland	1	1		
Germany	1	1		
Greece	2	2		
Ireland	1	1		
Russia	1		1	
Slovakia	1	1		
Slovenia	3	2	1	
Spain	2	2		
Ukraine	1	1		
Nonreforming country total	16	14	2	0
TOTAL	**34**	**24**	**5**	**5**

in CEE and in the Commonwealth of Independent States (CIS) (14); 7 came from countries in Western Europe and 4 from Latin America. The majority of answers came from experts (23), 5 were received from decisionmakers, and 5 were filled out by experts who were also decisionmakers in the process. The sample of countries that responded to the questionnaire does not include all the countries to which the questionnaire was sent.

This chapter is structured in the following way: The second section includes an analysis of the commitment building stage, a short review of the political economy literature, and a set of hypotheses concerning the environment necessary for successful pension reform. In the third section we focus on the process of coalition building and we analyze the role of social partners, society, and public relations in the reform process. The final portion provides a conclusion.

The Commitment Stage

Discussion of the Literature

The traditional political economy analysis of policy reform asserts a clear normative economic motivation for reforms. It explains how the opposition of various private interest groups is overcome and what institutional settings help policy reforms take place. The crucial assumption of this analysis is that there is a broad consensus that pension reform improves economic efficiency—similar to other policy reforms at the end of the 1980s and in the 1990s, such as trade liberalization and privatization.

As for the role of private interest groups, political economy of pension policy has been investigated mainly along two lines of distributional conflict: young versus old, and rich versus poor (or a combination of those factors). The age-oriented theory suggests that age distribution is a crucial determinant in voting for a public unfunded pension system (Browning 1975). This type of system will expand as the population ages because older workers face only a relatively short contribution period but nonetheless participate in the full benefit period. In those models aging leads to a further worsening of the financial position of pension schemes (Marquardt and Peters 1997).

These theoretical conclusions, however, contrast with actual reform experience. First, the probability of radical pension reform taking place seems to be independent of the age structure of the population because population aging varies substantially among countries that have implemented pension reform. For instance, Mexico is a very "young" country, whereas Switzerland is a relatively "old" country. Second, population aging generally is accepted as an important reason for pension reform. Thus, this theory does not explain why there is a turning point in pension reform, nor the extent of reform (parametric or systemic) or its timing. Similarly, theories focusing on the analysis of interest groups according to the second taxonomy (rich versus poor) can explain the rise of unfunded pension systems but not the switch toward capital funding (Tabellini 1991).

As for the impact of institutional arrangements, the authoritarian regime often has been emphasized when explaining the first case of pension system privatization in Chile. It is obvious, however, that the Chilean case cannot be generalized. First, other Latin American countries that were culturally similar to Chile had similar problems in their pension schemes and displayed many shortcomings in their democratic systems. Many of those countries have not implemented pension reforms. Second, systemic pension reform was implemented in many countries with extensive democratic traditions (Italy, Sweden, Switzerland, and the United Kingdom). The most recent systemic pension reforms have been implemented in transition countries in CEE with already well-established democratic institutions. This means that a low level of democracy is neither a necessary nor a sufficient condition for pension reform.

Another way to study the role of institutions might be to examine whether there is any relationship between systemic pension reforms and the country's constitutional system, as suggested in some public choice models of pensions. We can observe that reforming countries have different constitutional systems. Switzerland has a direct democracy; most Latin American countries have a majority presidential system; the United Kingdom is a parliamentary democracy with a majority system; and most of the other countries have a parliamentary democracy based on a proportional system (including CEE countries). Thus, voting systems do not seem to determine the chances for pension reform either.

The least investigated political factor behind pension reform has been ideology. The main reason for this is that despite its importance, it is difficult to identify the driving forces behind changes in ideology over time. There is, however, a general consensus that there was an ideological turnaround in the 1980s toward neoliberalism, which had an effect on the change in economic thinking (the retrenchment of the state) and the discussion of pension reform approaches. Augusztinovics (1999) claims that although systemic pension reform was originally not a subject of the so-called Washington consensus, it has become de facto a part of the widely accepted neoliberal reform package.

It is well documented that ideology influenced pension reforms in Latin America. Pierson (1994) claims that the United Kingdom's pension reform in 1986 also was ideologically driven. Although neoliberal ideology affected other reform processes in the former socialist countries, it seems to have had a limited impact on pension reform. None of the

"Thatcherites" in CEE (for example, Balcerowicz in Poland and Klaus in the Czech Republic) adopted systemic pension reform. By contrast, non-conservative governments, which often opposed neoliberal ideology, adopted reform in many cases. Another limitation of neoliberal ideology as an explanation for pension reform lies in the fact that the idea of the *mandatory* fully funded system is still contentious among neoliberal economists (Friedman 1999). Neoliberal ideology, therefore, can only explain why pension systems were adjusted—the reason was to prevent the buildup of a huge implicit debt—and why there should be more reliance on private saving.

The empirical literature on policy reform indicates that a crucial factor affecting reform commitment is leadership. Political economy approaches that draw on the private interests theory anticipate reform leadership only when it clearly can be linked to political self-interest. The empirical record of many policy changes put in place in the 1980s and 1990s contrasts with this logic (Williamson 1994). The case of pension reform is similar. It was often accomplished by influential technocrats and by politicians endowed with political power who had strong reform visions and were ready to carry out their ideas against interest group pressure (for instance, Marchenko in Kazakhstan, Bokros in Hungary, and Baczkowski in Poland). Despite its importance, leadership remains underemphasized in the theoretical literature and it often is treated as an idiosyncratic phenomenon.

In the light of this knowledge, our focus was first to investigate how strong the consensus is on radical pension reform. If there is no strong reform consensus, economists can hardly expect to be taken seriously by policymakers.[6] Second, we investigated what political factors—mainly institutional arrangements—can be significant for radical pension reform to occur and what is perceived as the genuine trigger for radical pension reform.

The Survey Results

The Pension Reform Consensus. In the case of pension policy, most economists support reforming old-fashioned pension schemes—mainly to strengthen the link between pension contributions and pension benefits (parametric reforms) and to support voluntary saving (the third pillar). Many countries have already implemented these steps, yet there is ongoing disagreement among economists about how much of the PAYG pillar should be replaced by mandatory capital funding. This dispute includes such issues as the extent of economic distortions (savings, labor market, capital market), insurance properties, and the optimal PAYG-fully funded (FF) mix.[7]

Our survey results show that mainly economic (or "technical") issues are considered relevant to pension reform. The question of whether pension reform is only a political problem was answered negatively by the prevailing majority of respondents (31 of 34, or 91 percent). We further investigated the degree of expert involvement in the discussion of pension reform. We asked respondents from nonreform countries if they agreed that experts' advice is used in the preparation of pension reform. Only 1 respondent (of 16) answered negatively. Similarly, we asked the respondents from reform countries to assess the extent to which experts were involved in preparing pension reform (using a scale of 0–5 with 0 being not at all and 5 being significantly). The average figure for the reform countries was 4.2. Thus, in both groups of countries pension experts have had an impact on policy discussion. This means that the introduction of radical pension reform cannot be explained by the ignorance of pension experts in nonreform countries, nor can it be explained by involvement by experts in countries that have enacted reform. Rather, an important explanatory factor behind the different reform results might be a lack of agreement among pension policy experts.

We asked if there was a consensus among experts on pension reform. The answer was ambiguous: 19 of 34 respondents answered negatively. To learn the substance of the pension reform controversy, we asked our respondents to identify the objectives of pension reform. We specified five reform objectives and asked them to rank each on a scale from 1 (highest priority) to 3 (lowest priority). The average values for each objective are summarized in figure 5.1. Thirty respondents answered that the most important goal of pension reform should be financial

Figure 5.1 What Should Be the Main Goal of Pension Reform?

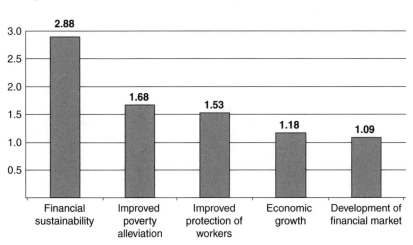

sustainability of the pension scheme. Two other reform objectives with the highest priority were improved poverty alleviation and improved protection of workers against decreases in income. Development of financial markets and economic growth were lower priorities and often were treated as external to the main reform objectives.

We also asked the respondents to give their definition of pension reform. We assumed that each respondent defines pension reform as an optimal mix of pension policy instruments intended to reach the goals of the reform. We gave them four options:

1. Introduction of a mandatory and at least partially fully funded pillar
2. Introduction of a NDC system
3. Parametric reform within the PAYG system
4. Any other option specified by the respondent.[8]

As indicated in figure 5.2, respondents' opinions about what constitutes pension reform differed. For 8 respondents pension reform meant only the introduction of the pillar that was at least partially fully funded; for 6 of them it meant only parametric change of the PAYG system; and for 1 respondent it meant the introduction of an NDC scheme. Eleven respondents answered that pension reform is a combination of the introduction of a fully funded pillar and either parametric reform or introduction of NDC. For 3 respondents, both parametric reform and the shift to NDC signify reform.

We also asked those respondents who answered that there was no consensus among experts on pension reform to specify the reasons for that disagreement. To our surprise, the main source of experts' disagreement

Figure 5.2   What Is Your Definition of Pension Reform?

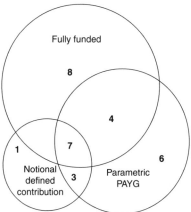

Figure 5.3   Reasons Why Experts Disagree about Pension Reform

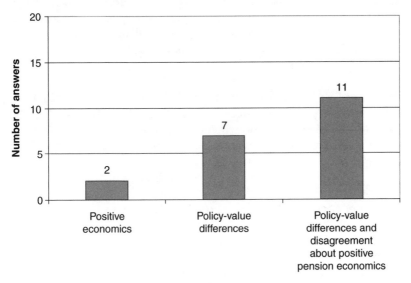

Note: Twelve countries reported expert agreement; 19 reported disagreement.

on reform policy is not considered to be differences in pure policy values (as one could expect) but differences in judgments about positive economics (2 answers) and positive economics cum policy values (11 answers). Among those who think that there is no expert consensus on pension reform, 7 respondents stated that only policy-value differences are important for the disagreement and 11 said that both policy values and positive economics played a role (figure 5.3). This would imply that both positive and normative (ideological) factors are behind experts' diverging opinions on the optimal pension reform.

When considering expert consensus, another important issue in the theoretical literature on pension reform is the question of whether radical reform involving a switch to capital funding is a zero-sum game or Pareto-improving. We asked, "Do you think that pension reform means a large intergenerational redistribution?" Ten respondents answered negatively and 17 answered positively, which indicates that there is no unanimous opinion on this point either, and that the majority of our respondents are not convinced that the claimed efficiency gains can compensate for the double burden of the PAYG-FF shift.[9]

What can be concluded from these results? Given the relatively high consensus about the objectives of pension reform (financial stability as the highest priority and a relatively low ranking of "pure" economic objectives like economic growth and development of financial markets), disagreement on how to reach those objectives is fairly striking.

Consensus among experts regarding systemic pension reform involving the introduction of a mandatory funded pillar (as proposed by the World Bank) is still missing. Thus, political opposition to pension reform might result not only from the defense of egoistic particular interests (as studied in traditional political economy models) but also from scepticism concerning its economic advantages.

The Role of Political Factors. Institutional economics has recognized that many policy outcomes depend on the identity of the agenda-setter. The results of our survey show that the leading institutions within both reforming and nonreforming governments were the ministries of labor (or analogous entities). Hungary was the only country in which the reform process was dominated by the ministry of finance. In some countries, pension reform was a responsibility shared among several government agencies (Argentina, the Russian Federation, and Mexico) (table 5.2).

Table 5.2   Institutional Agenda-Setters

Leading institution	Reform countries	Nonreform countries
Ministry of labor and social affairs (or analogous entity)	Moldova, Romania, Slovenia, Argentina, FYR Macedonia, United Kingdom, Switzerland	Slovakia, Greece, Spain, Czech Republic, Germany, Ukraine, Brazil
Ministry of finance	Hungary	
Ministry of labor and social affairs, ministry of finance, and social security agency (or analogous entity) simultaneously	Mexico	Azerbaijan
Ministry of labor and social affairs and ministry of finance simultaneously	Latvia	
Special arrangement	Poland (office of plenipotentiary for pension reform) Croatia (office of plenipotentiary for pension reform) Uruguay (special commission) Bulgaria (working group)	
Other		Russia (ministry of labor and social affairs and pension fund), Finland (labor market organizations), Ireland (ministry of labor and social affairs and social security agency)

The lead institution, however, cannot explain variations in reform outcomes from country to country. The only significant institutional difference between reformers and nonreformers was the existence of a special body dealing with pension reform in reform countries (Bulgaria, Croatia, Poland, and Uruguay), but those institutions were established only after a basic consensus for reforming the pension system was achieved.

The external institutional framework may have had a special role in the commitment building process. Orenstein (2000) discusses the role of international institutions as providers of "politically relevant policy innovations." Our survey asked about the specific role of such institutions in the reform process. The results show the involvement of international institutions in seventeen countries. According to the answers, the World Bank played the dominant role (active in 16 cases). Other active international agencies included the U.S. Agency for International Development (Bulgaria, Hungary, FYR Macedonia, Russia, and Ukraine) and local development banks (the Inter-American Development Bank in Mexico and the European Bank for Reconstruction and Development in Russia). The International Labour Organisation participated in reform processes in Bulgaria, the Czech Republic, Latvia, and Romania. There is, however, no systemic difference in reform outcomes that could be explained by the involvement of international financial institutions.

Some economists, political scientists, and politicians claim that pension reform is a direct result of conditions imposed by international financial institutions, particularly the World Bank. According to our survey, domestic experts dominated the reform process in 13 countries, and foreign experts took the lead in 6 countries (Azerbaijan, Latvia, FYR Macedonia, Moldova, Poland, and Romania). In Ukraine, domestic and foreign experts were equally important. Foreign expertise seemed to be more important in countries that reformed their pension schemes. With the exception of Argentina, the countries in which foreign experts made a strong impact were CEE reformers (Croatia, Hungary, Latvia, FYR Macedonia, Moldova, Poland, and Romania).

Despite that influence, international institutions and their experts cannot start the pension reform process alone against the will of domestic forces. This can be observed in respondents' rankings of the impact of different institutions in the reform process. As noted earlier, the institution with the highest average ranking was the ministry of labor (or an analogous entity). This ranking reflects the ministry's position as the main agenda-setter or coordinator of the reform process. The institution with the second highest ranking was the ministry of finance, and then, ranked almost equally, international institutions and domestic experts. Relatively speaking, financial markets had the weakest role. These findings are summarized in figure 5.4.

An interesting by-product of our study is the difference observed in the relative impact of institutions in three regions: CEE, EU (including

Figure 5.4   Importance of Selected Institutions to the Reform Process

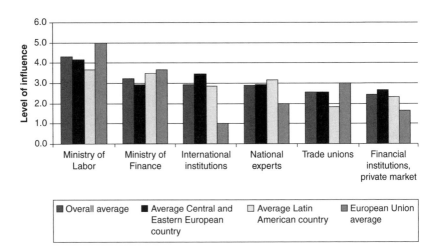

Switzerland), and Latin America. The ministries of labor and finance played a more important role in the reform process in the EU and CEE countries than in Latin America. International institutions played the most important role in CEE countries (even larger than the role of finance ministries), a smaller role in Latin America, and the smallest (almost nonexistent) role in EU countries. The role of domestic experts generally was perceived as more important than that of trade unions in CEE countries and in Latin America. The opposite situation was observed within the EU countries. In Latin American countries, the role of domestic experts was larger than in CEE countries.

In contrast to some political economy theories, which state that systemic pension reform is driven by international financial institutions or private financial institutions, our results show that pension reform is driven domestically, usually by ministries of labor. Ministries of finance have a weaker influence. Trade unions and domestic experts also play an important role—larger than financial markets and almost equal to the role played by international institutions. Our results reveal that the role of foreign experts is to convey new ideas and reform experience.

The Trigger of Radical Pension Reform. When and why some countries reform their pension systems while others do not was the main focus of our survey. When asked what triggered pension reform, 11 reform countries answered that it was mainly the financial crisis of the old pension scheme. In some countries, this led to a crisis of credibility for pension institutions. Extended contribution evasion worsened the situation (for example, in FYR Macedonia and Romania). Four respondents explicitly cited political and institutional factors as reform triggers (that is, the interests of commercial participants, World Bank efforts to educate and influence the government, the collapse of the former Yugoslavia, new democracy, and change of government). At first it seems obvious that financial crisis is perceived as the most important reform trigger. The issue that interested us was to what extent the fiscal problems of a pension scheme can be considered a sufficient condition for systemic pension reform.

We asked respondents in both reforming and nonreforming countries to assess the size of the fiscal problems in their pension schemes. Of the countries that answered the question, in 5 of the countries respondents assessed their fiscal problem as very large, in 6 countries as large, in 7 as moderate, and in 6 as low. Generally, the average size of fiscal deficit in reform countries was defined as large, whereas in the case of nonreform countries it was described as moderate. Reformers are overrepresented among countries in which the deficit in the pension scheme is perceived to be very large (4 reformers out of 5 countries) or large (4 out of 6). In those cases the unsustainable financial situation of the pension scheme was used as an argument to support unpopular radical actions (for example, in Latvia, FYR Macedonia, and Romania). One respondent stated this idea very clearly, saying that "the deficit also acts as a driving force to proceed with the planned reforms and even to take decisions that are not always popular."

To investigate what triggers pension reform more systematically, we did a probit analysis based on the survey results. We performed three regressions, taking the following set of variables as explanatory ones:

- size of fiscal deficit (on a scale of 1 to 4, with 1 being low and 4 being high)
- institution with the lead role in the reform process (ministry of labor, ministry of finance, other)
- main goals of pension reform[10] (on a scale of 1 to 3, with 1 being highest and 3 being lowest)
- definition of pension reform.[11]

The results of the analysis are presented in table 5.3. Of all factors taken into account, the size of fiscal deficit is statistically significant in all cases of regression. When the deficit is higher, there is a higher probability that a country will reform its pension system. This proves the statement made by most respondents that a pension system deficit influences reform activities. As the results of the third regression show, another

Table 5.3   Results of Probit Regression

	Regression 1	Regression 2	Regression 3
Scale of fiscal deficit	**0.7962**	0.5762	**0.6095**
	0.029	*0.030*	*0.019*
Institution leading the reform process	0.1442		
	0.744		
Goals of pension reform 1. financial sustainability of the pension scheme	−0.8053	−1.1166	
	0.462	*0.215*	
2. economic growth	0.1350	0.4274	
	0.746	*0.159*	
3. improved poverty alleviation	−0.0209	−0.0162	
	0.960	*0.954*	
4. improved protection of workers against drops in their incomes	0.3349	0.0908	
	0.357	*0.718*	
5. development of financial market	−0.2738	−0.3658	
	0.554	*0.279*	
Definition of pension reform 1. introduction of the mandatory fully funded pillar, at least partially	**1.3816**		**1,2589**
	0.088		*0.043*
2. introduction of notional defined contribution system	0.6893		0,7773
	0.420		*0.199*
3. parametric reform within the PAYG system	−0.5378		−0,5190
	0.504		*0.393*
Constant	−2.0881	−0.2885	**−2.1231**
	0.305	*0.797*	*0.025*
Log likelihood	−12.1603	−17.2991	−13.7210
Pseudo R^2	0.4152	0.2392	0.3402
Number of observations	30	33	30

Note: p-values are in italic type; statistically significant variables are in bold type.

variable with a significant impact on the probability of radical pension reform is the definition of the reform as involving the introduction of at least a partially funded pillar. For countries in which respondents defined pension reform in that way, reform is more probable.

If we investigate the direction of influence, we can observe a negative impact on the probability of reform in the case of two reform goals—economic growth and improved protection of workers (because numeric values were increasing as the importance of goals was decreasing)—and in countries where reform is defined as parametric changes to the PAYG system. These results, however, were not statistically significant.

Pension policy seems to be driven only by *current* financial considerations. This can be confirmed by responses to the question about intergenerational redistribution. Only 7 respondents answered that intergenerational redistribution was discussed in their countries and only 5 said that instruments showing a long-term intertemporal financial balance (like generational accounts) were applied in the reform discussion. This myopia about pension system financing was expressed very well in one of the answers to the question concerning the nature of the impact of the financial situation on reform activities: "Now when the system is in surplus no one dares to say anything radical."

The Process of Coalition Building

In this section, using qualitative responses from questionnaires as the basis, we analyze the roles of trade unions, society at large, and information campaigns in building a coalition for pension reform. This process is at least as important as the process of commitment building. If there is no coalition to support the proposal, it can be altered significantly or even rejected during the attempt to enact it. Rutkowski (2000) specifies several factors that can determine the success of the coalition building process, including working with the media, especially forming a core group of friendly journalists; and identifying key veto and proposal players and interest groups and integrating them into the process.

In our survey, respondents were asked to determine the turning point in their reform process. The milestones most frequently stated include reaching political agreement in parliament and finalizing dialogue with social partners. Members of parliament and trade unions can be the most important veto groups in the coalition building process and, according to our survey, only consensus between those groups can lead to the successful completion of the coalition building phase. Thus, the process should include both political parties and social partners. Because we assume that governments enjoy a majority in parliament before the reform is introduced, the most important issue is to convince the social partners and society to support the reform. The tools and outcomes of government actions in this field are analyzed below.

The Role of Trade Unions

Experience shows that the role and power of unions must be properly assessed when proposing reforms. Confrontational behavior by the government can lead to an exclusion of important interest groups (such as trade unions), which later can veto the reform proposal. Active negotiation with social partners is much more likely to achieve significant reform than is confrontation. For example, a national pact enabled the success of Italian pension reform. The Dini government involved trade unions in the reform process and succeeded in implementing substantial pension reform. The Berlusconi government in Italy and the Juppé government in France ignored social partners when preparing reform proposals, and reform failed (Culpepper 2000). Inclusion of social partners in the reform process also is used to explain the successful Dutch reform of the 1980s.

As the survey results show, agreement with trade unions was necessary in the implementation of pension reform. To gain the acceptance of the unions, countries usually had to compromise on some aspects of the reform. The results show that the role of unions is different among the responding countries. Unions' opposition was an important factor influencing reform actions in FYR Macedonia, Mexico, Slovenia, and Spain. In Latin American countries, the unions played a minor role in Argentina and Uruguay, although they had some influence in Mexico. These findings help explain why in Mexico members of the tripartite council were placed on the boards of Consar (a specialized institution collecting funded pillar contributions) and other institutions connected to the social security system.

The situation was more complex in CEE countries. In most of them (except Croatia and Moldova), unions were strong and they influenced reform activities. In the majority of countries, unions opposed at least part of the program. The most important area of opposition was the retirement age (because reform usually included a rise in the statutory retirement age and elimination of special privileges) as well as the introduction of a mandatory funded pillar. Because unions had significant veto power they could delay the reform process, as they did, for example, in FYR Macedonia. The largest trade union influence could be observed in Slovenia where unions managed to veto both the proposal to raise the retirement age and the introduction of a mandatory funded pillar. In Hungary, the unions influenced the reform process via the position of pay-as-you-go system managers.

Responses from the EU show that unions also had an influence on reform activities. They blocked all reform action in Greece, and in Spain a broad political consensus that included trade unions must be achieved to perform any reform action.

To move forward with reform, governments used public relations techniques. For example, in Mexico reformers remained active in the media by granting interviews and holding press conferences. Their aim was to counterattack similar activities carried out by trade unions. FYR Macedonia decided to negotiate an agreement with its social partners, and the resulting document, which formulated basic principles of the reform, was signed by all partners.

To summarize, in most countries trade unions and tripartite councils play a significant role in the reform process. It is important to include trade unions in discussions on pension reform options and issues. They can be supportive in those instances in which changes do not endanger the position of the work force (at least from the unions' perspective). Such a situation occurred, for example, in Poland where trade unions supported reform activities in the first stage of the legislative process, when the second- and third-pillar laws were discussed. Their initial support made it difficult for trade unions to explicitly oppose the second stage of reform in which PAYG system rules were changed, including an increase in the pension age and a reduction of replacement rates via a shift from a defined-benefit to a defined contribution system.

Most of the countries that implemented pension reform managed to reach a consensus with unions by compromising and amending the initial proposal. The scope of the amendments depended greatly on the political power of unions in a given country.

The Role of Society

Although trade unions often are thought to represent the working part of society, that is not always true. Unions sometimes have other interests relating to the social security system. For instance, in many European countries unions traditionally are involved in the management of PAYG systems. Additionally, public opinion is important from the politicians' perspective. Thus, gaining the acceptance of society and not only the trade unions is important in the process of reforming the pension system.

From the answers we obtained, we can draw the conclusion that only some countries tried to factor public opinion into the preparation of pension reform. Some actions were taken in Bulgaria, Latvia, FYR Macedonia, Poland, Romania, and Slovenia. Other countries either did nothing to increase public awareness or took limited action.

Typically, information about reform was disseminated through conferences, workshops, and public hearings. Because such methods are unlikely to reach every citizen, they are aimed at so-called opinion leaders who pass along their knowledge. Such actions are important in organizing further support and in gaining politicians' commitment to the reform process. Dialogue can be enhanced by organizing debates with representatives of society (trade unions, employers, pensioners, and so forth), as occurred, for example, in Romania. Another factor frequently mentioned by responders is cooperation with the mass media, which happened, for example, in Romania and Poland. In those countries, a professional public relations company was also used.

Opinion surveys and focus groups to assess a country's readiness for pension reform were carried out in Bulgaria, FYR Macedonia, and Slovakia. Other countries did not use those tools. We found that society's response to reform proposals depended significantly on the nature of preexisting policy legacies. In Latvia, where the old pension system offered only flat-rate benefits that did not reflect an individual's working history, society strongly supported a solution that drastically changed this policy. In Slovenia, however, society and its representatives opposed the suggested solutions that they believed would endanger the current system, which in their view worked quite well. The Polish example shows that a public opinion survey can help win political acceptance for pension reform by demonstrating the extent of public support for particular reform proposals.

In most countries reforms are conducted with limited attention to public opinion. Such a situation can stem from the following beliefs:

- It takes time and usually seems to have little or no effect.
- The pension system is difficult to communicate about and society would not understand its complexity ("show me a citizen who doesn't get lost in the conceptual and technical maze of pension reform.").
- The public is not interested in learning about pension system changes. Most affected participants are too young and too myopic to think about their future, and unions are more focused on preserving accrued rights than on changing the system to achieve long-term macroeconomic stability.

Only in some cases is the role of the public recognized and used to build a larger coalition for the support of further reform actions.

Public Information

When the crucial actors in the reform process are identified, there is a need to develop a consensus among them on the principles of the new pension system. One of the most important tools is the public relations and information campaign.

In the survey, only the countries that were considered "reformers" were asked about the goals, means, and results of public information campaigns. Some type of information campaign was done in most reform countries; in the other countries, it has been planned. Croatia and Spain did not conduct any such campaign. Generally, the goals of a campaign were to inform the public about the need for the changes, the new system rules, and the choices that participants were offered. In Hungary the campaign also tried to make people consider switching to the second pillar. Campaigns usually began during or after the completion of legislation as part of the implementation stage. In many countries information campaigns were carried out during the last phases of the coalition building stage (for example, Argentina, Bulgaria, Hungary, FYR Macedonia, Mexico, Moldova, Slovenia, and Uruguay). In Latvia and Romania, however, the campaigns were carried out or planned when at least part of the reform had been implemented. Popular media were used (TV, radio, and print) in most cases. Respondents pointed out that booklets and brochures were also important tools for disseminating information. Additionally, there were some local actions, including direct dialogues in the form of town hall meetings in Bulgaria and local conferences in Hungary.

Campaign assessments were not done in all countries. In those cases in which the public was asked about the information they received, results varied significantly. In most cases, public opinion was rather neutral and there was not a lot of attention paid to pension reform. The only positive assessment was recorded in Mexico. A positive public attitude also could be noticed in FYR Macedonia, although it was countered by the opposition of the trade unions.

Public information campaigns were carried out as an obligation that countries believed they had to follow. Usually, however, governments did not make a serious effort to reach the public, and the public itself was not interested in pension reform. Such a situation could lead to declining public support for pension reform in the longer run. That happened in Poland, for example, where initial enthusiasm about the changes has worn out and more negative voices now can be heard because of reported difficulties in the implementation of the reform and information about the reduction of future benefits.

Conclusions

In this chapter we analyzed the role of political factors in creating governmental commitment to implement pension reform and some aspects of the process of consensus building. To conduct the analysis we used a survey given to experts and decisionmakers from both reforming and nonreforming countries. In most countries, the necessary precondition for pension reform was crisis in the PAYG system. By almost unanimous agreement among responders, the size of fiscal problems influenced reform thinking and, it seems, gave a first push toward reform. This hypothesis is supported by the results of probit regression—the scale of the deficit and the definition of reform as "introduction of the mandatory funded pillar" are the only statistically significant variables that explain reform activities in the responding countries. Additional conditions, however, are necessary to complete the reform process. These conditions may be described as political factors, such as a need to separate from the previous regime and its legal framework, favorable political circumstances that enable experts to think about the reform concept, or some external influence such as one coming from international institutions such as the World Bank.

It seems that what matters most is the perception of the costs and benefits of pension reform in each individual country—a perception that often follows experts' advice. Our results indicate that there is no clear definition of pension reform globally, although most respondents agree that it involves some mix of a funded pillar and a modified PAYG system (including either parametric changes or a shift to the notional defined contribution principle). Another conclusion is that there is widespread disagreement among experts and politicians about the objectives and nature of pension reform.

Thus, any reform process requires a long period of coalition building accompanied by dialogue and negotiations among interested actors. Trade unions play an important role in this process, especially in the countries of Central and Eastern Europe. If the role of unions is strong, any reform concept must gain at least partial public acceptance—sometimes via an extensive media campaign to convince society and sometimes by negotiations to reach agreement with social partners.

Which institutions play the most important role in the reform process? Usually it is government (represented by the responsible ministry, generally labor). In the case of CEE countries, an almost equally important role is played by international institutions that provide technical and financial support for the reforms. Domestic experts and trade unions also take an important role. The role of private financial institutions is less important but not negligible.

An important part in coalition building also is played by public information. Most countries mount some kind of information campaign aimed at informing and educating society about new pension system rules and the choices that individuals have. In a few cases, the role of information campaigns is more specific—for example, to convince people to consider switching systems. Generally, the role of the public information effort depends on the country and its initial conditions. Most countries, even those that conduct public information campaigns, do not try to assess their outcomes. Rather, they treat the task as a necessity instead of a role that government must play in increasing public literacy in "the maze of the social security system."

Notes

1. The funded pillar in Latvia is planned to begin in 2002.

2. On Central Eastern Europe see Orenstein (2000) and Müller (2000); on Latin America, see Müller's contribution to this volume and references therein.

3. The main motivation for surveying both experts and decisionmakers was to get a larger set of data on the decisionmaking process than that available from studies made by particular countries.

4. For the text of the questionnaires, see the appendix to this chapter.

5. We are grateful to the organizers of the conference "Learning from the Partners" (especially to Robert Holzmann and Michal Rutkowski) for their help in disseminating the questionnaires through World Bank channels.

6. Well known are the jokes about "one-handed economists" or about "five economists with six opinions, two of them of Keynes."

7. For recent critical articles, see Orszag and Stiglitz (1999) and the debate among Barr (2000), Persson (2000), and Börsch-Supan (2000) for practical considerations.

8. Respondents could also specify any combination of options.

9. We suspect, however, that this question might have been misunderstood by many respondents because several answers were unclear and some respondents did not answer at all. The interpretation of the result should be viewed with extreme caution.

10. Based on question 10 in the questionnaire included in the appendix.

11. Based on question 11 in the questionnaire included in the appendix.

References

Augusztinovics, Mária. 1999. "The Economic Implications of Population Ageing in the ECE Region." Paper presented at the United Nations Economic Commission for Europe Spring Seminar on Reforming Pension Systems in the Transition Countries, April, Geneva.

Barr, Nicholas. 2000. "Reforming Pensions: Myths, Truths, and Policy Choices." IMF Working Paper, WP/00/139. Washington, D.C.

Börsch-Supan, Axel. 2000. "Was lehrt uns die Empirie in Sachen Rentenreform?" *Perspektiven der Wirtschaftspolitik* 1(4):431–51.

Browning, Edgar K. 1975. "Why the Social Insurance Budget Is Too Large in a Democracy." *Economic Inquiry* 13:373–88.

Culpepper, Pepper D. 2000. "The Sources of Policy Innovation: Sub-National Constraints on Negotiated Reform." Kennedy School of Government Working Paper 00-014. Cambridge, Mass.

Friedman, Milton. 1999. "Speaking the Truth about Social Security Reform." Cato Institute Briefing Paper 46. Washington, D.C.

James, Estelle, and Sarah Brooks. 1999. "The Political Economy of Pension Reform." Revision of paper presented at the World Bank Research Conference, September 14–15, Washington, D.C.

Marquardt, Marko, and Wolfgang Peters. 1997. "Collective Madness: How Ageing Influences Majority Voting on Public Pensions." Working Paper 79. Department of Economics, European University, Viadrina, Frankfurt Oder.

Müller, Katharina. 1999. *The Political Economy of Pension Reform in Central-Eastern Europe.* Cheltenham, U.K.: Edward Elgar.

Orenstein, Mitchell. 2000. "How Politics and Institutions Affect Pension Reform in Three Postcommunist Countries." World Bank Policy Research Paper 2310. Washington, D.C.

Orszag, Peter R., and Joseph E. Stiglitz. 1999. "Rethinking Pension Reform: Ten Myths About Social Security Systems." Paper prepared for the New Ideas about Old Age Security Conference, September, World Bank, Washington, D.C.

Persson, Mats. 2000. "Five Fallacies in the Social Security Debate." Institute for International Economic Studies, Seminar Paper 686. Stockholm University.

Pierson, Paul. 1994. *Dismantling the Welfare State? Reagan, Thatcher, and the Politics of Retrenchment.* Cambridge, U.K.: Cambridge University Press.

Rutkowski, Michal. 2000. "Bringing Hope Back: Pension Reform in Transition Economies." Presentation at the World Bank Pension Course, February, Budapest.

Tabellini, Guido. 1991. "The Politics of Intergenerational Redistribution." *Journal of Political Economy* 99:335–57.

Williamson, John, ed. 1994. *The Political Economy of Policy Reform.* Washington, D.C.: Institute for International Economics.

Appendix: Questionnaires

SURVEY ON PENSION REFORM POLICY

(To countries—reformers)

Note: Questions that were identical for both questionnaires are indicated in italics.

PLEASE NAME THE COUNTRY TO WHICH THE FOLLOWING INFORMATION IS RELATED (please state only one country; if you have relevant information on more countries and you want to share your experience, use another survey): _____

Please classify yourself:

O Expert
O Decisionmaker

1. *When did the discussion on pension reform start in your country?*

   _____

2. *What triggered the reform action? What was the critical point in the reform process?* _____

3. Which institution coordinated the reform process (ministry of finance, ministry of labor and social affairs, and so forth)? _____

4. Were international experts involved in the reform process? If yes, from which institutions? _____

5. Was the expertise dominated by the domestic or by the foreign experts? _____

6. What was society's role in the reform process? Were opinion surveys used to assess the readiness for pension reform? _____

7. *Was there any public information campaign about the reform in your country?* _____

   If yes:

   When was it launched (in relation to the pension legislation implementation)? _____

   What was the main goal of the campaign? _____

   What were the main media used? (TV, radio, print) _____

   How was it assessed by public opinion? _____

   If no:

   How was the public informed about the reform? _____

   Is an information campaign planned? _____

8. *What were, in your opinion, the most important events (turning points) in the reform process (that is, changes of government, new participants in the discussion, public protests)?* _____

9. *Please describe in one or two short sentences the main features of the reformed pension system in your country.* _____

10. What, in your opinion, should be the main goals of the reform? (please rank: 1 = highest, 3 = lowest)
    (i) _____ financial sustainability of the pension scheme
    (ii) _____ economic growth
    (iii) _____ improved poverty alleviation
    (iv) _____ improved protection of workers against drops in their incomes
    (v) _____ development of the financial market
    (vi) _____ other (specify): _____

11. *What is your definition of pension reform?*
    (i) _____ *introduction of the mandatory fully funded pillar, at least partially*
    (ii) _____ *introduction of notional defined contribution system*
    (iii) _____ *parametric reform within the PAYG system*
    (iv) _____ *other (specify):* _____

12. *Please rank the influence of the following on the reform process. (5 = strongest, 1 = weakest)*
    (i) _____ *ministry of labor*
    (ii) _____ *ministry of finance*
    (iii) _____ *trade unions*
    (iv) _____ *national experts*
    (v) _____ *financial institutions, private market*

13. *To what extent was the experts' advice used in the pension reform prepara-
    tion? (5 = significantly, 0 = not at all)* _____

14. a. *Do you agree that there is a pension reform consensus among experts?*
    _____

    If yes, what is its most important element? _____
    If no, what is the main reason for the disagreement?
    (i)   _____ *disagreement about positive pension economics*
    (ii)   _____ *policy-value differences*
    (iii) _____ *both (i) and (ii)*
    (iv)   _____ *other (specify):* _____

    b. *Do you agree that there is a pension reform consensus among decisionmakers?*

    If yes, what is its most important element? _____
    If no, what is the main reason for the disagreement?
    (i)   _____ *disagreement about positive pension economics*
    (ii)   _____ *policy-value differences*
    (iii) _____ *both (i) and (ii)*
    (iv)   _____ *other (specify):* _____

15. *Do you think that pension reform means a large intergenerational redistri-
    bution?* _____
    If yes, was this issue discussed in the reform process in your country?
    _____

    Which instruments were used to illustrate this issue? _____

16. *Do you agree that pension reform is only "a political problem"?*
    _____

17. *Does the existence of different schemes (for example, for the self-employed,
    for civil servants) influence the reform? (Yes/No? Please explain in a few
    words.)* _____

18. *Should countries have fragmented pension schemes or one universal
    scheme? Please explain your views.* _____

19. *Is there a tripartite agreement in your country? Does it influence the reform
    process? What was the role of unions? Please explain in a few words.*

20. a. *Is your pension system in deficit?* _____ *Please assess the
    size of the fiscal problem.*
    (i)   _____ *very large*
    (ii)   _____ *large*
    (iii) _____ *moderate*
    (iv)   _____ *low*

    b. *Does the fiscal problem influence pension reform activities?* _____

SURVEY ON PENSION REFORM POLICY

(To nonreforming countries; only for experts)

PLEASE NAME THE COUNTRY TO WHICH THE FOLLOWING INFORMATION IS RELATED.

If the survey is based on your experience in many countries, please list the most important ones. _____

3. In my country the experts' advice is used in the pension reform preparation.
    - (i) _____ agree
    - (ii) _____ disagree
    - (iii) _____ agree (with provisions)

4. Which domestic institution is playing the leading role in the pension reform process?
    - (i) _____ ministry of labor and social affairs
    - (ii) _____ ministry of finance
    - (iii) _____ social security agency
    - (iv) _____ other (specify):

5. Are international experts involved in the reform process in your country?
    - (i) _____ yes
    - (ii) _____ no
    - (iii) _____ no opinion

    If yes, from which institution(s)? _____

6. The experts' advice on pension reform in your country is more dominated by
    - (i) _____ the domestic experts
    - (ii) _____ the foreign experts
    - (iii) _____ equally by both of them.

10. What is society's role in the reform process? Are opinion surveys used to assess the readiness for pension reform in your country?
    _____

.

6
Social Policy Models in Transition: Why So Different from One Another?

Tito Boeri

Social policies in countries undergoing transition from central planning to a market system differ both in size and composition. The countries of the Visegrad group (the Czech Republic, Hungary, Poland, and the Slovak Republic) spend comparatively more on social protection and attribute a greater importance to nonemployment benefits (defined as unemployment benefits, social assistance, early retirement, disability benefits, and sickness benefits). Bulgaria and Romania devote a lower proportion of their gross domestic product (GDP) to cash transfers but have kept in place throughout the transition unemployment benefit systems that are more generous than those of Visegrad countries such as the Czech and Slovak Republics. The latter two countries, however, display more stringent employment protection regulations, which offer another type of insurance to their workers by imposing higher costs on employers who lay off employees.

Pension spending is also extremely varied across countries: The Russian Federation and the former Soviet Union (FSU) countries pay relatively low pensions but devote a much larger fraction of their social policy budget to pension transfers.

Differences among the models are even more apparent when it comes to the targeting of the various programs. For instance, nonpension transfers increase income inequality in Russia, whereas almost everywhere else they reduce it. In Hungary, Poland, and Slovenia unemployment benefits are targeted to poor people: a large percentage of working-age people whose incomes are below the poverty line receive these transfers.

Such differences are not simply the result of successes and failures in transition; they have deeply shaped different transition trajectories. For instance, the virtual absence of nonemployment benefits in Russia can help explain the low increase in unemployment in this country despite particularly severe output losses: wages, rather than employment, bore most of the weight of adjustment. The Visegrad countries, by contrast, display employment-to-output elasticities significantly larger than those of Russia because of the presence of safety nets that often constrain wage declines at the lower end of the earning distribution. The effects of the structure of nonemployment benefits on the wage distribution are also important to understanding the widening regional labor market imbalances in Central and Eastern Europe and a lack of interregional worker flows.

Is there anything surprising in the cross-country variation of social policy models? The social policy mix is different even among current European Union (EU) member countries. Differences in the composition and targeting of social spending have to do with historical factors because there is considerable inertia in adjusting institutions. Cultural roots are also important. We must take into consideration different languages, religious influences, and connections to Western Europe. Nonetheless, there is at least one feature of social spending which had to be created from scratch at the outset of transition: unemployment benefits. Although all transition countries sought to relieve state employers from their social responsibilities relative to their workers, unemployment benefits started off very different in design from one country to another.

Therefore, we will devote most of this chapter to the role and design of unemployment benefits. In doing so we will show that some gross mistakes were made in the design of this new policy instrument. Fortunately, there seems to be time to remedy such mistakes and to improve the efficiency of welfare systems in these countries. This is very important for the countries preparing for EU membership. While the "fatal attraction" of the EU forced Central and Eastern European countries to adopt a social policy model that favored labor reallocation, the accession process itself may cause serious problems unless social policies are reformed because the Visegrad model features low participation and a high social security burden on formal employment.

The plan for this chapter is as follows. The second section characterizes the main differences in social policy models, putting particular emphasis on the design of the new systems of unemployment benefits and social assistance. The third section offers a discussion of why the countries of the FSU chose a different design of nonemployment benefits than did the Central and Eastern European countries. The fourth section details the policy mistakes made within this broad perspective and discusses why they occurred. The final section discusses what the future may bring.

Identifying Differences in Social Policy Models

It is convenient to characterize welfare states in transition countries in terms of two extreme models. One is the model followed by the Visegrad countries that involves a large social policy expenditure and significant redistribution occurring via nonemployment benefits. The other is the Russian model that is characterized by low social policy expenditure, virtually no unemployment benefit system, and a minimum role for the state in reducing income inequalities and promoting social cohesion. The most striking sign of the absence of Russian public authorities in providing poverty relief is the fact that they allowed a huge stock of wage arrears in the budgetary sphere to build up. Between these two extreme models we have the Baltics, Bulgaria, and Romania.

Table 6.1 highlights social policy summary statistics, emphasizing primarily the relative importance of nonemployment benefits and their role in reducing inequalities in the distribution of earnings. For the most part, these were new cash transfers introduced at the outset of transition. From their design and targeting we can make important inferences as to why countries selected particular social policy models. The first two columns show the importance played by nonemployment benefits (defined as unemployment benefits, social assistance, early retirement, disability

Table 6.1 Nonemployment Benefits and the Distribution of Earnings

| | Nonemployment benefits | | Contribution of social transfers to changes in Gini | | | |
| | Relevance (1991–95) | | Nonpension | | Pension | |
	Percentage of GDP	Percentage of social expenditure	1990–92	1995–96	1990–92	1995–96
CEE countries						
Bulgaria	1.6	17.2	0.0	0.4	–1.1	0.8
Czech Republic	3.6	32.7	—	—	—	—
Hungary	2.4	32.3	0.2	–0.2	–0.9	1.4
Poland	5.0	31.8	0.2	–0.1	–3.2	3.4
Romania	1.9	27.5	—	—	—	—
Slovenia	2.7	29.5	—	–0.4	—	—
The Baltics						
Latvia	0.5	26.5	0.1	0.5	–2.2	–2.0
CIS countries						
Russia	0.6	10.9	2.5	2.3	4.5	3.7
Ukraine	0.3	3.3	—	—	—	—

— Not available.

Notes: "Earnings" denotes gross monthly earnings. "Income" denotes disposable per capita household income (net of taxes and including transfers).

Sources: Column 1, Boeri 2000; columns 3 and 5, Atkinson and Micklewright 1992; columns 4 and 6, Cornia 1996, Garner and Terrell 1998.

benefits, and sickness benefits) in terms of GDP share and as a percentage of social expenditure. The other columns evaluate the contributions of nonemployment benefits and pensions to changes in the Gini coefficients.

The table documents three points. First, the Visegrad countries spent much more on nonemployment benefits than did other countries, both as a proportion of GDP and as a percentage of the overall social policy budget. Second, most countries used cash transfers to contain the dispersion of earnings. This can be grasped by looking at the (more or less) implicit design features of unemployment benefits (which were explicitly flat in countries like Poland, whereas in Hungary they became a flat benefit de facto as a result of low indexation of benefits above the minimum). Low union coverage in the emerging private sector together with the lack of workplace unions also prevented the enforcement of the statutory minimum wages present in many of these countries. This led to nonemployment benefit minima taking the place of a minimum wage in these countries. Third, in Russia both pensions (which are supposed to operate mainly as intergenerational redistribution) and nonemployment benefits helped to *increase* inequalities, whereas in the Visegrad countries pensions served as an effective antipoverty device. Indeed, the Czech Republic, Hungary, and Poland did not experience an increase in the incidence of low-pay or a worsening of the relative position of the bottom decile, both of which occurred in Russia.

Table 6.2 illustrates trends in some standard measures of earning and income inequality. Although we acknowledge problems with

Table 6.2   Trends in Earning and Income Inequality

	Gini–Earnings		Gini–Income		P90/P10–Earnings		P90/P10–Income	
	1987–89	1993–94	1987–89	1995–96	1987–89	1993–94	1987–89	1993–94
CEE countries								
Bulgaria	0.21	0.28	0.22	0.32	2.56	—	—	4.33
Czech Republic	0.20	0.26	0.20	0.23	2.43	3.15	2.44	4.11
Hungary	0.27	0.34	0.21	0.23	3.14	3.72	2.81	2.66
Poland	0.21	0.28	0.25	0.36	2.43	3.38	3.07	3.92
Romania	0.19	0.28	0.24	0.26	1.94	3.49	—	3.18
Slovenia	—	—	0.20	0.22	—	—	—	—
The Baltics								
Latvia	—	—	0.23	0.33	—	—	—	—
CIS countries								
Russia	0.27	0.45	0.22	0.52	3.45	14.86	3.16	15.10
Ukraine	0.24	0.36	0.23	0.26	3.04	8.04	2.76	5.07

— Not available.

Notes: "Earnings" denotes gross monthly earnings. "Income" denotes disposable per capita household income (net of taxes and including transfers). "P90/P10" denotes the ratio of earnings income at the top (90th) decile to the bottom (10th) decile.

Sources: Columns 1, 3, 5, and 7, Atkinson and Micklewright 1992; columns 2, 4, 6, and 8, Cornia 1996, Garner and Terrell 1998, and Milanovic 1998.

cross-country comparisons of earning inequality measures, the table points to a much stronger increase in inequality within the countries of the Commonwealth of Independent States (CIS) than in the countries of Central and Eastern Europe (CEE). Within the latter group, the largest increases in Gini coefficients and in P90/P10 ratios were registered in Bulgaria and Romania. The data suggest that the driving force behind widening income disparities was the concentration of earnings.

We have discussed the possible role played by unemployment benefits in reducing earning dispersion from below. Another way in which nonpension transfers have affected inequality is via explicit redistribution in favor of poor households. Comparable studies of the Czech Republic and Slovakia (Garner and Terrell 1998) and of Russia (Commander, Lee, and Tolstopiatenko 1998) document that these diverging trends in inequality can be explained largely by differences in social transfer policies. Taxes also were important in generating different trends in inequality. In Russia, overall tax revenue has been declining steadily since the early 1990s. Tax compliance for entrepreneurial and self-employment income has been negligible. Employers avoided high payroll taxes totaling 40 percent of the wage bill by replacing wages with under-the-counter cash payments and in-kind payments. Because this left the government reliant on the value-added tax, tax incidence fell disproportionately on the middle and lower end of the income distribution (Commander, Lee, and Tolstopiatenko 1998). However, in Central Europe the untaxed informal economy was smaller (Lacko 1999) and reforms were implemented to make taxes more progressive over time. Using a Gini decomposition analysis, Garner and Terrell (1998) show that changes in tax payments over time have reduced inequality, other things being held constant, in the Czech Republic and Slovakia.[1] Whereas the CEE countries generally were effective in restructuring their transfers during the first four years of transition to offer a sufficient level of benefits targeted to the lower end of the income distribution, in the CIS the safety net is considered inadequate and is not means tested. In particular, Garner and Terrell show that after the Czech Republic restructured its safety net, the share of total income in the bottom decile that was receiving government transfers (including pensions, social assistance, family benefits, health benefits, and unemployment benefits) rose from 8.2 percent in 1989 to 16.8 percent in 1993. The beneficiary share for the top decile remained about the same, at 3.1 percent in 1989 and 3.2 percent in 1993. Meanwhile, in Russia and most of the FSU countries there are no national standards for providing social assistance, as well as a virtual absence of fiscal transfers across regions that would enable the poorest oblasts to pay social assistance of the last resort. Nominal replacement rates for low-income earners may appear similar to those provided in Central and Eastern Europe, but in real terms they are negligible for everybody. Russian pensioners were treated worse than their counterparts in CEE, as the average pension to average wage ratio was lower by about 20 percentage points in the CIS than in countries like the Czech Republic. However, Russian unemployed people were treated even worse in relative terms because they could have access to benefits offering replacement rates that were only one-fifth or one-sixth of those provided by nonemployment benefits in CEE.

The differences among social policy models and in the scope of redistribution within the working age group are relevant also from another perspective: the differences help explain labor market adjustment trajectories experienced by these countries since the beginning of transition. In Russia the bulk of adjustment involved wages, which meant strong aggregate wage declines (with a cumulative loss of 57 percent in the 1990–95 period) and widening earning differentials at all levels. In the CEE, notably in the four countries of the Visegrad group, aggregate wage declines were much less pronounced (averaging 19 percent in the 1990–93 period). Thus, in the CEE countries, employment carried the weight of adjustment. Bulgaria and Romania featured in intermediate positions in terms both of wage adjustment (–41 percent) and increases in earning inequality.

Explaining Differences among Models

There are at least three explanations for this fundamental asymmetry between Russia and many former Soviet Republics (the partial exception being the Baltics), and between Russia and the Visegrad countries. The explanations are

- differences in the degree of inequality aversion
- differences in the degree of economic development and access to international capital markets, which make it harder for Russia to sustain large social policy outlays
- the more or less strict conditionality and appeal of the EU social policy model relative to the transition countries.

Now we will discuss each of these explanations in some detail.

Differences in Preferences

There is not much literature on preferences for inequality in the former planned economies. Based on data from the 1999 International Social Survey Programme, Suhrcke (2001) documents that Russian citizens dislike income differences more than do nationals in CEE. Differences in preferences for inequality may be affected by personal experience: many Russians experienced severe downward income mobility in the 1990s. As documented by Atkinson and Micklewright (1992), however, at the onset of transition even the least unequal of the Soviet Republics displayed larger Gini coefficients than did any of the CEE countries.

The Gini coefficients that prevailed before the fall of the Berlin Wall may be interpreted as an indication of societal concerns over income distribution. Ten years later, however, they are a poor predictor of income inequality (Boeri 2000): initial conditions account for less than one-fifth of the cross-country variation in posttransition income inequality. Furthermore, the initial ranking of countries in terms of income inequality has been altered significantly throughout the transition: the Spearman rank correlation coefficient is 0.57, which is low, considering that we are comparing inequality indexes only a few years apart. Were Russia to preserve the same distance as Central and Eastern Europe in terms of income concentration, it would be characterized today by significantly lower Gini coefficients.

Problems in the Financing of Social Policies

There are large asymmetries in revenue collection between the CEE countries and the CIS: 1997 total tax revenues reached about 35 percent of GDP in the former and half of that level (roughly 18 percent of GDP) in the latter. Redistribution is costly. According to Branko Milanovic (1997), the elimination of absolute poverty in Russia in 1993–94 would have required (supposedly perfectly targeted) payments of US $6 billion per year, or approximately 3.5 percent of GDP. This is by far much more than resources allocated to antipoverty measures in Russia, where expenditure in social assistance throughout the transition never exceeded 0.4 percent of GDP.

To a great extent, current differences in revenue collection between CEE countries and the CIS are the result of developments originating in the early 1990s. Although tax revenues as a percentage of GDP declined throughout the region, the fall was much steeper in Russia and the other CIS countries than in CEE. Significantly, the decrease in revenues only marginally affected social security contributions, which are the main source of social policy financing. Payroll taxes were generally earmarked for the various extrabudgetary funds created at the beginning of transition, and this kept governments from using social security contributions for other purposes. For instance, the Russian National Employment Service, which is responsible for unemployment benefit payments and active policies, ran a comfortable surplus for several years. Hence, more generous unemployment benefits could have been paid in Russia at least until 1995 without requiring new levies or even improvements to revenue collection. Moreover, Russia did not decide to increase social security contributions after the rise of unemployment, as did countries of Central and Eastern Europe.

The strong decline in revenue collection in the CIS was largely a by-product of the delays with which tax structures in these countries were adjusted to market conditions rather than a legacy of the past. In other words, problems on the revenue side cannot be used to justify low social spending, notably low spending that favors the working-aged unemployed because governments could have selected better revenue collection methods.

The "Fatal Attraction" of Europe

We are left therefore with the third explanation—namely, the view that geographical proximity to Europe has played a crucial role in generating different social policy models. It often is claimed that accession is an "institutional factor" in its own right (Roland 2000; Fidrmuc 1999) and there are important reasons to share this view. The conditionality of the "European model" was stronger for the countries that had a chance to enter the EU. It is significant that the countries targeted for the first round of EU accession are those that have spent more on social policies, notably more on nonemployment benefits, throughout transition. This is high-lighted by figure 6.1, where we see that the former first-round candidates

Figure 6.1   The Generosity of Unemployment Benefits in Former First-Round and Second-Round Candidates for EU Accession

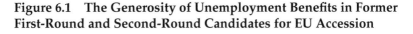
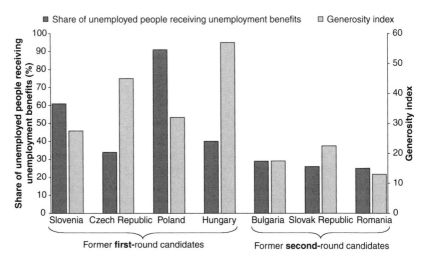

Note: Generosity index as an average of replacement rates of the 1st month of benefit receipt and the 60th month of benefit receipt.

Table 6.3   Summary of EU Recommendations in the Labor and Social Policy Areas

Country	Employment strategy	Labor law	Social dialogue	Equality of treatment and opportunities	Pension and health system	Health and safety at work
First-round EU candidates						
Czech Republic		NP	NP	NP		NP
Estonia	RA	RA	NP	NP		NP
Hungary		NP			RA	NP
Poland		NP	NP	NP		NP
Slovenia		NP		NP	RA	
Second-round EU candidates						
Bulgaria		NP	NP	NP	NP	RA
Latvia	—	NP	NP		—	NP
Lithuania		NP				NP
Romania		NP	NP	NP	NP	NP
Slovakia		NP		NP	RA	RA

— Subject not recommended in the report.
NP No further progress registered during the last year; only partial or insufficient alignment to the Acquis Communautaire of the European Union; more efforts in implementing reforms are needed.
RA Recommendation of immediate action.
Source: Reports from the Commission of the European Union (various countries) 1999.

for accession provided more generous unemployment benefits, both in terms of replacement rates (the summary generosity index) and greater coverage of this type of insurance scheme.

Moreover, the EU memoranda regarding the accession process (see table 6.3) make frequent references to the importance of labor law compliance for collective redundancies, which involve preferential access to unemployment insurance schemes.

Returning to Europe

Social policies in the CEE countries are poorly designed. There are not only the usual inconsistencies present in the West between various policy instruments, but the measures also are inadequate. Broadly speaking, there are too many schemes providing too few cash transfers to too many people. The plethora of family benefits is one example. With some schemes, administrative costs surpass the cost of payments distributed.

For these reasons it is important for prospective members to put their houses in order before joining the EU. The new EU candidates have relatively large welfare systems (accounting for per capita GDP levels) whose burden falls on a narrow tax base. Figure 6.2 shows that payroll taxes earmarked for financing pensions, unemployment benefits, sickness benefits, and other cash transfers (excluding social assistance, which typically is funded from general government revenues) amount to a *larger* fraction of the payroll than in the average EU country. At the same time, however, the accession countries spend *less* in proportion of their GDP than EU countries typically spend. One of *the* reasons—if not *the* reason—for this situation is the large size of the informal sector (Lacko 1999). There are indications that a vicious circle is in motion: A small tax base requires higher statutory social security contributions to fund social expenditures, and these high contributions induce an even larger number of employers to avoid contributing to social security. The problem cannot be solved with more efficient tax collection and tougher penalties for illegal behavior. Under the present conditions in CEE countries— relatively high, persistently stagnant, and regionally concentrated unemployment—strong repression of the informal sector may increase unemployment. Consider the combined effects of such a policy on both job destruction and job creation (Boeri 2000). An increase in repression of the informal sector may be perceived by newly created firms as a reduction in future benefits and therefore may backfire. This link between employment in the informal sector and unemployment is at the heart of

Figure 6.2   High Social Security Contributions and Relatively Low Social Spending

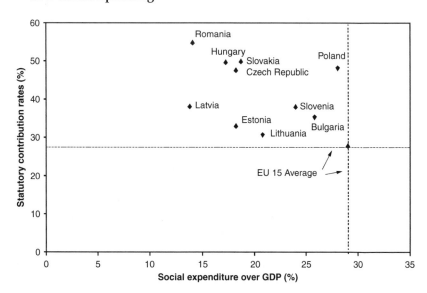

the policy dilemma faced by policymakers who realize that a more aggressive approach against the informal sector may result in a more depressed labor market.

Accession can make things worse in this respect because it may involve a greater role for institutions—like a higher coverage of collective bargaining—which compress wage distributions and make large compensating transfers to jobs that would otherwise be eliminated. This is the lesson learned from eastern Germany after re-unification.[2]

Thus, the EU cannot impose Western European welfare standards on the CEE countries, forcing them to bear all costs. That would slow their convergence to the EU average and reduce economic efficiency at a time when productivity growth is greatly needed. CEE countries' raising taxes to pay for a generous safety net simply may expand the large informal sectors in these countries. As mentioned previously, these countries already levy higher social security contributions as a percentage of wage bills, although they spend less in social policies than their EU counterparts. This situation results from low "wage shares" in CEE countries and from a sizable informal sector, which increases the gap between statutory and effective contribution rates.

An important in-kind contribution that current EU members can provide to the CEE countries relates to the design of the welfare system. Western European systems also are poorly designed. They impose distortions on the economy and may be headed for financial crises. Accession candidates cannot afford such a scenario. Therefore, CEE countries should refrain from copying the exact design of Western European countries. Instead, their systems should be designed to preserve work incentives and deter abuse.

Because of the large-scale reform process associated with entry into the EU, these countries have a one-time opportunity to design their systems correctly. For example, unemployment benefits should be paid on the condition that the recipient is actively seeking work. Part of the Czech Republic's success in maintaining low levels of unemployment in the early 1990s lies in a strict benefit administration combined with active labor market policies (Boeri and Burda 1995). The Czech Republic may provide a blueprint for other CEE countries, where wage distributions are now much less compressed than at early stages of transition. This makes it possible to introduce in-work benefits for low-paid jobs with relatively contained fiscal costs.

Political Constraints

Activation and "making work pay" features are absent from many Western European countries, and introducing them could require painful political compromises. Reducing some schemes while implementing new ones is also politically costly. Will CEE countries be able to meet these challenges?

Governments in the region missed a window of opportunity for substantial welfare reform at the outset of economic transformation. Countries could have used "periods of extraordinary politics" (in the words of Leszek Balcerowicz) to renege on commitments made by the previous regime. Faith in the virtues of the market mechanism also gave governments leverage to propose "low contributions—low pensions" deals to high wage earners because there was a widespread perception that returns from savings could have been significantly higher than those offered by public pensions. Thus, pension reforms should have been put at the top of transition countries' agendas.

It is still possible for these countries to change, but it is much more difficult now than it was then. Public opinion polls indicate that there are political constraints facing reforms aimed at rationalizing the welfare system. Figure 6.3 compares the results of two surveys. The first was carried out in February 2000 in France, Germany, Italy, and Spain by Fondazione Rodolfo Debenedetti (Boeri, Börsch-Supan, and Tabellini 2001). The second survey was conducted in Hungary in early 1996 (Csontaos, Kornai, and Toth 1998). Both surveys aimed at eliciting information on citizens' preferences as to the size of the welfare state and their awareness of the tax burden associated with its financing.

Figure 6.3   Public Opinion on the Size of the Welfare State

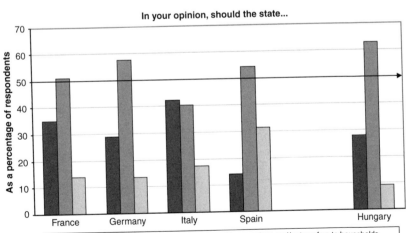

The results of the two surveys are surprisingly similar. First, citizens underestimated the actual cost of social welfare systems. When asked how much of their monthly wages go to various extrabudgetary funds, they answered with figures much lower than actual contribution rates (both for employee and employer). The second similarity is a strong preference for the status quo. More than 50 percent of citizens in all countries (except Italy) favored keeping the size of the system the same. This is in line with the "median voter" result: Political parties have adapted to the voters' preferences and electoral competition has forced them to offer the policies preferred by the majority of voters. An alternative interpretation is that citizens' preferences adapted to the status quo. In either case, the fact that people are so poorly informed about the costs of the system suggests a loophole for CEE countries. The survey indicated clearly that citizens who were better informed about the costs of the system were more open to reform. Thus, if governments can better inform their citizens, they can change the balance in favor of reforms.

Final Remarks

Formerly planned economies entered transition with very different social policy models. The countries of the former Soviet Union did not have a safety net and allowed earning differentials, notably top to bottom decile ratios, to become almost five times as large as they were at the beginning of transition. The nations of Central and Eastern Europe had, instead, institutions in place that compressed wage structures, preventing earning and income inequality from reaching the levels attained by Russia. The driving force of the social policy model adopted by the CEE countries was the "return to Europe." We now can say that the second model was the more successful, but that is not necessarily the case for the future.

Redistribution is a luxury good and CEE countries should resist the pressures to adopt the same social policy model of countries that have much higher per capita income levels. Before actually returning to Europe and fully entering the EU, they should improve the effectiveness of their welfare system in redistributing and broadening the tax base.

Reforming welfare systems in these countries, however, is proving to be as difficult as it was in Western Europe. There is evidence of status quo bias in the preferences of citizens of the accession countries. Under such conditions, reforms should be devised and packaged carefully to gain majority support and commitment.

Notes

1. Using the same methodology, Commander, Lee, and Tolstopiatenko (1998) conclude that changes in tax payments from 1992 to 1996 have contributed to the increase in inequality over time in Russia.

2. Needless to say, unification is more than the accession to an economic union.

References

Atkinson, A., and J. Micklewright. 1992. *Economic Transformation in Eastern Europe and the Distribution of Income.* Cambridge, U.K.: Cambridge University Press.

Boeri, T. 2000. *Structural Change, Welfare Systems and Labour Reallocation: Lessons from the Transition of Formerly Planned Economies.* Oxford, U.K.: Oxford University Press.

Boeri, T., A. Börsch-Supan, and G. Tabellini. 2001. "Would you like to Shrink the Welfare State? The Opinions of European Citizens." *Economic Policy* 32(April):7–50.

Boeri, T., and M. Burda. 1995. "Active Labour Market Policies, Job Matching and the Czech Miracle." *European Economic Review* 40:805–17.

Commander, S., U. Lee, and A. Tolstopiatenko. 1998. "Social Benefits and the Russian Industrial Firm." In S. Commander, Q. Fan, and M. Schafer, eds., *Enterprise Restructuring and Economic Policy in Russia.* Washington D.C.: World Bank.

Commission of the European Union. 1999. Country Reports on the State of Accession Negotiations.

Cornia, G. A. 1996. *Economic Policy in Traditional Economies.* London: Kluwer.

Csontaos, L., J. Kornai, and I. G. Toth. 1998. "Tax Awareness and Reform of the Welfare State: Hungarian Survey Results." *Economics of Transition* 6:287–312.

Fidrmuc, J. 1999. "The Political Economy of Reforms in Central and Eastern Europe." Center Dissertation Series, Tilburg University, The Netherlands.

Garner, T., and K. Terrell. 1998. "A Gini Decomposition Analysis of Inequality in the Czech and Slovak Republics during the Transition." Centre for Economic Policy Research Discussion Paper 64. London.

Lacko, M. 1999. "Hidden Economy: An Unknown Quantity? Comparative Analysis of Hidden Economies in Transition Countries in 1989–95." Johannes Kepler Universitat Linz Working Paper 9905, Linz, Austria.

Milanovic, B. 1997. "A Simple Way to Calculate the Gini Coefficient and Some Implications." *Economics Letters* 56(1):45–59.

Roland, G. 2000. *Transition and Economics, Politics, Markets and Firms.* Cambridge, Mass.: MIT Press.

Suhrcke, M. 2001. "Preferences for Inequality: East Vs. West." UNICEF—Innocenti Working Paper, No. 89.

7

Mapping the Diffusion of Pension Innovation

Mitchell A. Orenstein

Multipillar pension reform is a global phenomenon. First implemented in Chile in 1981, multipillar reforms, involving the partial or full replacement of pay-as-you-go (PAYG) state pensions by systems of privately managed individual accounts, have spread rapidly in Latin America, Western Europe, and the post-communist countries of Central and Eastern Europe. The first instances of multipillar reform in Asia are now evident. This chapter puts these developments in perspective by comparing the current spread of multipillar reform with the earlier diffusion of first pension system adoptions between 1889 and 1994. This chapter will suggest that viewing this phenomenon as the diffusion of a new policy idea helps us better understand the global context of pension reform, as well as the reasons for and mechanisms of its spread.

Multipillar Pension Reform

Multipillar pension reform represents a new paradigm in pension system design by relying on multiple pillars of pension provision, including the state budget, state insurance programs, and private pension funds. Particularly, the idea that states can discharge part of their responsibility for insuring adequate pensions by mandating employee savings in individual, privately managed pension savings accounts, is new and revolutionary.

Grateful acknowledgment is made to the American Council of Learned Societies and to the John D. and Catherine T. MacArthur Foundation for their sponsorship of this research. Thanks also to Michael Cain, Estelle James, Michael Mintrom, Joan Nelson, Kathryn Sikkink, Jacqui True, Kurt Weyland, and participants at the American Political Science Association and World Bank/IIASA conference panels for their comments and advice on earlier drafts.

First developed by the "Chicago boys" team of economists in Chile and implemented in 1981, under the authoritarian rule of General Augusto Pinochet, whose reputation for social care was suspect, partial privatization of state pension systems was not widely accepted at first within the global social policy community. Many experts questioned, and continue to question, whether multipillar systems really work to achieve some of the major goals of pensions, particularly protecting people from poverty and exploitation by fee-hungry investment managers (Beattie and McGillivray 1995; James 1996; Queisser 2000). Another element slowing the acceptance of the Chilean reform was the fact that it had come, after all, from Chile, a semiperipheral middle-income country in the global economy. However, Chile proved to be a powerful example in Latin America and a model case for advocates of neoliberal policies, and soon Western European countries with long-established welfare systems were experimenting with reforms inspired by the Chilean model.

In 1994 the World Bank published *Averting the Old Age Crisis: Policies to Protect the Old and Promote Growth,* a major report that set forth a series of well-substantiated arguments in favor of multipillar pension reforms. *Averting the Old Age Crisis* argued that pension systems should ideally have three pillars: a state-managed, redistributive pillar providing a basic pension to secure against poverty; an earnings-related pension supported by mandatory lifetime contributions to individual pension savings accounts that are privately managed; and a pillar of voluntary private schemes, including supplemental industry, corporate, and mutual benefit plans. Such highly visible support and coherent argumentation for the multipillar model from a major international organization added significantly to the legitimacy and acceptability of these proposals in countries around the world. By 1999 Katharina Müller, a contributor to this volume, had coined the term the "new pension orthodoxy" to capture the extent to which multipillar reforms had become a dominant new policy paradigm. This new paradigm is not fully accepted by all parties to the debate, but it clearly represents a new phenomenon in global approaches to old-age provision and is increasingly the norm in countries around the world.

Policy Invention and Diffusion

As a new policy invention in the process of diffusion to countries around the world, multipillar pension reform is amenable to analysis from the multidisciplinary literature on diffusion of innovation (Rogers 1995). A diffusion perspective is useful because it enables us to situate multipillar pension reform as a global policy trend and it points to several causal mechanisms for its spread that are often ignored in the traditional political economy of policy reform literature. Using the diffusion perspective to complement a political economy analysis, therefore, can lead to a fuller understanding of the process by which policy innovations spread and a greater understanding of the international dimension of reform (Dolowitz and Marsh 2000). Such understandings are critical for global policy advocates who seek to promote the diffusion of their own policy innovations, as well as for scholars who analyze global social and institutional change.

The political economy of pension reform literature usually begins from the premise that path dependencies created by existing political institutions and policy structures constrain the development of new domestic policies (for example, Pierson 1994). Radical change is explained through a model of shock and response in which domestic policymakers tend to enact policy change when faced with a crisis (Bates and Krueger 1993, p. 452; Nelson 1990). A crisis forces decisions on policymakers who are otherwise inclined to maintain the status quo. In particular, a crisis forces them to decide on a policy response from among a relatively well-known set of internationally available policy options. The political economy literature usually assumes these options to exist and poses the question, why do policymakers choose one or another response—often one that is economically sub-optimal? The answer usually involves politics, which is understood as a competition for resources among self-interested actors and interest groups, rather than as a competition among supporters of different policy ideas. In this model, policy ideas are generated non-problematically by economists and problems in implementing them are generated by politics.

The diffusion literature starts from a somewhat different vantage point and with a somewhat different concept of the origins and genesis of policy reform. Diffusion studies emphasize that some class of policy changes arises from the creation and spread of new ideas. Such changes cannot take place until these new policy ideas are invented and tested in a specific environment. When invention has occurred, innovations may be undertaken in other countries. Interestingly, the diffusion literature suggests that crisis is not a sufficient condition for policy innovation. Necessity may be the mother of invention, but invention does not always occur when needed. The diffusion literature thus makes a substantial contribution to our understanding of the political economy of reform by injecting a new self-consciousness about how new policy ideas are generated in global discourse (see, for instance, Deacon 1997; Queisser 2000). A second notable contribution of the diffusion literature is that it has generated highly robust results about which states are more likely to adopt innovation earlier. A variety of studies (primarily of policy diffusion among the 50 states of the United States) have shown that states that are larger, more industrial, and economically more prosperous tend to adopt policy innovations before states that are smaller and poorer (Walker 1969; Gray 1973; Welch and Thompson 1980). This situation usually is explained by the fact that richer states have more slack resources (Cyert and March 1963), rendering policy experimentation easier and the risk of failure less severe. The diffusion literature also has reported strong regional effects, suggesting policy emulation among states in the same region or peer group. Berry and Berry (1999) list three main mechanisms: emulation of neighboring states, emulation of regional leader states, and emulation of global peer states. Studies have shown strong evidence to confirm regional patterns of innovation diffusion, with smaller states tending to follow the examples of regional or global leaders (Walker 1969; Gray 1973; Collier and Messick 1975). The third substantial contribution of the diffusion literature is to shed light on mechanisms of policy diffusion. These mechanisms include interstate competition for economic resources and legitimacy (Berry and Berry 1999), the role of interstate organizations (Walker 1969; Welch and Thompson 1980) or "epistemic communities" (Haas 1992) in spreading ideas and information about policy reform, and the role of regional models in demonstrating policy feasibility (Walker 1969). As we will see, these findings receive further confirmation below in this investigation of diffusion of pension reform ideas over time.

The diffusion approach taken here is historical and comparative. Most diffusion studies employ event history analysis (Berry and Berry 1999, p. 190) to analyze a set of policy adoptions over a given period of time. In contrast, this study investigates policy adoptions during two time periods by comparing the diffusion of multipillar pension reform since 1981 with the earlier spread of national pension systems in the years 1889 to 1994. This historical comparison of two episodes of diffusion in one policy domain (Burstein 1991) enables us to better understand which features of multipillar pension reform diffusion are particular to an episode and which features reflect relatively timeless patterns. A simple visual mapping technique is used to allow us to see individual countries in the data, while illustrating causal mechanisms. Such visual display of quantitative information follows principles articulated and exemplified by Tufte (1992). Another peculiarity of the policy diffusion literature is that most of its early works concern diffusion among the 50 U.S. states. Global studies of policy innovation diffusion are relatively few (Collier and Messick 1975; True and Mintrom 2001). This study shows, however, that approaches and insights derived from the study of diffusion among the 50 states can be applied usefully to the analysis of global policy diffusion.

One cautionary note: Diffusion models do not explain everything about the political economy of reform and cannot be seen as a complete paradigmatic replacement of this rich literature (Dolowitz and Marsh 2000). For instance, the diffusion literature has very little to say about how innovations are altered during the process of adoption in particular states (Rogers 1995), a question that is central to the political economy of reform literature, including my own previous work on pension reform (Orenstein 2000). I do not mean to underestimate the importance of this problem or suggest that the diffusion literature can serve fully to replace the literature on the political economy of reform. What I do claim is that the diffusion literature emphasizes a commonly overlooked set of causal mechanisms for policy innovation and provides a different picture of the policy reform process—one that is appropriate for analyzing the diffusion of new policy ideas. By so doing, this diffusion literature can make a substantial contribution to our understanding of global policy reform processes.

The First Phase (1889–1994)

Researchers seldom have looked at the spread of welfare state institutions around the world as an instance of policy diffusion. Notable exceptions are Collier and Messick (1975) and Rodgers (1998). But most accounts of welfare state development come from the growing literature on historical institutionalism (Weir and Skocpol 1985; Esping-Andersen 1990; Skocpol 1992; Pierson 1994). These institutionalist accounts have emphasized the deep historical roots of welfare state institutions in particular national contexts and the importance of national path dependencies in explaining their development. This chapter seeks to challenge the perception that welfare states grow from primarily national roots by showing that international emulation has been a critical factor in determining the course of welfare state development globally.

The first pension system was invented in Germany and implemented by Bismarck in 1889. The Bismarckian model was important in Europe (Bonoli 2000, pp. 10–11), putting pressure on other European states to respond similarly—or differently—to increased worker demands and state imperatives for greater old-age security. As table 7.1 and figure 7.1 show, pension systems were adopted across Western and Central Europe before the first world war, with Eastern European and some Latin American states, plus South Africa, adopting in the interwar period. But the major explosion of pension systems around the world occurred in the wake of the Second World War and under the influence of the international principles articulated by the International Labour Organisation (ILO) in its Declaration of Philadelphia in 1944 (ILO 1944). Those principles included the creation of unified, national pension insurance systems under a central social security administration, to provide a specified set of benefits, including disability and old-age pensions (ILO 1944, p. 20). The ILO, in conjunction with major countries including the United States, vigorously promoted these aims in regional conferences

Table 7.1 Global Spread of Pension System Adoption, 1889–1994

	Europe/Antipodes/US/CA	Latin America/Carribean	Africa/Middle East	Asia
1880s	*DE*			
1890s	*DK, NZ*			
1900s	*AU, AT, BE, IS, UK,* **CS,** *IE*			
1910s	*FR, IT, NL, SE, ES,* **RO,** *LU*			
1920s	*CA,* **BG, EE, HU, LV, LT, PL, RU, YU,** GC	**CL, EC**	**ZA**	
1930s	*FI, NO, US, GR, PT*	**BR, PE,** TT, **UY,** BB		
1940s	**AL,** *CH,* **TR,** MC	**AR, CO, CR, DO, GY,** *MX,* **PA, PY, VE**	**DZ,** GQ	*JP*
1950s	CY, JE, LI, MT, SM	**BO, HN, JM, NI, SV,** BS	**BI, EG, IQ, GN, IR, IL, LY,** MU, **MA, RW, SY, ZR, CV**	**CN, ID, IN, MY, PH, SG, LK, TW**
1960s	AD	**CU, HT, GT,** BM, GD	**BF, CM, CF, CG, CI, ET, GA, GH, KE, LB, MG** **ML, MR, NE, NG, SA, TG, TN, TZ, UG, ZM**	**NP, VN,** FJ, FM, MH, PW
1970s		AG, **BZ,** DM, LC, VC, VG	**BJ, TD, JO, KW, LR, OM, SD, SN, SZ, BH,** SC, ST	**HK,** *KR,* **PK,** KI, SB, WS
1980s			**GM, YE**	PG, VU
1990s			**ZW, BW**	**TH**

Notes: Bold indicates country with over 1m population in 2000. Italics indicate high-income OECD country. Countries listed alphabetically by category.

ISO 3166 Country Codes: AD = Andorra, AG = Antigua, AL = Albania, AR = Argentina, AT = Austria, AU = Australia, BB = Barbados, BE = Belgium, BF = Burkina Faso, BG = Bulgaria, BH = Bahrain, BI = Burundi, BJ = Benin, BM = Bermuda, BO = Bolivia, BR = Brazil, BS = Bahamas, BW = Botswana, BZ = Belize, CA = Canada, CF = Central African Republic, CG = Congo, CH = Switzerland, CI = Ivory Coast, CL = Chile, CM = Cameroon, CN = China, CO = Colombia, CR = Costa Rica, CS = Czechoslovakia, CU = Cuba, CV = Cape Verde, CY = Cyprus, DE = Germany, DK = Denmark, DM = Dominica, DO = Dominican Republic, DZ = Algeria, EC = Ecuador, EE = Estonia, EG = Egypt, ES = Spain, ET = Ethiopia, FI = Finland, FJ = Fiji, FM = Micronesia, FR = France, GA = Gabon, GC = Guernsey (my abbr.), GD = Grenada, GH = Ghana, GM = Gambia, GN = Guinea, GR = Greece, GT = Guatemala, GQ = Equatorial Guinea, GY = Guyana, HK = Hong Kong, HN = Honduras, HT = Haiti, HU = Hungary, ID = Indonesia, IE = Ireland, IL = Israel, IN = India, IQ = Iraq, IR = Iran, IS = Iceland, IT = Italy, JE = Jersey (my abbr.), JM = Jamaica, JO = Jordan, JP = Japan, KE = Kenya, KI = Kiribati, KR = South Korea, KW = Kuwait, LB = Lebanon, LC = St. Lucia, LI = Liechtenstein, LK = Sri Lanka, LR = Liberia, LT = Lithuania, LU = Luxembourg, LV = Latvia, LY = Libya, MA = Morocco, MC = Monaco, MG = Madagascar, MH = Marshall Islands, ML = Mali, MR = Mauritania, MT = Malta, MU = Mauritius, MX = Mexico, MY = Malaysia, NE = Niger, NG = Nigeria, NI = Nicaragua, NL = Netherlands, NO = Norway, NP = Nepal, NZ = New Zealand, OM = Oman, PA = Panama, PE = Peru, PG = Papua New Guinea, PH = Philippines, PK = Pakistan, PL = Poland, PT = Portugal, PW = Palau, PY = Paraguay, RO = Romania, RU = Russia, RW = Rwanda, SA = Saudi Arabia, SB = Solomon Islands, SC = Seychelles, SD = Sudan, SE = Sweden, SG = Singapore, SM = San Marino, SN = Senegal, ST = St. Tome & Principe, SV = El Salvador, SY = Syria, SZ = Swaziland, TD = Chad, TG = Togo, TH = Thailand, TN = Tunisia, TR = Turkey, TT = Trinidad and Tobago, TW = Taiwan, TZ = Tanzania, UG = Uganda, UK = United Kingdom, US = United States, UY = Uruguay, VC = St. Vincent, VE = Venezuela, VG = Virgin Islands, VN = Vietnam, VU = Vanuatu, WS = Samoa, YE = Yemen, YU = Yugoslavia, ZA = South Africa, ZM = Zambia, ZR = Zaire, ZW = Zimbabwe.

(Altmeyer 1945, pp. 720–21; ILO 1948a, 1948b), through the dispatch of consultants (Acosta 1944, p. 46), the publication of reform templates (Acosta 1944; Schoenbaum 1945), and the articulation of principles by major world leaders, including U.S. president Franklin D. Roosevelt (ILO 1945). Earlier reforming countries also were encouraged to revise their often fragmented systems of pension provision to meet the new standards. All of this was done in the context of creating a world order that would guarantee peace. Considering these facts, it is strange that analysts have tended to ignore the extent to which pension systems reflect global trends.

To enhance our understanding of this phenomenon, I have charted in table 7.1 the first adoption of a pension system in the 152 countries listed in the U.S. Social Security Administration's publication, *Social Security Programs throughout the World* (SSPTW), 2001 Web edition. I have coded each country according to the International Standards Organization's (ISO 3166) two-letter economy codes, also available on the Web. This provides a standard plot size for each country on the chart, enabling visual quantitative comparisons. I use the date of adoption of pension systems reported in SSPTW, which is usually the date of first pension legislation rather than the date of reform implementation. These dates are used advisedly because in several countries legislation was adopted well before pension systems actually were created. Other anomalies may exist. However, I did not attempt to correct the SSPTW data, but instead chose to use a single standardized source to avoid errors of bias, as has long been the standard in the field (Collier and Messick 1975, p. 1302). Countries are listed alphabetically by decade of adoption and region. Three of these regions are purely geographical, whereas the first one, "Europe/Antipodes/ United States/Canada," is more cultural and economic in nature. It represents the high-income Organisation for Economic Co-operation and Development (OECD) nations minus Japan, including the industrial countries that have long been governed by settlers of European origin. These countries can be considered a single cultural/economic region for purposes of policy innovation and dissemination.

Note that by focusing on the first establishment of national pension systems, table 7.1 aggregates pension systems of three distinct types. Scholars of European welfare states have identified two ideal types of early pension systems in Europe (Bonoli 2000, pp. 10–11). First, Bismarckian social insurance systems emphasized providing workers a pension that reflected a proportion of their income while working. Second, the Danish (1891) or later Beveridgean (U.K.) model was essentially an extension of the poor laws, and emphasized poverty relief and the maintenance of basic minimum living standards. Financing for these two types of systems differed in accordance with their goals. Whereas the Bismarckian system relied on contributions from employers, employees, and the state, Denmark's 1891 system was general tax financed by general taxes. France, Italy, the United States, and Switzerland initially followed the social insurance model, but New Zealand, the United Kingdom, Sweden, and Norway initially followed the Danish poverty-prevention tradition. These two pension system types were quite different at first, but most national systems tended to adopt elements of both over time (Bonoli 2000, 12). The result is that now "the guarantee of a minimum income combined with a partial replacement of earnings is a common feature to almost all pension systems," although Germany and Denmark remain exceptions to that rule (Bonoli 2000, p. 13). A third distinct type of pension system was the national provident fund, a central savings fund administered by the government that generally provided a lump-sum benefit at retirement. These were popular in Asian and some African countries under British colonial influence (Gillion et al. 2000, p. 501). As this brief discussion suggests, a more detailed analysis of the spread of each of these types of systems internationally might yield interesting results and an even more nuanced view of cultural and regional patterns of pension system diffusion. The aggregate analysis presented here, however, focuses on arguably the main event in this first phase of reform—the establishment of a broad, national pension system where none existed before.

The diffusion literature has tended to focus on four factors to explain policy innovation and diffusion—state wealth, size, industrialization, and geographic region. A first-order question, therefore, is whether these variables also explain the creation and diffusion of pension systems, beginning with Bismarck's reforms in 1889. The basic answer is yes.

Table 7.1 shows strong evidence for many of the key findings of the policy diffusion literature. First, level of economic development is highly correlated with the timing of pension system adoption (Walker 1969; Collier and Messick 1975). The average high-income OECD country established a pension system approximately 40 years before the average non-OECD country. Collier and Messick (1975), however, note that later adopters tended to adopt at much lower absolute levels of economic development. Second, country size is also an important factor. In each region of the world, large countries innovated before small countries (countries with fewer than 1 million people in 2000 are not set in bold type in table 7.1). Also, the regional variable is a strong influence. Pension reform diffused for 30 years in Europe and the high-income OECD countries before being adopted in Latin America. African and Asian countries innovated approximately 20 years later than did their counterparts in Latin America, creating a regional cascade effect. One reason for this, of course, is the earlier history of statehood in Latin America, which suggests that "stateness" (Linz and Stepan 1996) also may be a relevant variable in international comparison.

It is likewise interesting to note that international diffusion of pension systems follows the usual distribution pattern for adoption of innovations—a few countries are pioneers, followed by a steep increase in the rate of adoption, with a few laggards filling in at the end. When charted cumulatively, this results in an S-curve (see figure 7.1). The curve resembles similar curves for the United States, which have been explained by the confluence of a large number of interrelated factors that determine policy adoption and the learning and interaction effects between adopting states (Gray 1973, pp. 1175–176).

Finally, an intraregional cascade effect is visible, particularly through the graphic approach in table 7.1. In Europe it is notable that the first countries to innovate were mainly Anglo-Saxon countries, with Germany being the policy creator. Denmark and New Zealand came next, followed by Australia, Austria, Belgium, Iceland, the United Kingdom, Ireland, and Czechoslovakia, which at that time was part of the Austro-Hungarian Empire. Next came the Mediterranean and Romance countries, France, Italy, Spain, Luxembourg, and Romania, along with the Netherlands and Sweden, during the 1910s. Pension innovation spread to Eastern Europe only in the 1920s, after 30 years' gestation in the West (see also Collier and Messick [1975, p. 1312] for a graphic display). At the same time, the innovation jumped to the leading Latin American countries, including Chile and Brazil, in the 1920s and 1930s. Most large, industrial Latin American countries adopted by the end of the 1940s, and the smaller nations and Caribbean countries followed in the 1950s and 1960s. Only small island nations were left in the 1970s. In Africa, too, the first innovator was South Africa. The first in Asia was Japan in the 1940s. On those two continents most of the major countries followed within 20 to 30 years; the smaller and more peripheral states adopted systems last. This intraregional cascade strengthens the finding that wealth, size, and region are key factors determining policy innovation, with the larger, wealthier, more industrial countries in each region innovating first, and reform then spreading out concentrically from core to periphery. This underlines the global importance of a relatively stable set of regional policy innovation leaders, just as Walker (1969) found in the United States.

One big question to arise from table 7.1 is what causes the interregional diffusion of pension system ideas? Culture and regional example appear to be important. It is notable that pension systems were restricted to Europe and the Anglo-Saxon countries for 30 years before diffusing first to Latin America and then to Africa and Asia simultaneously. However, table 7.1 provides evidence that the existence and activities of international organizations operating in a policy area also may be critical. We know that in 1919 the ILO was founded to spread international labor standards. We observe that slow interregional diffusion was the norm

Figure 7.1   Cumulative Adoption of First Pension Systems Worldwide

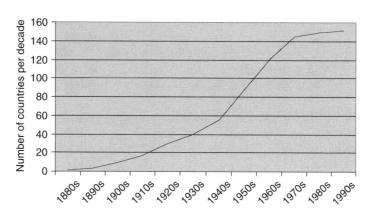

until 1919 when pension system establishment began a process of inter-regional diffusion. There is also a sharp upturn in the rate of diffusion in the 1940s (figure 7.1), with the publication of the Declaration of Philadelphia and the ILO's global campaign to spread its new welfare state model.

Activities of the ILO were a major factor in the export of pension ideas to the rest of the world (Collier and Messick 1975, p. 1305; Craig and Tomeš 1969), particularly after the Second World War. The ILO's actions encompassed the setting of international norms of social protection, gen-eration of reform templates, provision of consultants and consulting advice, and the use of high-level regional meetings to popularize its ideas and approach. Most crucially, the ILO's 1944 Declaration of Philadelphia won the endorsement of the major victorious powers as the template for a new, peaceful, postwar social order. It makes for impres-sive reading and was highly inspirational at the time of its publication. The Declaration of Philadelphia was significant not only for its high-level political support (ILO 1944, 1945), but also for the way it set strong, highly idealistic, but widely agreed and specific norms for full employ-ment and social protection after the war (ILO 1944), although it should be noted that pension provision was only one element in this vision. The ILO energetically distributed information about its program through high-profile regional meetings that brought top political leaders together to discuss specific social policy challenges (ILO 1948a, 1948b). The ILO provided legislative reform templates, in the form of detailed informa-tion about reform programs in leading states (Schoenbaum 1945), regular updates about the progress of reform in different countries (Acosta 1944), and reports by regional leader countries about their activities in spreading reform in their region (Altmeyer 1945). The ILO also provided expert advice to reforming countries (Acosta 1944, 46), including actuarial support. All in all, the organization played a major role in the establishment of social welfare states, articulating a global vision for social reform and creating momentum behind the first phase of pension system adoption in countries around the world.

The Second Phase (1981–2041)

What is different about this second phase of pension reform? What do we learn by comparing it with the first phase of pension system diffusion? I find four main ways in which the second phase differs from the first phase of reform. First, the content of reform differs. Whereas the first episode of reform involved the establishment of first pension systems in the context of broader social system development, the second phase involves reforming pension systems created in the first wave. Second, the inventing country is different, and differently situated in the global economy. When Chile moved to privatize its pension system in 1981, it was a semiperipheral developing country, whereas Germany—the leader in the first phase—was a leading industrial economy. Third, the rate of diffusion of multipillar pension reform has been faster. It is spreading at approximately two times the rate of first adoptions, and the speed of interregional transfer is particularly pronounced. Fourth, the leading international organization involved in formulating and spreading reform is different: The World Bank, rather than the ILO, is dominant in the spread of multipillar reform, reflecting shifts in global discourse on social and economic policy. There are also significant similarities between the first and second reform phases, including the fact that country income and region remain significant determinants of reform. This section will discuss these differences and similarities in turn.

Perhaps the overriding difference between multipillar pension reform and the establishment of first pension systems is that multipillar reform is a second-phase reform. Because most countries in the world have established pension systems already, the multipillar movement involves changing the organization of pension commitments rather than founding wholly new systems. Multipillar reforms therefore are less ambitious in scope, and they necessarily react to what came before them.

In particular, multipillar reforms reflect an attempt to remedy some of the problems of the previous ILO model, which called for the establishment of unified, defined-benefit pensions run by a central social security administration. These systems relied primarily on some form of PAYG pension financing. In PAYG systems, current-year pension contributions are used to pay current-year pension outlays. Social security administrations use actuarial methods and manipulation of various pension parameters to ensure a relatively predictable or "defined" benefit to all pensioners, usually consisting of a target "replacement rate" of previous income. This system contrasts with fully funded, defined-contribution plans in which employees and possibly employers contribute to individual savings accounts. In funded systems, contributions are defined but benefits are uncertain, depending on investment results.

Although ILO model pension systems represented a major advance over a past in which few states felt an obligation to ensure old-age security (Gillion et al. 2000, p. v), experience revealed some characteristic problems of these systems. First, social security administrations in much of the developing world faced serious administrative problems from corruption, politicization, and low state capacity (Gillion et al. 2000, p. 9). It proved difficult for such administrations to operate PAYG pension systems adequately and to avoid political pressures to promise more benefits than were realistically payable (World Bank 1994). As a consequence, people lost faith in national pension systems. The problem was particularly acute in Latin America (Gillion et al. 2000, p. 541) and formed an important backdrop to the Chilean reform and its decision to rely more heavily on private sector managers. Second, PAYG pension systems involve intergenerational transfers of income that become difficult to manage when the population is aging (World Bank 1994). When the working-age population is growing and employment levels are high (a central goal of the ILO's Declaration of Philadelphia) (ILO 1944), PAYG pension systems provide a generous income for the first retiring generation. But as people spend longer in retirement and the proportion of workers to pensioners narrows, as it has in many industrial countries, PAYG pension systems face serious fiscal challenges. The population aging problem is most acute in developed Western countries and the former socialist countries of Central and Eastern Europe. A third problem of state PAYG pension systems is that their benefits are tied mainly to wage growth in the economy. This worked well in the postwar boom when wage levels rose dramatically. But more recently wages have stagnated in relative terms while returns to capital have increased. This means that funded pension systems did better than state PAYG pension systems (World Bank 1994).

Multipillar pension systems seek to diversify retirement income sources (Chlon, Góra, and Rutkowski 1999) and separate the various social goals of pension systems into different mechanisms of financing. In the World Bank model (World Bank 1994), the first pillar of pension provision should be state-financed and redistributive, providing a basic income for all who have worked a requisite period of time.

Relatively simple administrative means can be devised for countries with low policy capacity, to ensure that all workers receive at least some minimum income. A second pillar of pension provision should be mandatory and provide income-related benefits. As opposed to the older ILO model, which emphasized PAYG benefit financing, advocates of multipillar reform suggest that these income-related benefits should be fully funded, privately managed, and accumulated in individual pension savings accounts. In theory, this strategy reduces reliance on inefficient state social security administrations and enables systems to take advantage of more efficient private sector management. Finally, a third pillar of voluntary private pension schemes may be created on a variety of different models with state tax incentives.

The Chilean system was a particularly radical version of what later became the multipillar model. The Pinochet government mandated a complete replacement of the former PAYG state pension system founded in 1924 with a system of mandatory, fully funded, defined-contribution individual savings accounts managed by private pension fund administrators (AFPs). Workers' previous contributions to the state system were recognized through the issuance of individual "recognition bonds" that paid a 4 percent real interest rate (Gillion et al. 2000, p. 542). The new Chilean system also provides a minimum guaranteed pension to retirees whose pension accounts fall below this minimum level and who have worked at least 20 years, as well as a means-tested public assistance program for indigent elderly people (Gillion et al. 2000, p. 542). This constituted the first pillar of the new multipillar system. Since Chile, most reforming countries have chosen a partial rather than a full replacement of the previous PAYG system.

Multipillar pension reform was shaped by perceived problems with the older ILO model as well as by its original model. Why was Chile the policy inventor rather than a core capitalist economy like Germany in the first wave, and what impact did this have? Chile's first-mover status may reflect the globalization of economic policy discourse and the ways in which developing countries have become laboratories for experimentation with different economic principles (Deacon 1997). The Pinochet regime clearly drew on the latest economic ideas of the industrial world, particularly from those current at the University of Chicago, in formulating its pension system. This may signal the growing impact of "epistemic communities" (Haas 1992) of like-minded professionals in global economic policy, whom Haas and others have argued are central in the dissemination of policy advice. It also suggests that innovative policy thinking now may be more available to developing countries than in previous periods. In any case, it is clear from the past 20 years' experience (table 7.2) that reform no longer starts in the rich, Anglo-Saxon OECD countries and radiates out to the less industrial world. Instead, most

Table 7.2 Global Spread of Multipillar Pension Reform, 1981–2001

	Europe/Antipodes/US/CA	Latin America/Carribean	Africa/Middle East	Asia
1980s	*CH, NL, UK*	CL		
1990s	*AU, DK,* **HU, PL,** *SE*	**AR, BO, CO, MX, PE, SV,** UY		**KZ**
2000s	**BG, EE, HV, LV**	CR, NI		HK

Notes: Bold indicates country with over 1m population in 2000. Italics indicates high-income OECD country. Countries listed alphabetically by category.

ISO 3166 Country Codes: AD = Andorra, AG = Antigua, AL = Albania, AR = Argentina, AT = Austria, AU = Australia, BB = Barbados, BE = Belgium, BF = Burkina Faso, BG = Bulgaria, BH = Bahrain, BI = Burundi, BJ = Benin, BM = Bermuda, BO = Bolivia, BR = Brazil, BS = Bahamas, BZ = Belize, CA = Canada, CF = Central African Republic, CG = Congo, CH = Switzerland, CI = Ivory Coast, CL = Chile, CM = Cameroon, CN = China, CO = Colombia, CR = Costa Rica, CS = Czechoslovakia, CU = Cuba, CV = Cape Verde, CY = Cyprus, DE = Germany, DK = Denmark, DM = Dominica, DO = Dominican Republic, DZ = Algeria, EC = Ecuador, EE = Estonia, EG = Egypt, ES = Spain, ET = Ethiopia, FJ = Fiji, FM = Micronesia, FR = France, GA = Gabon, GC = Guernsey (my abbr.), GD = Grenada, GH = Ghana, GM = Gambia, GN = Guinea, GR = Greece, GT = Guatemala, GQ = Equatorial Guinea, GY = Guyana, HK = Hong Kong, HN = Honduras, HT = Haiti, HU = Hungary, HV = Croatia, ID = Indonesia, IE = Ireland, IL = Israel, IN = India, IQ = Iraq, IR = Iran, IS = Iceland, IT = Italy, JE = Jersey (my abbr.), JM = Jamaica, JO = Jordan, JP = Japan, KE = Kenya, KI = Kiribati, KR = South Korea, KW = Kuwait, KZ = Kazakhstan, LB = Lebanon, LC = St. Lucia, LI = Liechtenstein, LK = Sri Lanka, LR = Liberia, LT = Lithuania, LU = Luxembourg, LV = Latvia, LY = Libya, MA = Morocco, MC = Monaco, MG = Madagascar, MH = Marshall Islands, ML = Mali, MR = Mauritania, MT = Malta, MU = Mauritius, MX = Mexico, MY = Malaysia, NE = Niger, NG = Nigeria, NI = Nicaragua, NL = Netherlands, NO = Norway, NP = Nepal, NZ = New Zealand, OM = Oman, PA = Panama, PE = Peru, PG = Papua New Guinea, PH = Philippines, PK = Pakistan, PL = Poland, PT = Portugal, PW = Palau, PY = Paraguay, RO = Romania, RU = Russia, RW = Rwanda, SA = Saudi Arabia, SB = Solomon Islands, SC = Seychelles, SD = Sudan, SE = Sweden, SG = Singapore, SM = San Marino, ST = St. Tome & Principe, SV = El Salvador, SY = Syria, SZ = Swaziland, TD = Chad, TG = Togo, TH = Thailand, TN = Tunisia, TR = Turkey, TT = Trinidad and Tobago, TW = Taiwan, TZ = Tanzania, UG = Uganda, UK = United Kingdom, US = United States, UY = Uruguay, VC = St. Vincent, VE = Venezuela, VG = Virgin Islands, VN = Vietnam, VU = Vanuatu, WS = Samoa, YE = Yemen, YU = Yugoslavia, ZA = South Africa, ZM = Zambia, ZR = Zaire, ZW = Zimbabwe.

Sources: Palacios, Robert and Montserrat Pallarès- Miralles, International Patterns of Pension Provision, Washington, DC: The World Bank, 2000, and own research.

pension system innovation in the early years of the second phase has occurred in middle-income, semiperipheral countries like Chile, Uruguay, Argentina, Poland, and Hungary. The fact that Chile was the inventing country may account for this, as well as for the strong regional diffusion in Latin America. It should be noted that at least one middle-income, semiperipheral country, New Zealand, also was a leader in the first phase of pension system adoption. However, this trend toward innovation at the semiperiphery seems more pronounced in the second phase of multipillar reform.

A third difference visible between tables 7.1 and 7.2 is the speed of diffusion, particularly interregional diffusion. In the first phase, it took more than 30 years before pension reform spread out of Europe. In the second phase, mandatory funded pension systems spread from Chile to three industrial West European countries within a few years, and to Central and Eastern Europe in the next decade, again before most capitalist core countries had adopted the innovation. This provides evidence that policy ideas travel faster now, perhaps because of the increasingly powerful role international organizations play in spreading policy ideas across regional boundaries. It is notable that the ILO joined the first phase of pension innovation in 1944, after 55 years of diffusion. The World Bank joined in the promotion of multipillar reform 13 years after it was first invented in Chile. Current trends indicate that second-phase innovation is spreading at approximately twice the rate of the first wave. If this trend continues, it will take approximately 60 years for multipillar pension reform to sweep the globe (1981–2041), with the peak occurring somewhere in the 2000s and 2010s.

A fourth difference between the two episodes of reform lies in the international organization leading the charge. Whereas the first establishment of pension systems worldwide was influenced by the normative and substantive platform of the ILO, the aims and methods of multipillar pension reform have been articulated in large part by the World Bank (World Bank 1994; Chlon, Góra, and Rutkowski 1999; Holzmann 2000). This reflects broader changes in economic policy thinking since the Second World War, mainly the decline of Keynesianism and the rise of neoliberalism, represented most vigorously by the International Monetary Fund and the World Bank in international policy discourse (Deacon 1997). Although it would be an exaggeration to say that either the ILO or the World Bank acted alone as a global policy advocate in either phase,[1] the leadership role these organizations have played has been important in setting the tone of reform. Walker (1969) observed that interstate organizations play a great role in the diffusion of policy innovations among states by spreading information and experiences of reform to others. The World Bank certainly has played that role in the current reform phase, organizing conferences and publishing books about the political economy of reform; sending pension officials from reforming countries to Chile and other places where reform has already taken place; and generally accelerating the growth of knowledge about reform processes, methods, and outcomes. In addition, the World Bank has sent its experts to reforming countries, such as Hungary and Poland, to help with technical aspects of reform.

These differences are important for putting the contemporary diffusion of multipillar pension reform in context. They demonstrate the extent to which globalization and particularly the international spread of ideas has accelerated. However, there are also some striking similarities between the two phases of reform. First, consistent with the diffusion literature, country wealth remains a significant determinant of innovation in the second phase. As noted previously, most early innovators have been middle-income developing countries like Poland, Hungary, Argentina, and Uruguay. High-income industrial countries also are well represented among the early reformers, but there are only a few poor countries, such as El Salvador and Kazakhstan. On average, wealthier countries remain more likely to innovate despite their higher preexisting pension commitments. This contradicts a major finding of the historical institutionalist literature (compare Pierson 1994) that suggests that wealthier countries with more established welfare programs and systems of interest representation will face greater political obstacles to reform. Such obstacles undoubtedly exist but their effects are overwhelmed by the greater capacity for policy innovation in rich states.

Regional example remains an important predictor of pension reform adoption in the second phase. Latin America, which had the powerful example of Chile, experienced the most rapid spread of innovation during the second decade of reform. Chilean experts appear to have played a major role in this, spreading reform ideas and policies by consulting with regional neighbors. Other factors—for instance, language and perceived social similarities—probably supported this development. Similarly, it is notable that the first two decades of multipillar pension reform were restricted to Latin America and Europe, with the exception of Kazakhstan and Hong Kong, which were until the 1990s part of major European empires. This suggests that diffusion is far more likely to occur within regions, whereas interregional diffusion remains difficult. Other regional effects also are evident. One particularly striking feature is that the first reforming regions in the first phase were the same as the first reforming regions in the second phase—Europe/Antipodes/United States/Canada and Latin America—although in a somewhat different order. In addition, it is interesting that Chile was not only the first country to adopt multipillar pension reform, but also the first Latin American country to adopt a pension system in 1924. This suggests that there may be enduring reasons that particular regions and countries are more innovative in social policy (following Walker 1969), and that we may need to rethink the main obstacles to innovation. Although many authors have emphasized the size of implicit pension debt and other path dependencies as obstacles to innovation, the primary obstacles actually may be cultural or ideational.

In particular, the absence of Asian and African countries from the first 20 years of multipillar pension reform raises important questions about the relative impact of different determinants of reform. A path-dependency perspective might suggest that countries with less entrenched pension systems of the old model should be more likely to adopt the new model more readily. But national path-dependency explanations of pension reform cannot adequately explain the timing of policy innovation. Instead, innovation timing appears to track global trends, regional models, and the actions of global policy actors in spreading these innovations. The next section develops the hypothesis that reform timing is driven in part by a "global politics of attention" (Orenstein and Haas 2000). Because global policy actors cannot focus equally on all regions of the globe at once, because of scarce resources, their decisions about where to focus their attention may help determine patterns of diffusion in the second phase of pension innovation.

National Path Dependency or Global Policy?

Until now, the literature on the political economy of reform has focused on political and economic obstacles to change at the national level. Political scientists, notably Pierson (1994), have shown that political institutions and policy structures create path dependencies that make it hard to change national policies. The political economy literature emphasizes that a crisis is needed to place reform on the agenda. Even then, economists have shown fairly conclusively, countries with high implicit pension debt tend only partially, rather than fully, to replace their preexisting pension systems with a private, funded pillar (for example, James 1998). This is because high implicit pension debt makes it harder for countries to finance the transition to a funded system. Current literature on the political economy of pension reform suggests that preexisting policies, policy structures, and institutions play a significant role in shaping subsequent reform efforts (see also Weir and Skocpol 1985; Müller 1999; Orenstein 2000), thereby creating enduring differences in national policy structures.

However, the global policy diffusion patterns identified here seem to challenge this literature in important ways. First, it seems that these publications underplay the extent to which policy innovation is a global process driven by the diffusion of policy ideas (Rodgers 1998). Crisis, except in a most general sense, does not appear to be a sufficient condition for multipillar pension reform. Many countries experience pension system crises, and only some adopt multipillar reforms. In addition to crisis conditions, new policy ideas were necessary for multipillar reform to take place. In particular, the invention of multipillar reform arose from global trends in economic policy discourse, as they played out at the University of Chicago in the 1970s and 1980s.

Although publications on the political economy of reform focus on the importance of domestic economic and political variables in explaining policy adoption, both phases of pension reform analyzed in this chapter suggest that countries reform in response to global and regional models, under the influence of norms and ideas spread by the leading international organizations and epistemic communities of the day. Historical-institutionalist theories and path dependencies may explain a lot about why countries adapt innovations in specific ways to suit national conditions (compare Orenstein 2000), but they must be combined with a diffusion perspective to explain the important questions of why countries innovate in the first place and on what basic model they do so. Rather than locating the explanation for social policy change at the international or domestic level, the political economy literature needs a serious effort to integrate an international perspective with historical-institutionalist and path-dependency accounts. It is likely that these different approaches are not mutually exclusive, but rather complementary, tending to explain different parts of the phenomenon. Some of the chapters in this volume have already begun this work. For instance, Chlon and Mora study the influence of international financial institutions (IFIs) in domestic policy processes, and Mueller relates the influence of IFIs to levels of country indebtedness. More needs to be done, in particular to understand how internal processes of IFI decisionmaking may affect the diffusion of innovation.

Global Politics of Attention

Let us consider alternative explanations for why Asian and African countries have lagged behind in both phases of reform. This is a serious puzzle indeed because the path-dependency literature strongly suggests that the most amenable places for multipillar pension reform would be the late-reforming countries of Africa and Asia, with their smaller implicit pension debts and less-developed programmatic political networks. Why have these countries not been the first to embrace multipillar reform? There are several possible explanations. First, there may be long-standing structural features of the African and Asian states that make them slower policy innovators. This possibility has beguiled the U.S. literature from the beginning, when Walker (1969) showed that California, New York, Massachusetts, and New Jersey on average adopted policy reforms much sooner than did Mississippi or South Dakota, across a wide variety of policies and policy areas. Perhaps the same is true globally—perhaps the European and (North and South) American countries uniformly adopt policy innovations earlier because of more favorable structural conditions. If so, this would have to be shown across more policy areas, and a good explanation would be interesting and potentially important for global policy advocates.

A different but complementary explanation for this phenomenon might focus on the role of international organizations. Following Walker (1969), let us assume that the interregional diffusion of policy innovations is driven in large part by international organizations and other global policy advocates who play a major role in the spread of policy ideas and models. It is possible that international organizations have neglected the African and Asian countries in the second phase of pension reform to date, despite the relatively positive chances of reform there. If that is true, a global politics of attention may be driving policy diffusion and its spread may depend in part on where global policy advocates happen to focus their substantial policy resources, as well as on domestic factors. International organizations may make decisions on where to target their attention based on their evaluation of a country's importance in the global economy, their evaluation of the seriousness of its pension crisis, their evaluation of a country's likelihood and political will for reform, or other factors. Although many chapters in this volume suggest that domestic factors drive pension reform processes, there is some evidence to suggest that international organizations can affect the initiation of reform in developing countries. A previous study of Central and Eastern Europe showed that certain social sector reforms in the region started simultaneously in several countries after the World Bank began to devote significant resources to promoting these programs (Orenstein and Haas 2000). Several other studies have suggested that the World Bank's high degree of attention to pension reform in Central and Eastern Europe has facilitated adoption of multipillar innovations in the region (Müller 1999; Orenstein 2000). In other regions, such as Latin America, the World Bank and other international organizations and bilateral aid agencies played a supporting role in pension reform (see Müller in this volume), perhaps accelerating the pace of diffusion.

The global politics of attention perspective raises questions about the priorities and internal decisionmaking processes of global policy advocates. For instance, why has the World Bank focused so much attention on promoting pension policy diffusion in Central and Eastern Europe and not on African and Asian countries where the relative impact of its resources could be greater? Are Central and Eastern European states seen as targets of opportunity because of ongoing economic transformation and the impending European Union accession process, which increase chances for reform? Are Central and Eastern European countries seen by others as global pension reform leaders and thus potentially influential models? Is the World Bank supporting a European Union agenda at the expense of reform in poorer developing countries? Do the larger pension systems of European states make them the most important targets for reform, despite the greater political challenges? Whatever the reasons, it would seem important to investigate further the link between the internal processes of global policy advocates and global patterns of policy diffusion.

Conclusions and Recommendations

This chapter has found that level of economic development, size, regional example, and activities of global policy advocates have influenced the diffusion of pension innovations around the world. There also are significant differences between the first and second phases of reform, notably that in the second phase the content of reforms has been different, the first reforming country was a semiperipheral one, the speed of diffusion is higher, and the leading international organization is different. The adoption of multipillar reforms by the countries that led the first phase may have been slowed by higher implicit pension debt, but such historical path dependencies cannot adequately explain policy adoption decisions globally. In addition to domestic factors, this chapter suggests that the invention and spread of new ideas, the presence of regional examples, and a global politics of attention are driving the second wave of multipillar pension innovations.

Several policy recommendations may be drawn from this historical study of pension innovation. First, the World Bank and other global policy advocates in social policy and other areas should focus their attention on achieving reform in regional example countries because surrounding countries often take their cues from these regional leaders. Second, diffusion of innovation may be faster if global policy advocates identify and pursue reform on several continents at the same time. Third, global policy advocates should consider putting their limited resources to best use by focusing their attention on those regions that for historic or cultural reasons appear to innovate later than others. In summary, global policy advocates appear to be a major force in the interregional diffusion of policy ideas and would benefit from a careful and systematic analysis of where and how their resources are best employed.

Note

1. Chlon and Mora in this volume show the United States Agency for International Development, the European Bank for Reconstruction and Development, the Inter-American Development Bank, and the International Labour Organisation also to be important in the

second phase. In the first phase, the U.S. Social Security Administration provided technical assistance, primarily to countries in Latin America (Altmeyer 1945).

References

Acosta, César R. 1944. "Social Legislation in Paraguay." *International Labour Review* 50(1/July):40–46.

Altmeyer, Arthur J. 1945. "The Progress of Social Security in the Americas in 1944." *International Labour Review* 51(6/June):699–721.

Bates, Robert H., and Anne O. Krueger. 1993. "Generalizations Arising from the Country Studies." In Robert H. Bates and Anne O. Krueger, eds., *Political and Economic Interactions in Economic Policy Reform: Evidence from Eight Countries.* Oxford, U.K.: Blackwell.

Beattie, R., and W. McGillivray. 1995. "A Risky Strategy: Reflections on the World Bank Report *Averting the Old Age Crisis.*" *International Social Security Review* 48:3–4.

Berry, Frances Stokes, and William D. Berry. 1999. "Innovation and Diffusion Models in Policy Research." In Paul A. Sabatier, ed., *Theories of the Policy Process.* Boulder, Colo.: Westview Press.

Bonoli, Giuliano. 2000. *The Politics of Pension Reform: Institutions and Policy Change in Western Europe.* Cambridge, U.K.: Cambridge University Press.

Burstein, Paul. 1991. "Policy Domains: Organization, Culture, and Policy Outcomes." *Annual Review of Sociology* 17:327–50.

Chlon, Agnieszka, Marek Góra, and Michal Rutkowski. 1999. "Shaping Pension Reform in Poland: Security through Diversity." World Bank Social Protection Discussion Paper 9923. Washington, D.C.

Collier, David, and Richard E. Messick. 1975. "Prerequisites Versus Diffusion: Testing Alternative Explanations of Social Security Adoption." *American Political Science Review* 69(4/December):1299–1315.

Craig, Isabel, and Igor Tomeš. 1969. "Origins and Activities of the ILO Committee of Social Security Experts." *International Social Security Review* 22:

Cyert, Richard M., and James G. March. 1963. *A Behavioral Theory of the Firm.* Englewood Cliffs, N.J.: Prentice Hall.

Deacon, Bob. 1997. *Global Social Policy.* London: Sage Publications.

Dolowitz, David P., and David Marsh. 2000. "Learning from Abroad: The Role of Policy Transfer in Contemporary Policy-Making." *Governance: An International Journal of Policy and Administration* 13(1):5–24.

Esping-Andersen, Gøsta. 1990. *The Three Worlds of Welfare Capitalism.* Cambridge, U.K.: Polity Press.

Gillion, Colin, John Turner, Clive Bailey, and Denis Latulippe, eds. 2000. *Social Security Pensions: Development and Reform.* Geneva: International Labour Organisation.

Gray, Virginia. 1973. "Innovation in the States: A Diffusion Study." *American Political Science Review* 67(4):1174–185.

Haas, Peter M. 1992. "Introduction: Epistemic Communities and International Policy Coordination." *International Organization* 46(1):1–35.

Holzmann, Robert. 2000. "The World Bank Approach to Pension Reform." *International Social Security Review* 53(1):11–34.

ILO (International Labour Organisation). 1944. "The Twenty-Sixth Session of the International Labour Conference, Philadelphia, April–May 1944." *International Labour Review* 50(1/July):1–39.

———. 1945. "Franklin Delano Roosevelt." *International Labour Review* 51(5/May): 559–63.

———. 1948a. "Preparatory Asian Regional Conference of the International Labour Organisation, New Delhi, 27 October–8 November 1947." *International Labour Review* 57(5/May):425–37.

———. 1948b. "Regional Meeting for the Near and Middle East of the International Labour Organisation, Istanbul, November 1947." *International Labour Review* 58(1/July):1–17.

James, Estelle. 1996. "Providing Better Protection and Promoting Growth: A Defence of *Averting the Old Age Crisis*." *International Social Security Review* 49(3):3–17.

———. 1998. "The Political Economy of Social Security Reform: A Cross-Country Review." *Annals of Public and Comparative Economics* 69(4/Devember):451–82.

Linz, Juan, and Alfred Stepan. 1996. *Problems of Democratic Transition and Consolidation*. Baltimore: Johns Hopkins University Press.

Müller, Katharina. 1999. *The Political Economy of Pension Reform in Central-Eastern Europe*. Cheltenham, U.K.: Edward Elgar.

Nelson, Joan M. 1990. "Conclusions." In Joan M. Nelson, ed., *Economic Crisis and Policy Choice: The Politics of Adjustment in the Third World*. Princeton, N.J.: Princeton University Press.

Orenstein, Mitchell A. 2000. "How Politics and Institutions Affect Pension Reform in Three Postcommunist Countries." World Bank Policy Research Working Paper 2310. Washington, D.C.

Orenstein, Mitchell A., and Martine Haas. 2000. "The Global Politics of Attention and Social Policy Transformation in East-Central Europe." Paper presented to the American Association for the Advancement of Slavic Studies Annual Conference, November 9–12, Denver.

Palacios, Robert, and Montserrat Pallarès-Miralles. 2000. *International Patterns of Pension Provision*. Washington, D.C.: World Bank.

Pierson, Paul. 1994. *Dismantling the Welfare State? Reagan, Thatcher, and the Politics of Retrenchment*. Cambridge, U.K.: Cambridge University Press.

Queisser, Monika. 2000. "Pension Reform and International Organizations: From Conflict to Convergence." *International Social Security Review* 53(2):31–45.

Rodgers, Daniel. 1998. *Atlantic Crossings: Social Politics in a Progressive Age*. Cambridge, Mass.: Harvard University Press.

Rogers, Everett M. 1995. *Diffusion of Innovations*. 4th ed. New York: Free Press.

Schoenbaum, Emil. 1945. "A Programme of Social Insurance Reform for Czechoslovakia." *International Labour Review* 51(2/February):141–66.

Skocpol, Theda. 1992. *Protecting Soldiers and Mothers: The Political Origins of Social Policy in the United States*. Cambridge, Mass: Harvard University Press.

True, Jacqui, and Michael Mintrom. 2001. "Transnational Networks and Policy Diffusion: The Case of Gender Mainstreaming." *International Studies Quarterly* 45:27–57.

Tufte, Edward. 1992. *The Visual Display of Quantitative Information*. Cheshire, Conn.: Graphics Press.

U.S. Social Security Administration. 2001. Social Security Programs throughout the World. Web edition available at http://www.ssa.gov/statistics/ssptw/2001/English.

Walker, Jack L. 1969. "The Diffusion of Innovations among the American States." *American Political Science Review* 63(3/September):880–99.

Weir, Margaret, and Theda Skocpol. 1985. "State Structures and the Possibilities for 'Keynesian' Responses to the Great Depression in Sweden, Britain and the United States." In Peter Evans, Dietrich Rueschemeyer, and Theda Skocpol, eds., *Bringing the State Back In*. Cambridge, U.K.: Cambridge University Press.

Welch, Susan, and Kay Thompson. 1980. "The Impact of Federal Incentives on State Policy Innovation." *American Journal of Political Science* 24(4/November): 715–29.

World Bank. 1994. *Averting the Old Age Crisis: Policies to Protect the Old and Promote Growth*. Oxford, U.K.: Oxford University Press.

About the Authors

Author's name: Agnieszka Chlon-Dominczak
Position: Director of the Statistics and Forecasting Department
Institution: Ministry of Labour and Social Policy
Nationality: Polish

Agnieszka Chlon-Dominczak is a Director of Statistic and Forecasting Department at the Ministry of Labour. She was a member of a pension reform team in Poland that was responsible for preparation of the 1999 reform. She has published on the Polish pension reform issues.

Author's name: Robert Holzmann
Position: Director, Social Protection
Institution: The World Bank
Nationality: Austrian

Robert Holzmann is the Director of the Social Protection Department of the World Bank. Until 1997 he was professor of economics at the Universities of Saarland (Germany) and Vienna (Austria) and guest-professor at universities in Chile, Japan and the USA. As principal administrator at the OECD (1985-87), he wrote a comprehensive report on public pension reform in industrialized countries. At the IMF (1988–1990), he was working on fiscal and social security issues of Central and Eastern European transition economies, and he researched intensively on the economic and financial market effects of the Chilean pension reform.

Author's name: Legros Florence
Position: Professor
Institution: CEPII
Nationality: French

Florence Legros is professor of economics at the university of Paris-IX-Dauphine, and deputy director of Cepii (Center for economic prospective and international information) in Paris. She is also member of the council for retirement pension schemes advising the prime minister and has widely published about pensions schemes and ageing economics.

Author's name: Landis MacKellar
Position: Project Leader, Social Security Reform
Institution: International Institute for Applied Systems Analysis,
                    (IIASA), Laxenburg, Austria
Nationality: U.S.A.

Landis MacKellar is an economist specializing in economic demography. Since 1998, he has been leader of the Social Security Reform Project of the International Institute for Applied Systems Analysis (IIASA), Laxenburg, Austria. From 2000-2002, he served as Executive Director of the International Union for the Scientific Study of Population, an international association of 2000 members in 120 countries with its secretariat in Paris.

Author's Name: Marek Mora
Position: Research and teaching assistant
Institution: University of Leipzig, Institute for Economic Policy
                    Research
Nationality: Czech

Marek Mora is research and teaching assistant at the University of Leipzig, Germany. He has been cooperating with the Czech Ministry of Labour and Social Affairs on the preparatory works of the Czech pension reform. He has published several articles on pension reform issues. He works as external advisor to the Czech Minister of Industry and Trade.

Author's name: Katharina Müller
Position: Research Fellow
Institution: German Development Institute (DIE)
Nationality: German

Katharina Müller is research fellow at the German Development Institute, Bonn, Germany, and has published widely on pension reform in Latin America and Eastern Europe.

Author's Name: Steven Ney
Position: Research Fellow
Institution: The Interdisciplinary Centre for Comparative
                   Research in the Social Sciences (ICCR)
Nationality: British

Steven Ney is a Research Fellow at the Interdisciplinary Centre for Comparative Research in the Social Sciences in Vienna. A policy analyst by training, he has looked at European and international policy-making in a number of policy domains including environmental policy, science and technology policy, and social policy. Recently, Steven Ney's research has concentrated on the politics of pension reform in Europe, has coordinated a number of collaborative research projects about the issue.

Author's name: Mitchell A. Orenstein
Position: Assistant Professor of Political Science
Institution: Maxwell School of Syracuse University
Nationality: USA

Mitchell A. Orenstein is assistant professor of political science at the Maxwell School of Syracuse University and faculty associate of the school's European Union Center. He is the author of a book entitled *Out of the Red: Building Capitalism and Democracy in Postcommunist Europe* and other works on the political economy of Central and Eastern Europe and welfare states in transition.

Author's Name: Michal Rutkowski
Position: Sector Manager
Institution: The World Bank, Europe and Central Asia
                      Region
Nationality: Polish

Michal Rutkowski is a Sector Manager for social protection in the World Bank. He leads a group of 40 professionals working on pensions, labor market and social assistance reforms in 27 countries of Central and Eastern Europe and former Soviet Union, as well as in Turkey. In 1996-97 he was a director of the Office for Pension Reform in the Government of Poland and the comprehensive pension reform package was then designed under his guidance and partially legislated. He has published widely on the issues of labor markets, wages, pensions, and social security in transition economies and has advised several governments on social protection issues.

Index

Note: f indicates figures and t indicates tables